"In close tracking of the impact of fervent, ┊
the four 'Praying through the Window' gl┊
am convinced there is substantial evidence ┊
in *The Peacemaking Power of Prayer.* I commend it to your prayer┊
and consideration."

  —Luis Bush, International Director,
  AD2000 & Beyond Movement

"This is a remarkable book focusing on the awesome power of strategic prayer in arenas of human conflict. It is written by two men of God who have experienced first-hand what they are writing about. I believe you will be challenged, inspired, and blessed as you read it."

  —Dr. Paul Cedar, Chairman, Mission America

"The church globally is making a fresh discovery of an ancient biblical reality—strategic prayer transforms troubled societies, a truth that remarkably comes alive in *The Peacemaking Power of Prayer.*"

  —Dr. Dick Eastman, International President
  Every Home for Christ

"John Robb and Jim Hill relate graphically the immense power of prayer to change 'the affairs of men.' When God's people share together their deep concerns before God's throne of grace, these remarkable testimonies will be an encouragement to every reader."

  —Ted W. Engstrom, World Vision

"The present prayer awakening sweeping through the global Church is at the prompting of our sovereign God. *His* will is that *we* pray. Then, and only then, can the powder keg called Planet Earth be diffused. James Hill and John Robb are helping us respond to this reality."

—Jack W. Hayford, D.Lit., Pastor/President,
The Church on the Way, The King's Seminary, Van Nuys, California

"If you have any doubts that prayer is the most powerful weapon for advancing the kingdom of God, I hope that you read this book. *The Peacemaking Power of Prayer* is not just wishful thinking, but it will convince you by field-based experience that effective prayer really opens the door for God's will to be done on earth as it is in heaven."

—C. Peter Wagner, Chancellor, Wagner Leadership Institute

248

4997

We dedicate this book to our brothers and sisters in Christ who prayerfully seek to bring his peace to conflicts currently raging around the world.

We also dedicate it to our wives, Brenda Hill and Lori Robb, and to our parents, Kenneth and Phyllis Hill and John and Peggy Robb, thanking them for their unfailing support, as well as to the late Kjell Sjoberg from whom we have learned so much about praying for the healing of nations.

0–8054–2291–9

Published by Broadman & Holman Publishers, Nashville, Tennessee

Dewey Decimal Classification: 248
Subject Heading: PRAYER

Unless otherwise noted, Scripture quotations are from the New American Standard Bible, © The Lockman Foundation, 1960, 1962, 1963, 1968, 1971, 1972, 1973, 1975, 1977, 1995. Citations marked NIV are from the Holy Bible, New International Version, © 1973, 1978, 1984. Citations marked RSV are from the Revised Standard Version of the Bible, © 1946, 1952, 1971, 1973.

Library of Congress Cataloging-in-Publication Data

Robb, John D.
    The peacemaking power of prayer : equipping Christians to transform the world / John D. Robb, Jim Hill.
        p. cm.
    ISBN 0–8054–2291–9 (pbk.)
    1. Intercessory prayer—Christianity. 2. Ethnic relations—Religious aspects—Christianity. 3. Peace—Religious aspects—Christianity. I. Hill, Jim, 1948– II. Title.

BV220.R63   2000
248.3'2—dc21   00–023059

1 2 3 4 5 04 03 02 01 00

CONTENTS

"He makes wars cease to the ends of the earth; he breaks the bow and shatters the spear, he burns the shields with fire. Be still, and know that I am God; I will be exalted among the nations, I will be exalted in the earth."

PSALM 46:9–10

"For when you did awesome things that we did not expect, you came down, and the mountains trembled before you. Since ancient times no one has heard, no ear has perceived, no eye has seen any God besides you, who acts on behalf of those who wait for him."

ISAIAH 64:3–4

FOREWORD

Bosnia. Kosovo. Cambodia. Rwanda. Each of these places has come to symbolize the horrific potential for evil that dwells in the human heart. Each has been the scene of unspeakable cruelty between rival factions, cruelty that has devastated these nations' social structures as well as the lives of millions of men, women, and children.

The pages that follow make clear, however, that there is more to these stories than hatred, bloodshed, and misery. While these tragedies have been gruesome manifestations of sin's awful powers—and of the true intentions of our great enemy, Satan—they have also proved to be opportunities for the surpassing greatness of God's power to be demonstrated. And this book shows in no uncertain terms the means by which God's power has been brought to bear in these seemingly impossible circumstances: concentrated believing prayer.

For three decades now, it has been my privilege to serve the Lord with Samaritan's Purse, the relief and evangelism organization founded by Dr. Bob Pierce (who also founded World Vision). In the ministry I have seen again and again that prayer is the indispensable key to responding effectively to human need, both physical and spiritual.

Maximum prayer produces maximum results—whether we are feeding the hungry, treating the sick, or comforting the frightened. Prayer fuels our efforts to use the wars and other calamities of this world to show hurting people God's love and invite them to place their faith in Jesus Christ. And as the authors of this insightful volume document, prayer is also pivotal in defusing lethal conflicts and bringing about healing and reconciliation.

The Peacemaking Power of Prayer will challenge you to take seriously the spiritual battle raging in the world around us. It will drive home to you afresh that "the effective prayer of a righteous man can accomplish much" (James 5:16, NASB). And it will encourage you to make greater use of the weapons Almighty God has made available to all who trust in His Son.

God bless you as you read . . . and pray.

FRANKLIN GRAHAM, PRESIDENT
SAMARITAN'S PURSE
BOONE, NORTH CAROLINA

PREFACE

This book has arisen out of an experience in war-torn Bosnia, which we feel must be shared more widely. We believe that a specially coordinated prayer effort by Christians inside the country and around the world during August 1995 was used by God to bring an end to the conflict. If that is true, this experience has profound implications for the reconciliation of human conflicts everywhere. Similar accounts of transformation through united prayer also occurred in Cambodia and Rwanda, so we have included those stories as well. An externally organized prayer effort for Kosovo supported by networks of believers has also, we believe, been a major factor in the process of restoring the peace and the return of the refugees to their homes.

It was our privilege to participate in these initiatives in most cases as part of international teams and to witness firsthand how God worked in answer to his people's prayers. We want to share those experiences and the lessons we learned with you. As colleagues serving together in World Vision, a Christian humanitarian agency, we have written with a special audience in mind: people who are concerned enough about a suffering, divided world to pray for its healing and restoration of wholeness. We hope it will be encouraging and instructive, not only to those who already pray, but also to those who are just beginning to see that prayer can have a transformative impact. In addition, we hope this book will present a helpful model for those going on prayer journeys into conflict situations and for those involved with ethnic reconciliation, conflict mediation, and humanitarian relief efforts.

It has been a joy and challenge to collate our different perspectives into one book. John supplies the biblical and theological reflection on prayer and spiritual warfare in the early chapters along with the chapter on the roots of the Bosnia conflict. Jim chronicles the account of our prayer initiative inside Bosnia as well as the unfolding Kosovo story. Then John returns to tell his experience with the Cambodia and Rwanda initiatives. Though we each contributed different pieces, we worked together as a close partnership, editing the entire manuscript to its present form.

JAMES HILL AND JOHN ROBB
AUGUST 1, 1999

ACKNOWLEDGMENTS

We want to thank Greg Ash, Elaine Mercer, Eleanora Walton, and Col. Henry III and Charity Barber who partnered in prayer with us during this project; Barnabas Mam, Antoine Rutayisire, Solomon Nsabiyera, and Augustin Ahimana for their updates from Cambodia and Rwanda; our fellow team members and local leaders; and Jim Brown and Jan Thornton, who provided helpful comments on the manuscript.

SETTING THE STAGE

It was August 1995 during the height of Bosnia's civil war. Every diplomatic and military effort to bring peace had failed. In two of the nation's cities, Mostar and Tuzla, local Christians from every ethnic group gathered in desperation to seek the healing of their land.

The invitation was straight to the point. Who from among this company of forty-eight believers would be the first to step forward to start the process toward healing and forgiveness? Eyes looked around the room of this little house-turned-church in Tuzla, Bosnia-Hercegovina's second largest city, to see who from the gathering would step forward. In the room were Croats, believers from a Muslim background, Serbs, Americans, Germans, one from Britain, and one from Finland—a variety to be sure, considering this city was in the middle of a war zone. However diverse, they all had one thing in common: they came together for prayer because they knew that only God could heal this land.

From the left side of the room, a handsome man in his fifties rose quietly, approached the podium, and began:

> I am Serb. I live here in Tuzla. I have lived here before and during the war. I never felt hatred against the Muslim or the Croat side. My friends are still my friends. One neighbor had an unrighteous attitude because I was a guard in the military. The Serbs/Chetniks [nationalist irregulars] have done criminal things. From war in places by the river Drina, there was killing and slaughtering. There was killing, robbery; concentrations camps by Banja Luka, and other places. Persons, Muslims and Croats, were cleansed from Serb

areas. I from this pulpit call on my brothers and sisters, the Croats and Muslims. I ask them to forgive the Serbs. Forgive all of what happened because all Serbs are not criminals. I believe they need to be forgiven, and I confess on behalf of the Serb nation that I am ready to forgive all Croats and Muslims—what they have done until now. I call all Serbs to come and agree with me and ask for a solution so we can all live as we did till now. Thank you.

Our international team leader returned to the podium. "Will you who are Muslim and Croat, on behalf of your people, forgive the Serbs and what they have done?" The answer came from all over the room: "Yes." And the Holy Spirit began to move in Tuzla just as he did in Mostar a few days earlier—prompting forgiveness and healing, setting the stage so that intercession for the land could begin.

INTRODUCTION

Ethnic conflict is the great reemerging scourge of our time. As the forty-year superpower rivalry between the United States and the Soviet Union fades into memory, we are witnessing a troubling new phenomenon on the world scene—the eruption of conflicts based on ethnic and religious allegiance. Without the moderating influence that the Cold War powers exerted over the nations in their respective camps and even over the nonaligned countries, age-old divisions between peoples have resurfaced in harsh, violent forms. These divisions are often fueled by differing cultural and religious values that are manipulated by power-hungry political leaders to produce destructive wars and, in some cases, even genocide, as with Bosnia and Rwanda.

Many are worried and have prophesied a dark new period of chaos in international relations which already threatens to destabilize the "new world order." In his book *Pandemonium: Ethnicity in International Politics,* Senator Daniel Patrick Moynihan writes: "It appeared to me that the world was entering a period of ethnic conflict, following the relative stability of the Cold War. . . . As large formal structures broke up, and ideology lost its hold, people would revert to more primal identities. Conflict would arise based on these identities."[1] Harvard political scientist Samuel Huntington agrees: "The years after the Cold War witnessed the beginnings of dramatic changes in peoples' identities and the symbols of those identities. Global politics began to be configured along cultural lines. People are discovering new but often old identities and marching under new but often old flags which lead to wars with the new but often old enemies."[2] He quotes the strident words of the nationalist demagogue in

Michael Dibdin's novel *Dead Lagoon*, which capture the spirit of ethnic chauvinism and polarization: "There can be no true friends without true enemies. Unless we hate what we are not, we cannot love what we are. These are the old truths we are painfully rediscovering after a century and more of sentimental cant. Those who deny them deny their family, their heritage, their culture, their birthright, their very selves."[3]

Gojko Vuckovic, who himself hails from war-torn former Yugoslavia, describes the increasing prevalence of ethnic conflict. For those of us who think that the ravages of strife between peoples cannot visit our own nation, he warns: "Ethnic conflict in the aftermath of the Cold War has become one of the most important social and political phenomena present in almost all societies."[4] For those of us who live in the United States, prolonged racial or ethnic strife has been up to now someone else's problem. However, the ethnic makeup of the country is changing rapidly. According to the U.S. Census Bureau, America's population in 2050 will be 50 percent larger than in 1995. Overall, whites will decline sharply from three-quarters to just over half of the total, with Asian, African, and especially Hispanic Americans increasing accordingly.[5] Such a loss of demographic equilibrium could result in greater tension and open conflict. The Rodney King episode in Los Angeles and the sudden eruption of mass rioting and mayhem between ethnic groups that followed should serve as a warning that we Americans are not immune from ethnic conflict. More recently, the burnings of predominantly black churches as well as the senseless beating and dragging to death of a black Texas man by two white ex-convicts demonstrate that such tensions are still very much a part of our society and can erupt again at anytime.

As if to validate Jesus' words that as the end of history approaches there will be "wars and rumors of wars" (Matt. 24:6; Mark 13:7), Vuckovic charts the intensifying occurrence of wars through the centuries—471 conflicts since A.D. 170, which have taken more than 100 million lives. However, *90 percent of these deaths have happened in this century*, and now there is a new wave of warfare exploding in the 1990s that has the

2

potential of being even more destructive because it is ethnically based. Of the eight thousand identifiably separate cultural groups on earth, five thousand could potentially demand the right of self-determination and creation of their own state. Vuckovic worries, "With the current progressive trend toward ethnic mobilization and claims for implementation of rights for self-determination, the threat of ethnic violence and war is greater than ever."[6] Already in 1993 there were forty-eight such ethnic wars going on, most of these in the former Soviet Union where 164 "territorial-ethnic claims and conflicts concerning borders" burst into thirty armed struggles.[7] Indonesia, West Bank, Armenia, Chechyna, but also Rwanda, Somalia, South Africa, India, Sri Lanka, Canada, and Belgium are just a few of the nations in which such conflicts are either brewing or have broken out in violence. The conflict in Bosnia-Hercegovina, one of those featured in this book, lasted more than four years, claimed more than a quarter of a million lives, and made 3.7 million refugees. It demonstrated the destructive potential of only one such conflagration.

As we stand at the threshold of a new century and millennium, surely one of the greatest questions we humans face is how to defuse and heal future conflicts between peoples in tension. As seen in Bosnia, Rwanda, and elsewhere, hoped-for answers such as promoting greater democratization or relying on UN and NATO intervention are not adequate solutions. In our humanistic self-confidence we delude ourselves if we think that real peace can be negotiated when the unresolved hatreds and bitternesses of generations continue to fuel the rage and demand payback between ethnic groups.

Based on our experience in facilitating special prayer initiatives, this book will suggest a new approach for the healing of conflict between peoples that includes the use of spiritual resources, what we have chosen to call *strategic prayer*. Strategic prayer takes the God of the Bible at his word. If believers meet the conditions of his Word, he promises to answer, to enter the fray against the spiritual forces of darkness and destruction, and to bring hope and healing as they rely on him. This kind of praying does not preclude normal human attempts to resolve conflict, such as diplomacy, conflict mediation, and even the use of military force, but rather it helps them to be effective.

All human progress has occurred through the adoption of new paradigms or ways of thinking about reality which have enabled human beings to be more effective in dealing with the challenges we face. The grim and frightening specter of proliferating ethnic conflict cries out for the development of a new paradigm that brings supernatural resources to bear upon this most dangerous and deadly of challenges that humanity currently faces. Prayer initiatives will help to move the world toward that time when "he will judge between the nations and will settle disputes for many peoples. They will beat their swords into plowshares and their spears into pruning hooks. Nation will not take up sword against nation, nor will they train for war anymore" (Isa. 2:4).

1

THE TRANSFORMING
POWER OF PRAYER

Prayer is the only possible substitute for violence in human relations.
JACQUE ELLUL

Christ has left the devil only whatever power unbelief allows him.
HEINRICH SCHLIER

*Those who pray do so not because they believe certain intellectual
propositions about the value of prayer, but simply because the
struggle to be human in the face of superhuman powers requires it. . . .
The act of praying is itself one of the indispensable means
by which we engage the Powers.*
WALTER WINK

A major theme of Scripture is the history-changing, world-changing power of prayer. Repeatedly throughout the Old Testament, God's people cried out to God out of their deep oppression and need and saw his transformation of their circumstances. In the bondage of slavery to Pharaoh, the Israelites "groaned . . . and cried out, and their cry for help because of their slavery went up to God" (Exod. 2:23). In answer to their anguished prayer, God raised up a deliverer who led them out of their sufferings in Egypt and formed them into a new nation.

Over and over again the book of Judges describes the same cycle of disobedience by God's people leading to times of foreign oppression and misery. Humbled and despairing, the Israelites would then cry out to the Lord, and he would raise up a deliverer to restore their freedom and give them the possibility of a new future. In each case, their desperate crying out to the Lord came just before he raised up a deliverer (Judg. 3:9, 15; 4:3; 6:7). There are other examples, such as the invasion of the Moabites and Ammonites during the reign of Jehoshaphat (2 Chron. 20) or the Assyrians' attack during the time of Hezekiah (Isa. 37), in which whole-hearted prayer brought the intervention of God and changed the history of the nation.

In the New Testament, the teachings of Christ and the apostles often underlined the limitless possibilities of prayer. Jesus said, "I will do *whatever* you ask in my name, so that the Son may bring glory to the Father. You may ask me for *anything* in my name, and I will do it" (John 14:13–14, italics added). The apostle Paul proclaimed that God is "able to do immeasurably more than all we ask or imagine according to his power that is at work within us" (Eph. 3:20). The apostle James, drawing upon the example of Elijah the prophet, exhorts us: "The prayer of a righteous man is powerful and effective" (James 5:16). Scripture, therefore, unequivocally leads us to believe that our prayers in faith will actually make a difference and that we have not begun to realize the potential of connecting with the Almighty in this way. E. M. Bounds, author of many books on the power of prayer simply puts it, "Prayer can do anything that God can do."[1]

In spite of the clear exhortations of Scripture to pray in all circumstances, why don't we do so? We (the authors) believe that a weak theology of prayer contributes to a misunderstanding of prayer's potential. This is exacerbated by a materialistic culture that blinds us to how the spiritual world interacts with the material one. For these reasons we tend to neglect prayer—to our own detriment and that of our world. We, therefore, need to go back to the creation of the world and humankind to better understand the vital importance prayer plays in the whole scheme of things.

As recorded in the first chapter of Genesis, God gave humans the responsibility to "have dominion" over the earth. In other words, people were meant to serve as his vice regents, caring for the planet and all the other creatures upon it (Gen. 1:28–30). In the worst of tragedies, through the deception and disobedience of Adam and Eve, this dominion passed to Satan, who became the "god of this age" (2 Cor. 4:4) and the "prince of this world" (John 12:31; 14:30; 16:11). Subsequently, his influence became so strong that the apostle John wrote that "the whole world is under the control of the evil one" (1 John 5:19). This tragic rebellion on the part of our first father and mother opened the door to the destroyer and the powers in league with him. Disease, death, war, and the destruction of God's beautiful created order has been the result.

The good news is that God's calling of us as his vice regents has never been revoked. When we are "born again" and filled with the Spirit, placing ourselves under his lordship, we are given the power and privilege of being his children. Then, as we pray, we reassert our God-given dominion over the world, ruling and reigning with Christ. That is why the apostle Paul uses the past tense when he describes how, having been made alive with Christ, we have been raised up with him and are even now seated with him in the heavenly places. It is because we in the Body of Christ are already joined to him as our living head that, in this present spiritual union, we can experience his incomparably great power for us who believe, sharing in his authority over the demonic realm (Eph. 2:6; Luke 10:19). Though we are not sitting beside Jesus physically, we are seated with him spiritually, because the Holy Spirit links us together even now. Therefore, when we pray, we exercise the authority and dominion that he originally meant for us to have in him. This is the utterly stupendous power of prayer—a privilege all God's children have.

Dr. Hugh Ross, an astrophysicist, describes the "extradimensional" aspects of prayer that enable believers to transcend the limits of space and time: "Through prayer we can cross the space-time manifold of the cosmos and converse with God in this extradimensional realm. Because prayer is extradimensional in its reach, it must be considered the most powerful capacity God has made available to us in our current dimensional context."[2] Philosopher Blaise Pascal simply puts it this way: "God has instituted prayer so as to confer upon his creatures the dignity of being causes."[3]

Our prayers are utterly essential for the outworking of God's good purpose on earth. He is, of course, all powerful, but he has limited himself to work in partnership with human beings to whom he has given the oversight of the earth. Scripture makes it clear that we are in a dynamic, ongoing relationship with God, not subject to blind faith, fatalistically accepting whatever comes. Through the exercise of the authority Jesus gives us in prayer, we can change our world and its future. Richard Foster says, "We are not locked into a preset determinist future. Ours is an open, not a closed, universe. We are colaborers with God. As the Apostle Paul put it—working with God will determine the outcome of events."[4]

Our prayers can even change what God intends so that he decides on a course of action other than that which might have been taken had we not prayed. When the people of Nineveh cried out to God in repentance, he compassionately relented from bringing judgment upon them (Jon. 3:6–10). When Hezekiah cried out to God after Isaiah's prophetic announcement of the king's imminent death, the Lord heard his prayer and added fifteen years to his life (Isa. 38:2–5). Theologian Karl Barth puts it this way: "God does not act the same way whether we pray or not. Prayer exerts an influence upon God's action, even upon his existence. This is what the word 'answer' means."[5]

In 1994, during the height of the Bosnian conflict, a church group from Washington, D.C. made a ten-day visit to the Bosnian countryside. During their time there, they said they had "looked into the face of evil" but did not want to evade what they were seeing through "escapist prayer."[6] The idea that prayer constitutes an escape from reality demonstrates a tragic misunderstanding of the nature of prayer and reveals a basic unbelief that limits what God could have done to change the awful conditions they saw.

The tragic unbelief that God cannot and will not intervene in the horrific and depressing circumstances we observe around the world often keeps us from calling upon him. French prelate and writer François Fenelon said, "Of all the duties enjoyed by Christianity, none is more essential and, yet, more neglected than prayer." E. M. Bounds adds, "Everything depends on prayer, yet we neglect it—not only to our spiritual hurt, but also to the delay and injury of our Lord's cause on the earth."[7]

Unbelief springs from the limited concept of God we carry in our imaginations. Astrophysicist Ross thinks we underestimate God's power to act to the degree of trillions times trillions of times.[8] Theologian Wink says, "Miracle is just a word we use for things the Powers have deluded us into thinking that God is unable to do."[9] Clearly, our God is too small!

SOCIAL HEALING AND TRANSFORMATION THROUGH INTERCESSORY PRAYER

Secular media has largely omitted reporting on the role prayer has played in the great social and political transformations of our time, such as the fall of the Berlin Wall and reunification of Germany, the Romanian revolution and the overthrow of Ceaucescu, or the birth of the new South Africa. In all three of these cases, believers were actively praying for God's intervention and transformation during the times of conflict and social turmoil that preceded the positive changes that later occurred.

Recently, as Christians across Rwanda—supported by thousands of believers elsewhere in the world—have been praying for the reconciliation and healing of their tortured land, a marvelous thing has been happening. Hardened extremists, who took part in the 1994 genocide and terrorist attacks since that time, are coming out of the jungles to give themselves up and to ask forgiveness for their crimes. And, in some cases, those who lost family members in the rampage are now providing meals and other forms of caring for those who actually killed their relatives! God is at work in a profound manner healing inner wounds through the giving and receiving of forgiveness. (See chapter 10 for a more complete report of the beautiful, hopeful developments occurring in that nation through united prayer.)

Dr. Larry Dossey, a medical doctor who wrote *Healing Words: the Power of Prayer and the Practice of Medicine*, refers to more than one hundred scientific experiments, many conducted under laboratory conditions and termed "good science," that have conclusively demonstrated that "prayer brings about significant changes in a variety of living beings." He calls these experiments the "best kept secrets in medical science."

As intercessors prayed, positive changes were observed in such cases as high blood pressure, the healing of wounds, heart attacks, headaches, and anxiety. The experiments also found that the effects of prayer were not dependent upon distance or any other physical barrier. "Nothing seemed capable of stopping or blocking prayer." Even when an object was placed in a lead-lined room, shielding it from electromagnetic energy, the effect still occurred. Dossey concludes: "The evidence is simply overwhelming that prayer functions at a distance to change physical processes in a variety of organisms, from bacteria to humans."[10]

Dr. Dossey's conclusions about the power of intercessory prayer to affect everything from microorganisms up to human beings are not applied by him to larger social organisms such as human communities, but obviously his findings have deep implications for the healing and transforming of troubled societies like Bosnia. If the prayers of intercessors can produce physiological changes, can't they also be used by God to produce societal, structural changes, including the end of conflict and the restoration of social health?

We believe that it was the prayers of thousands of intercessors joined to those of local believers that turned the tide of the Bosnian conflict during August 1995 and that will bring ultimate healing and restoration. Intercessory prayer, in which believers intercede before God on behalf of their society, plays a decisive role in bringing his healing and transformation. This is why God seeks to raise up intercessors who will "stand in the gap" for their land and people.

In the book of Ezekiel, the prophet describes the terrible degeneration of the Jewish people and the city of Jerusalem. The city had become a "city of bloodshed," and its people had given themselves over to "detestable practices"—abusing the aliens, ill-treating the fatherless and the widow, committing lewd acts, accepting bribes, practicing extortion, and profaning the worship of God (22:1–29). In that context, God looked for a person "among them who would build up the wall and stand before me in the gap on behalf of the land so that I would not have to destroy it" (Ezek. 22:30). Tragically, he found no one! Terry LeFevre writes: "Prayer is the means by which the gap between God and the human world is overcome. If we do not pray, this widens into an abyss . . . to pray means to overcome distance . . . to heal the break between God and the world."[11]

Confronting similar conditions, God told Isaiah that he has put "watchmen" on the walls of Jerusalem who are to call on the Lord and give themselves no rest until he makes their city "the praise of the earth" (Isa. 62:6–7). Watchmen normally functioned as the guardians of ancient cities, watching out for possible invasion and thus protecting their people from destruction. But these particular watchmen are assigned the positive, transformational role of intercessors who unceasingly call on the Lord in prayer until he changes the nature of their people and city so that they will be called the "Holy People, The Redeemed of the LORD . . . Sought After, The City No Longer Deserted" (Isa. 62:12). As Walter Wink notes, "History belongs to the intercessors who believe the future into being. . . . Even a small number of people firmly committed to the new inevitability on which they have fixed their imaginations can decisively affect the shape the future takes. These shapers of the future are the intercessors who call out of the future the longed-for new present."[12] Ellul appears to agree: "Prayer goes with action, but it is prayer which is radical and decisive. . . . In this combat, the Christian who prays acts more effectively and more decisively on society than a person who is politically involved with all the sincerity of his faith put into the involvement."[13]

Perhaps more than any other metaphor in Scripture, Ezekiel's vision of the "valley of dry bones" shows God's capacity and desire to breathe new life and hope into the most hopeless and devastating of situations as his people play their part. It was as the prophet spoke forth the words God gave him in prayer that tendons, flesh, and new life came onto the old, dry, dead bones. A friend, Don McCurry, recounted his experience in visiting the African country of Guinea shortly after the Marxist dictator Sekou Toure had seized power. The cruel tyrant had kicked out all but two of the expatriate missionaries and had begun torturing his political opponents. In desperation, the two remaining missionaries, joined by twelve national pastors and McCurry, met to intercede for the nation and for the overthrow of this bloodthirsty, illegitimate ruler. Within one year, Toure was replaced by a benign leader who reversed Toure's policies and invited the missionaries back.

Prayer leaders in the New York City area have noted the "transformational effect" of ministries like the Lord's Watch, a twenty-four-hour prayer vigil that has occurred every month since 1995. It is supported by more than 4,000 people from 120 churches. They notice that a city known for its dangerous social climate has seen "the most significant drop in crime" in its history over the last two years to become "the safest city in America with a population of 1,000,000 or more." They attribute this to the strong intercessory prayer in the city for its welfare.[14]

After conversations with World Vision staff and Christian workers in many countries, we (the authors) are convinced that no real transformation occurs—people coming to Christ and adopting the values of his kingdom—apart from the united intercession of God's people. Jesus gave us a startling promise in Matthew 18:18–19, which we used in Bosnia and have also claimed in other prayer initiatives: "I tell you the truth, whatever you bind on earth will be bound in heaven, and whatever you loose on earth will be loosed in heaven. Again, I tell you that if two of you on earth agree about anything you ask for, it will be done for you by my Father in heaven." In these verses, the Lord has virtually given us a blank check that we can cash by uniting in prayer with other believers. In this way, *anything* becomes possible for us — even changing the history of nations.

PRAYER AS SPIRITUAL WARFARE

The apostle Paul, as we have seen, viewed prayer as one of the believer's main weapons in the struggle with the powers. This is a consistent biblical theme. In God's deliverance of his people from the bondage of Egypt, he used the prayers of Moses to unleash a series of plagues that were designed to bring judgment on all the gods of Egypt (Exod. 12:12) and to demonstrate that he alone was God to both Israelites and Egyptians. Moses was primarily an intercessor — one who had learned to hear the voice of God during forty long years in the wilderness — and his prayers were used to mediate a great dual deliverance: Israel from the bondage of physical slavery to Pharaoh and the Egyptians from the bondage of spiritual slavery to false gods.

Moses took a stand against the four-hundred-year slavery of his people, and by so doing defied the human and spiritual powers that kept them in bondage. "Intercession is spiritual defiance of what is — in the name of what God has promised. Intercession visualizes an alternative future to the one apparently fated by the momentum of current contradictory forces," says Wink. He adds, "The act of praying is itself one of the indispensable means by which we engage the powers. . . . Prayer is never a private act, it is rather the interior battlefield where decisive victory must first be won before any engagement in the outer world is even possible."[15]

In this warfare, it is clear that Moses learned to depend on the Lord of hosts to fight for him. He also taught this principle to the people of Israel. "The LORD will fight for you; you need only to be still" (Exod. 14:14). "The LORD your God, who is going before you, will fight for you" (Deut. 1:30). Tragically, Israel later disregarded this principle of depending on the Lord at Kadesh Barnea, where they initially pulled back in unbelief, then went ahead in presumption and were soundly defeated by their Amorite enemies (Deut. 1:41–46).

By recapturing this principle, King Jehoshaphat of Judah prevailed over a three-nation alliance of enemies. He and other leaders sought God, declared a national fast, gathered their people to pray in unity, and trusted in God's promises and sovereign power. They opened themselves to hearing the prophetic word, acted on it in obedience, refused discouragement and fear, and sang God's praise in the face of the enemy. The result was that God intervened, throwing their enemies into confusion, and the fear of God came upon all the neighboring nations (2 Chron. 20).

Another aspect of spiritual warfare seen in the case of Jehoshaphat and also in Joshua's conquest of Canaan is receiving a battle plan from God. Both objective data and subjective leading from the Lord informed Joshua's strategy. He had sent spies in to do some research on the situation in Canaan. He also repeatedly heard from the Lord as to what tactics should be used to conquer specific cities (Josh. 5; 6; 8). King David also practiced this prayerful dependence on the Lord for understanding what strategy should be used in his battles against the Philistines (1 Chron. 14:10, 13–16). As William Law says, "Prayer is a mighty instrument, not for getting man's will done in heaven, but for getting God's will done on earth."[16]

The experiences of these Old Testament heroes in their struggles with physical enemies is a picture of the spiritual struggle the Church has with the powers in our day. We are to take back territory for Christ in nations, societies, and human institutions that the evil one has taken as part of his usurped, illegitimate dominion. Clarence Shuler, national manager of Black Pastors' Ministries for Focus on the Family, says, "If people really want to pray and impact their cities, they have to go back and read the history of their cities and counties so they can pray against the strongholds where there are situations that have been rooted in the past. Once we know these things, we can pray specifically for them and begin to see results."[17]

God's promise to Joshua that he would give him every place where he put the sole of his foot has become the inspiration for a new form of prayer that has become more and more prevalent in the 1990s—the *prayer journey*. C. Peter Wagner, who has done much to encourage this kind of prayer ministry, defines a prayer journey as primarily focusing on the breaking down of strongholds. He defines a *stronghold* as "a set of circumstances in the context of human life that furnished demonic principalities and powers a legal base on which to establish a center of operations." "Planning a prayer journey," he says, "is a declaration of war against Satan."[18] We agree that this emphasis is certainly often a part of prayer journeys; however, we also believe that the main focus must be the positive one of praying for God's shalom to come upon the particular nation or society being visited. We believe that as we pray for his kingdom to come and his will to be done, the Lord of Hosts himself will move against the powers, restricting them and weakening their influence in that place.

This is definitely the approach our team has taken in various prayer initiatives. We have focused on the obvious need of reconciliation between ethnic groups, and prayed for the coming of peace. In that process, we have been led to come against the powers of darkness, division, ethnic hatred, violence, and war. But the great majority of the time has normally been spent praying out God's blessing, healing, delivering, and transforming as we walked, drove, and met with local people. As we have cast ourselves upon the Lord, seeking to listen to him and obey his direction, we have often received the assurance that he was answering and that he was fighting the battle for us. (Later chapters describe our experience of prayer initiatives in fuller detail.)

2

DISCERNING THE UNSEEN POWERS
AND THEIR ROLE IN HUMAN CONFLICT

Hadija Petrovic, a Bosnian Muslim woman who lost both her husband and eighteen-year-old son in the war, was trying to make sense out of a senseless conflict when she said, "I don't know what got into them and what got into us . . . who knows?"[1] Indeed, what could have gotten into Bosnian Serbs, Croats, and Muslims—friends and neighbors sharing the same language, living in relative harmony for decades, even intermarrying in considerable numbers. How could they throw all of this away, turning the graceful, picturesque villages and hills of their nation into one of the worst battlefields and the scene of the worst atrocities since the Nazis? The sheer irrationality of so much of the violence and destruction is what impresses visitor after visitor. It was as if some external power had possessed the combatants to abandon themselves to the work of destruction. Indeed, we believe this is what happened. To look at Bosnia is to see not only the work of rage-filled human beings but also the mark of what the Bible calls the "powers of this dark world" and the "spiritual forces of evil in the heavenly realms" (Eph. 6:12).

These powers, which are most likely angels who joined in Satan's rebellion against the Most High, are now assisting the devil in his efforts to deceive and destroy humankind. Author and professor Peter Wagner describes this alliance: "Satan delegates high-ranking members of the hierarchy of evil spirits to control nations, regions, cities, tribes, people groups, neighborhoods and other significant social networks of human beings throughout the world."[2] They are called "powers" because they exercise strong influence in our world. Heinrich Schlier writes: "Principalities do not merely possess power; they are power . . . pure power . . . power, capacity, dominion in person."[3] For three weeks they even successfully withstood the angel of the Lord bringing an answer to the prayers of Daniel the prophet (Dan. 10). According to the teaching of Paul, Jesus disarmed them, triumphing over them through the cross (Col. 2:15). However, it is also clear from the apostle's teaching that he and other Christians continued to battle against them. They applied the victory of Jesus' cross in the warfare through living in God's strength, putting on the armor of right living and thinking, and using the Word of God and prayer in the Spirit as offensive weapons (Eph. 6:10–18).

How do these spiritual powers continue to exercise their influence on earth? Jesus made it clear that one of the major works of Satan is lying to people. He is the liar and murderer from the beginning (John 8:44). Deception and destruction are linked in the Lord's description of the evil one. He and his allied powers of darkness deceive people in order to destroy them. The apostle Paul warned the Galatians that the *stoicheia*, his term for "worldly powers," wished to control them as they had before these believers had experienced freedom in Christ. Paul taught that this control was exercised through deceptive philosophies based on human tradition as well as through false religious rituals, festivals, and taboos, all of which relate to those patterns of thinking and cultural values with which people guide their lives (Gal. 4:8–9; Col. 2:8, 16–23). Because Satan, "the god of this age has blinded the minds of unbelievers" (2 Cor. 4:4), these accepted ways of thinking can become "strongholds" through which he and his confederates exert control over people's attitudes and actions (2 Cor. 10:4).

Paul uses the Greek word *hupsoma,* translated as "high thing" (2 Cor. 10:5, KJV). It was an astrological term, "the sphere in which astrally conceived powers hold sway."[4] Francis Frangipane correctly identifies such strongholds as within the mind. They are "the spiritual fortresses wherein Satan and his legions hide and are protected." He adds, "These fortresses exist in the thought-patterns and ideas that govern individuals . . . as well as communities and nations."[5] Conversely, it is prayer and petition with thanksgiving that bring the protective peace of God, which guards the hearts and minds of believers in Christ Jesus (Phil. 4:6–7). Otherwise, hearts and minds are laid bare to the wiles of the enemy, susceptible to every kind of lie and deceit.

How does this domination of individuals and societies happen? Schlier explains: "This domination usually begins in the general spirit of the world or in the spirit of a particular period, attitude, nation or locality. . . . Men inhale it and thus pass it on into their institutions and various conditions. In certain situations it becomes concentrated. Indeed it is so intense and powerful that no individual can escape it. It serves as a norm and is taken for granted. To act, think or speak against this spirit is regarded as nonsensical or even as wrong or criminal."[6] For example, visitors to Nazi Germany in the late 1930s described "a palpable evil in the air of a pervading atmosphere that hung over the entire land, full of foreboding and menace."[7] Some who visited Rwanda just after the outbreak of genocide described the same feeling about something oppressive in the air, a consciousness of brooding spiritual evil. I (John) felt the same thing during visits to Liberia and Sierra Leone shortly before the civil wars broke out in those countries, and it was in the air while we were in Bosnia. There was something in the air that spoke of tension, fear, and violence begging to be unleashed.

The powers first seek to incarnate themselves in people and human institutions in order to carry out their ultimate intention of destruction. In the Gospels we see plain evidence of their desire to control human beings and even animals. Those who were demonized had to be restrained, or they would hurt themselves or others. The demons Jesus drove out of the

Gadarene demoniac pled with him to be allowed to enter the herd of pigs, which they did to the resulting immediate destruction of the pigs.

We also should note the powers' influence over human authorities. The Jewish Sanhedrin falsely accused Jesus, and the Roman procurator openly violated his own system of justice by executing an innocent man to please a rabid crowd. John the Baptist and the apostles faced the same kind of violent opposition from the rulers, as did other early Christians under Nero and succeeding emperors. Theologian Walter Wink, in his exhaustive study of the principalities and powers, describes how they exert influence over institutions by becoming incorporated within them: "The Powers possess an outer, physical manifestation (buildings, portfolios, personnel, trucks, fax machines) and an inner spirituality, or corporate culture, or collective personality. The Powers are the simultaneity of an outer, visible structure and an inner spiritual reality."[8] Speaking of the way the German people came under the influence of Nazism through the grip of Hitler and the SS, wartime pastor Martin Niemoller said, "You cannot understand what has happened in Germany unless you understand that we were possessed by demonic powers . . . we let ourselves be possessed."[9] It is this latter kind of collective or corporate type of possession by the dark powers that is the most insidious and destructive type of demonization, and we believe it is most relevant to what happened in Bosnia, Kosovo, Rwanda, Cambodia, and other areas of destructive human conflict around the world.

For a fuller treatment of how satanic power is organized to influence nations and their institutions, see "Perceiving Satan's Agenda and Operation" in appendix A.

UNDERSTANDING THE ROOTS AND
NATURE OF THE BOSNIA CONFLICT

Ｉf we are to get to the roots of human conflict such as the one that
occurred in Bosnia, we need to sharpen our sense of spiritual discernment. It is not enough just to understand the economic, political, and
cultural dynamics that underlie such conflicts. As we have seen, if we
accept the biblical worldview, we need to acknowledge the role of spiritual forces and powers that are hostile to both God and human beings.
There are even some with a secular humanistic perspective who lean in
that direction. Richard Holbrooke, the leading diplomat who negotiated
the Dayton Peace Accords and currently the U.S. ambassador to the UN,
seems to admit the existence of such a dark force, though he offers no
answers for containing it. In his book *To End a War*, he plaintively wonders: "How could adults do such things to their neighbors and former
classmates? After a while the search for explanations failed. One simply

had to recognize that there was true evil in the world." He finds psychologist Carl Jung's comment appropriate to Bosnia: "We stand face to face with the terrible question of evil and do not even know what is before us, let alone what to pit against it."[1]

One of the gifts of the Spirit listed in 1 Corinthians 12 is the ability to discern spirits. Hendrik Berkhof says that "this involves especially the discerning of the powers which hold the hearts and actions of men under their sway in specific times and places."[2] We desperately need to pray for this gift in order to understand how the powers are operating and how to discern their methods of manipulating leaders and their peoples, pitting them against each other in order to get what they ultimately want: the shedding of human blood and the destruction of those made in the image of God.

THE UNDERPINNINGS OF THE CONFLICT

As we seek to understand the nature of the conflict in Bosnia, we see how Satan and his forces used economic and political developments, and especially religious and nationalistic ideologies full of lies and myths, to mold the thinking of the major human players who ignited the Bosnian inferno.

GREED FOR POWER AND TERRITORY BY POLITICAL LEADERS

> The devil led him up to a high place and showed him in an instant all the kingdoms of the world. And he said to him, I will give you all their authority and splendor, for it has been given to me, and I can give it to anyone I want to. So if you worship me, it will all be yours. (Luke 4:5–7)

In 1967, Josip Tito, the post World War II leader of Yugoslavia, proudly announced: "For fifty generations, going back 1,500 years, every generation has wasted its youth in war. No generation has escaped this devastation. But now, fifty-one will, for I, Tito, and Communism have brought this enmity between our peoples to a close!"[3] Until 1980, when he died, Tito managed to enforce this policy on his ethnically diverse nation of six republics and two autonomous provinces. But after his death, the economic and political infrastructure that had held Yugoslavia together began to dissolve in the years from 1989 to 1991 as tensions developed over the sharing of economic resources. At that time, in parts of the country inflation was running at 1,000 percent; people were unable to pay for basic needs like electricity; many faced poverty and hunger; and crime increased sharply. By 1990 the economy had disintegrated to the point where unemployment was more than 15 percent and the foreign debt was running at more than $22 billion.[4] Slovenia and Croatia, which together represented 55 percent of the gross national product, then decided to declare their independence and pull out of the Yugoslav Federation. The government of Bosnia later followed suit, provoking the clash with its own Bosnian Serb population and their supporters in Belgrade that soon led to war.

The anxious quest by unscrupulous political and military leaders to hold on to power was a major reason for the conflicts that developed during the breakup of Yugoslavia. As Serbian army generals and political leaders saw the federal communist party dissolving, they tried to preserve the old structures in an attempt to maintain their privileges as the nation's elite. Inventing the slogan, "Whenever there are Serbs, it is Serbia," they sought to create a "Greater Serbia." It was this grab for power and territory that resulted in war with Slovenia, the occupation of one-third of Croatia, and ultimately its worst manifestation—the war in Bosnia.[5] Richard Holbrooke, commenting on the origin of the conflict in Bosnia, said that it was the result of "bad, even criminal, political leaders who encourage ethnic confrontation for personal, political and financial gain."[6] Peter Kuzmic, theologian and seminary president from Croatia, emphatically denies the Balkanist view that this was primarily "ethno-religious warfare." Instead, he affirms it was a "territorial war in which political leaders with sick ambitions to enlarge their territories regardless of human cost, manipulated both ethnic and religious sentiments to achieve their inhumane goals."[7] One of these leaders who possibly bears the greatest blame for the conflict that brought carnage to Bosnia is Slobodan Milosevic, the president of Serbia. In 1989, at the six-hundredth anniversary of the defeat of the Serbs by the Ottoman Turks, he promised the more than one million Serbs who had gathered a glorious new future based on a revived Serbian nationalism. "The fact that we are the big nation in this region is not a Serbian sin or shame," he proclaimed. He also bemoaned the past "humiliation of Serbia" and hinted that war might be needed to right this wrong. Milosevic's fiery demagoguery mobilized the Serbs—then afflicted with as much as a 2,600 percent inflation rate— to recover the proud Serbian Empire they had enjoyed in the fourteenth century.

Another Serb leader, Radovan Karadzic, sought to implement this vision of a "Greater Serbia" within Bosnia itself. In an interview with *Svetigora*, an Orthodox journal, this psychiatrist-turned-war-criminal revealed some of the twisted thinking patterns that motivated him, General Ratko Mladic, and other co-conspirators to plunge their land into its genocidal nightmare. Communism, Karadzic stated, was used by the former Yugoslav state to keep Serbs in servitude, deceiving them with Tito's slogan of "brotherhood and unity." In his effort to bring about what he called the "complete restoration of the Serb empire," he claimed that he acted at God's behest and on his guidance: "I am convinced that God will show me which way to take and what to do." True, he and his political party had played a part in bringing "freedom" to the Serbs, but he maintained: that "All else is *God's* work. And *God* probably brought us freedom. . . . We have a firm belief that we are on *God's* right path and that [Bosnian Serb] folk will pay their debt to Serbdom and Orthodoxy. Our deaths, suffering, and endurance we accept as *God's* grace; *God* gave us the gift of faith to accomplish this end if he permits and, if he permits, we will save Serbia and Montenegro from devastation."

In the same interview, Karadzic styled himself as the defender of "our tribe and our church" and said, "God graced me to do something in my life that is significant, so significant that I think it was worth being born and to live and die to help my people." With either astonishing blindness or cruel sarcasm, he suggested his work was that of bringing healing: "We aim at healing, and healing requires wholeness. There is no wholeness without spiritual and worldly unity."[8] Notice the stark deception by which he assumed God's sanction for the genocidal acts he and other Serbs were carrying out, thereby elevating such barbarous deeds to a noble, spiritual mission. The destructive influence that gripped him was camouflaged by holy language. However, one of his poems more openly revealed his underlying motivation: "I'm born to live without a tomb, this divine body will not die. It's not only born to smell flowers but also *to set fire, kill and reduce everything to dust.*"[9]

PREVALENCE OF LIES, MYTHS, AND STEREOTYPES

One of the ways ethnic chauvinists like Milosevic and Karadzic spread the virulent strains of their expansionist propaganda along with their hatred for other ethnic groups was through co-opting the media. Terry Moffitt writes, "Before the first shot was ever fired in the Balkans, words of hatred instead of bullets were the firepower that volleyed from television sets, daily newspapers and street-corner meetings. People who had lived together in peace for more than forty years were taught to abhor each other, causing prejudicial divisions to erupt into bloodshed."[10] Former ambassador to Yugoslavia, Warren Zimmerman agrees, "The virus of television spread ethnic hatred like an epidemic through Yugoslavia."[11] Serb radio broadcasts spread the lie that Muslims planned to put Serb women in their harems. A cartoon in a Serb newspaper depicted a Muslim imam and a Croat bishop arguing over a Serb baby boy, with the bishop wanting to baptize him and the Muslim wanting to circumcise the child. In the second frame, the Catholic bishop is gouging out the child's eyes and the Muslim is stretching out the little boy's foreskin under a large knife.

As in Rwanda, where the Hutu extremists used the media so effectively first to dehumanize their Tutsi opponents as "cockroaches" and then to mobilize the population to eliminate them, so in Bosnia the

media served a similar purpose, disseminating negative ethnic stereotypes that served the purpose of both the political leaders and the powers of darkness. Political leaders, intellectuals, and the media distorted
facts in order to further their own cause. In this way the various people
groups were captured by myths and spread lies about themselves and
one another.

Paul Mojzes identifies the four major myths that mainly affected the
Serbs, but also to some extent the Croats and Muslims as well. The first
was the "myth of land and blood": foreigners were responsible for the evil
that befell their people; therefore, they must defend themselves from
attempts to steal the purity of their ethnic identity. Secondly, there existed
a "crucifixion and resurrection syndrome," the idea that through steadfast-
ness their people could turn past defeats into victories. They learned a glorified, romanticized view of their ethnic history through the singing of epic
songs rather than through objective study. A third myth was "time . . .
understood mythologically rather than chronologically." Concepts of the
past and present became intermingled in the thinking of people so that
past grievances—even decades or centuries old—were considered the
cause of present suffering. This myth evoked the constant need to relive
past traumas, making it impossible to experience real catharsis and renewing the demand for payback in blood. A fourth myth Mojzes identifies was
a "glorification of war and violence as the best way to keep or reclaim
one's freedom."[12] We just saw how this myth affected the thinking of
Radovan Karadzic.

Volatile, degrading terms were used to denigrate opposing ethnic
groups. Bosnian Muslims were referred to as "Turks," reminding Serbs of
their defeat at the hands of the Ottoman Empire in the fourteenth century
and raising the specter of a similar threat in the present. Serbs were called
"Chetniks," those nationalist guerrillas of World War II who carried out
atrocities against non-Serbs. Croats were labeled "Ustashe" after a fascist
group allied with Hitler's Nazis.

A major stereotype capitalized on by power-hungry leaders wanting
to ethnically cleanse territory to expand their holdings was the idea that

the Balkans were a place where ancient, recurring tribal enmities made the current barbarous conflict inevitable. "Balkanism" was used to justify violence and genocide because people in this region were "fated by history or genetics to kill one another." Serb nationalists in particular disseminated this line of thinking, contending that this was a "civil" or "ethnic" war in which outsiders should not interfere. Sadly, Western policymakers largely believed this propaganda, and early in the war concluded that intervening strongly to stop the conflict would be fruitless.[13] This last deception was the most tragic of all since it hindered a decisive international response that might have saved more than two hundred thousand lives.

LACK OF REPENTANCE AND FORGIVENESS FOR A BLOODY PAST

A 1913 Carnegie Endowment inquiry into past Balkan wars produced four hundred pages documenting "unspeakable savagery," including a record of horrible atrocities stretching back to the eleventh century: pillaging, rapes, eradication of whole villages, and arson.[14] Unfortunately, this frightful legacy of bloodshed and cruelty carried on into the twentieth century. World War I, which resulted in an estimated twenty million killed in Europe, began with the shots "heard around the world." They were fired in Bosnia by a Serb nationalist when he assassinated Archduke Ferdinand in Sarajevo on June 28, 1914. Many of the war's ensuing battles were fought on the soil of Serbia and Macedonia.

World War II brought the Nazi invasion and dismemberment of Yugoslavia, with more than one million casualties. Bosnia-Herzegovina became a "land of tears," with many bloody battles involving burning, raping, pillaging, and extensive massacres. No one was spared, not even babies or elderly people.[15] After World War II, Serbs, Croats, and Muslims had to live together, and any discussion of wartime atrocities was forbidden under the stern policies of the Tito era. However, the customary law of the Balkans, the vendetta—"an eye for an eye," or better yet, "two of your eyes for one of mine"—was still in operation.[16] Sabrina

Ramet, a political scientist from the former Yugoslavia, has characterized this time: "Interethnic hatreds hardened, feeding on bitter recollections of the inter-war kingdom and the war. . . . The past has never been laid to rest in Yugoslavia . . . *the wounds of the past have never healed*" (italics added).[17]

The memory of losing close relatives and friends is still a painful open wound for many Serbs. Jasenovac, near the border of Croatia and Bosnia, was the site of the largest death camp for Serbs, Jews, Gypsies, and dissident Croats. It was run by Croat fascists known as the Ustashe. "The brutality of the Ustashe was such that even some Nazis complained about it."[18] Between 60,000 and 750,000 Serbs were killed at Jasenovac. The reason for the huge discrepancy in the numbers is that both Serb and Croat nationalists have manipulated them: Serbs exaggerating the numbers of those killed, and Croats minimizing them.

Croat religious and political leaders never publicly repented of the Jasenovac genocide. The Croat Roman Catholic Church was slow to condemn the role of some of its priests in inciting and, in some cases, even carrying out killings of Serbs. Instead of truly empathizing with the possibly hundreds of thousands of Serbs killed, they only acknowledged these crimes as "errors." As late as the early 1980s, Croat bishops refused to even dialogue with Serb Orthodox clergy on this issue. Serb nationalists also blamed Bosnian Muslims for what happened at Jasenovac even though they fought on all sides, not only with Croat Ustashe, but also with Serb Chetniks and communist Partisans. Serb propagandists ignored this fact, choosing only to emphasize that because some Muslims had fought with the Nazi SS and Croat Ustashe, they as a people were all guilty of anti-Serb crimes.

It is somewhat understandable that in the absence of public remorse, people on every side would fear that opposing ethnic groups at some point might repeat the genocidal acts of World War II. Mojzes writes, "With extremely few exceptions, no remorse or sense of their own wrong doing characterizes the ethnic religious groups. They find blame with everyone and all, except their own group."[19]

A bloody past, coupled with an unwillingness to repent, sets up a cycle of vengeance and rage:

> They're the enemy—all of them. They deserve what they're
>   getting.
> Why?
> Because of what they did to us in the past.
> How far in the past?
> During the war.
> Which war?
> The Second World War. They had concentration camps, too,
>   you know; we did not invent genocide.
> But you weren't even alive then.
> That's all right. I heard about it.
> Where will it end?
> Not with me.[20]

The word *forgive* in the original language of the New Testament means "release." When we forgive, we release others and ourselves from the cyclical need to get even. Henri Nouwen wrote, "When not forgiving, I chain myself to a desire to get even, thereby, losing my freedom."[21] By not repenting or forgiving, we also open ourselves up to coming under the domination of the powers whose desire is to foment and perpetuate this cycle of killing and counterkilling from generation to generation.

Prayer team colleague Kjell Sjoberg told us of a city in Brazil that had been afflicted with ongoing violence and bloodshed throughout its history. At the foundation of the city, indigenous Indian people who protested the building of a railway through their land had been ruthlessly massacred by the railway company. Only when the great grandson of the man who ordered the killing asked forgiveness of the victims' descendants did the cloud of darkness lift from the city and the recurrent violence begin to end.

In Bosnia, unfortunately, no such forgiveness was offered, and Serbs' unforgiven grudges against Croats and Muslims, coupled with fears of another genocide at their hands, became a rationale for carrying out their own preemptive genocide. During the Bosnia War, after announcing among themselves that Muslims and Croats were about to exterminate Serbs, they themselves did this very thing to their enemies.[22]

THE ROLE OF RELIGIOUS NATIONALISM

What makes nationalism so pernicious, so death-dealing, so blasphemous, is its seemingly irresistible tendency toward idolatry. In the name of this idol, whole generations are maimed, slaughtered, exiled and made idolaters. One hundred million lives have been offered on the altar of this Moloch thus far in the twentieth century. Nationalism is not, in its essence, a political phenomena; it is a religious one.
—WALTER WINK[23]

Possibly more than any other factor, religious nationalism was used by the powers to pit the peoples of Bosnia against each other for the intended destruction of all. Walter Wink is right to ascribe a demonic aspect to nationalism and also to characterize it as having a religious quality. Paul Marshall would agree: "Nationalism is the belief that the major source of human identity, perhaps even the ultimate source of human identity, is membership in a cultural grouping called a nation."[24] If national self-interest becomes the major guiding principle for the way we live, we are in danger of substituting our nation for God and our national ideology for his moral principles. When this happens, anything is possible, even genocide, and the powers get what they want. This is what happened in Bosnia.

Richard Holbrooke recounts his teenage visit to the place in Sarajevo where the Serb zealot fired those shots that ignited World War I. The sidewalk inscription said, "Here on June 28, 1914, Gavrilo Princip struck the first blow for Serbian liberty." Speaking more perceptively than he perhaps realized, Holbrooke wrote that "the spirit behind" this inscription had been "revived, murderously so" during the Bosnian war.[25]

Religion, when mixed with nationalism, has the capacity to blind people to the real purport of their actions. Some of the greatest acts of barbarity in history have been committed by those devoted to their national religion. In the case of Bosnia, as the war went on, it took on more religious characteristics with imams and Christian clergy accompanying their troops into battle, blessing and praying for their victory.[26]

Religious nationalism infected the thinking of all three peoples, but the Serbs were preeminently captured by it. The Serbian Orthodox Church took a central role, becoming "a servant of religious nationalist militancy" as its clergy in many cases supported those who carried out genocidal acts, ritually celebrating ethnic cleansing and the destruction of mosques. Serbian Orthodox leaders sat as elected representatives on the Bosnian Serb parliament that oversaw the war effort. After the killing camps became known, the same leaders denied that they existed: "In the name of God's truth and on the testimony from our brother bishop from Bosnia-Herzegovina and from other trustworthy witnesses, we declare, taking full moral responsibility, that such camps neither have existed nor exist in the Serbian Republic of Bosnia-Herzegovina." They also leapt to the defense General Ratko Mladic when he was indicted by the International Criminal Tribunal for war crimes.[27]

One wonders how Christian leaders could be so blinded by narrow ethnic interests and so traitorous to the main teachings of Jesus Christ — loving God first and foremost and our neighbors as ourselves. Instead, their only concern seems to have been their own victimization as a people which also made them oblivious to the crimes their soldiers were carrying out against unarmed civilians.

The Serbian Orthodox bishops still struck this note as late as May 1995: "Always consistently on the side of justice and freedom, we see our people today without justice and freedom. . . . Today, we see our people cast out, expelled into the desert of the twentieth century, accused of the sins of others. . . . The Serbian nation is deprived of its rights, despite a sea of blood shed for its freedom and dignity."[28]

Bosnian Serb soldiers relied on heavy use of religious symbolism as they did their work of destruction. Passing alcoholic drinks and making the sign of the cross, they would sing: "Serb brothers, wherever you are with the help of Almighty God for the sake of the Cross and the Christian faith and our imperial fatherland, I call you to join the battle of Kosovo." Three-fingered hand gestures representing the Trinity, wearing sacred pictures on their uniforms, kissing the priest's ring before and after carrying out atrocities, and participating in special religious ceremonies after cleansing towns of their Muslim inhabitants were some of the other ways religious practice was integrated into their acts of war.[29]

With probing scholarship, Michael Sells, a Serbian American, turns the searchlight on the dark origins of the religious national methodology that possessed his people and by which they rationalized the worst acts of genocide. He writes, "At the heart of the agitation by Serb radicals against the Muslims of Yugoslavia, there has been a mythology which presents Slavic Muslims as Christ killers." This mythology he traces back to the medieval passion plays commemorating the sufferings of Jesus on Good Friday. From the time of the first crusade in 1096, the assertion that Jews were "Christ killers" provoked recurrent attacks on Jewish communities throughout Europe.[30] Serb nationalists of the last century then redirected this same animus against Slavic Muslims, and their descendants revived it in the 1980s. "Christoslavism," the belief that Slavs are by nature Christian and that conversion to another faith such as Islam is traitorous, provided the basis in Serb minds for their religious nationalist struggle.[31]

During the nineteenth century, Serb writers transformed Prince Lazar, the Serb leader killed by the Ottoman Turks in 1389, into a Christ figure, surrounded by a group of disciples partaking of a last supper and betrayed by a Judas. "Lazar's death" according to Sells, "represents the death of the Serb nation which will not be resurrected until Lazar is raised from the dead and the descendants of Lazar's killers are purged from the Serbian people." Slavs who converted to Islam were portrayed as the Judas who betrayed the Serb nation.[32]

The Mountain Wreath, considered by many Serbs as the most important piece in their literature, glorifies the extermination of Slavic Muslims at the hands of Serb warriors. During the drama, warriors suggest celebrating Pentecost by "cleansing" the land of non-Christians. A chorus chants: "The high mountains reek with the stench of non-Christians." A warrior states that the struggle will not end until "we or the Turks (Slavic Muslims) are exterminated." Sells observes that *The Mountain Wreath* "moves the conflict from the realm of blood feud into a cosmic duality of good and evil." The Muslims have two choices, "either be baptized in water or in blood." The drama ends on Christmas Eve with the killing of Slavic Muslim men, women, and children. After the massacre, Serb killers take Communion. Sells concludes, "Killing Turks or Turkified ones becomes not only worthy—but sacred.[33] Here lies both the inspiration and justification for the unspeakable tortures, the horrors of ethnic cleansing, and the wholesale murder of Bosnian Muslims from 1992 to 1995 at the hands of devoted Serb nationalists. The misguided religious national mythology of *The Mountain Wreath* became a stronghold of twisted thinking that the great destroyer manipulated at will in a cavalcade of horrors.

THE FACE OF THE DEMONIC: GENOCIDE

According to the Geneva Conventions of 1948, to commit genocide is to "destroy in whole or in part, a national, ethnic, racial or religious group . . . a coordinated plan of different actions aiming at the destruction of essential foundations of the life of national groups." This includes cultural institutions, language, security of property, liberty, health, dignity, and human life.[34]

Acts of genocide were clearly carried out in the war in Bosnia, but the idea that every side was guilty of genocide is wrong. According to the definition just given, this crime—this worst of all crimes—consists of a "coordinated plan" that informs and guides its execution.

It is true that Croats and Muslims were guilty of atrocities against Serbs, but as Michael Sells has demonstrated, the great majority of atrocities and those that reflected a systematic policy were carried out by the Serbs. The line that "everyone is guilty" was the stance taken by Slobodan Milosevic and other Serb leaders to generalize and relativize guilt so that they would not be held accountable for the specific atrocities they had perpetrated.[35]

It was the Serb policy of "ethnic cleansing" that thoroughly dehumanized their victims, forcing them into cramped concentration camps without toilets and showers to endure weeks without proper food, water, or hygiene. Besides the derisive term *Turks*, they called their Muslim captives *balije*, which may be related to the term for spit or mucus. Prisoners who lived to tell about it said their Serb captors often spit this word at them.[36]

In each area they conquered, the Bosnia Serb nationalists established killing camps for prisoners who were either beaten to death over hours and days or were massacred outright. The first inhabitants targeted were intellectual and cultural leaders because the Serbs wanted to destroy the future cultural strength of their enemies. They also organized the systematic rape of women and girls in order to destroy their potential as child-bearers, knowing that in the patriarchal tradition, the shame of rape makes it difficult for those so abused to become accepted as wives and mothers.[37]

Serb militia commanders also treated their own troops and citizens with brutality. They used alcohol to break down the inhibitions of soldiers before ordering them to commit atrocities. Pigs were used to show young soldiers how to cut throats, and they were forced to watch killings, rapes, and tortures. If they refused to participate, they risked death. Serb citizens who refused to support attacks on Muslims were killed. An elderly man was beaten to death because he didn't want to be separated from his close Muslim friends. A seventeen-year-old girl had her throat slit for protesting the shooting of a Muslim. Those who helped non-Serb neighbors were put into camps with them.[38]

The World Vision program director in Sarajevo described how during the siege of that city the zoo animals had not been fed and were dying. Responding to the plaintive cries of these caged animals, local residents ventured out with food and water only to be cut down by Serb snipers who were waiting for anyone foolish enough to help these desperate creatures.

Upon hearing this, his interviewer wrote, "No one could tell me Satan didn't exist. Only he could inspire someone to use the pleas of a starving animal to lure the merciful into the sights of his gun."[39]

PASSIVITY AND WEAKNESS BY WESTERN GOVERNMENTS

After the world discovered the depths of Nazi brutality and genocide during the Holocaust, the world's leaders proclaimed that "never again" would they let this kind of thing happen. However, only fifty years later, the United States, European nations, and Russia largely stood by and watched Nazilike acts of genocide being committed in Bosnia without forcefully putting a stop to it—until almost 300,000 lives were lost. Irvin Staub of the *New York Times* wrote, "To prevent genocide, it is essential for 'bystander nations' to react early with strong statements of disapproval and by withholding aid with boycotts and sanctions, if necessary." Instead, he said, "hesitation, wavering and hand-wringing . . . allowed the continuation of violence in Bosnia."[40]

Richard Holbrooke criticizes "Euro-passivity" and also blames the Europeans for their inability to act unitedly. However, the slowness and vacillation of his own U.S. administration's policy seems to escape his analysis. According to him, there were so many tumultuous events—such as the fall of the Berlin Wall, the break up of the Soviet Union, and the Persian Gulf War—that the American government was too fatigued to get involved in a nation without much strategic value. If anyone on the American side deserved blame, he thinks it was the earlier divided, confused Bush administration that blundered by refusing to commit American military and diplomatic power early in the crisis.[41]

No doubt because Holbrooke was working for the Clinton administration, he did not want to highlight the weakness and incompetence so many others have noted. As one critic wrote: "American policy on Yugoslavia, 1991–1995, was many things—indecisive, muddled and ignorant." But above all—and especially in the first two years of the

Clinton administration—it was cruel.[42] Fouad Ajami notes, "The mix of equivocation and spin that [constituted] Clinton's policy towards Bosnia," and "damage control" seemed to be the only things that really mattered in the Clinton administration's approach since Bosnia was a place of no importance to American interest.[43]

Peter Kuzmic rightly pointed out that if NATO had aggressively targeted Serb military positions at the beginning of the war more than two hundred thousand lives could have been saved. The reason they waited so long, he ascribes to a "vacuum in global leadership." He relays the poignant question of a Sarajevan Muslim friend: "When will the Christian conscience of the most moral nation in the world awaken and come to our rescue?"[44]

The really disturbing thing about the passivity of Western governments was that their delay in acting forcefully occurred in the face of detailed information about the crimes being carried out against unarmed civilians. Western leaders knew only too well about the ethnic cleansing, mass rapes, and genocide that was going on. "How is it that genocide in Bosnia has been tolerated given the information 'super highway' in the 1990s?" ask authors Cushman and Mestovic. "The visibility of this genocide leaves one with the troubling thought as to whether cognizance of genocide and moral condemnation of it even matter anymore."[45]

Knowing that genocide is a crime under international law and not acting to stop the crime and punish those responsible makes Western governments complicitous in what happened. Whether or not it was in their self-interest to get involved, they had a compelling moral interest to do so. Their delayed, reluctant response is reminiscent of Cain's hardhearted retort to God, "Am I my brother's keeper?" (Gen. 4:9). Charges of complicity by Western powers gain further substance due to their refusal to lift the UN embargo on weapons so that the Bosnian Muslims could properly defend themselves. Serb nationalists relied on a cache of Yugoslav army weapons that gave them at least a twenty-to-one advantage over the Bosnian Muslim army. On September 25, 1991, the UN Security Council, in its resolution, gave the Milosevic regime and Bosnian Serbs what they wanted when all five permanent members of the council voted to embargo the flow of arms into Bosnia.

Michael Sells describes the impact of the embargo upon the war in Bosnia: "This was not war, but organized destruction of largely an unarmed population. With weapons and weapons factories under their control, and with the arms embargo in place and stubbornly maintained for years, Serb militants were able to carry out their program with impunity."[46]

Other attitudes in the West blunted a compassionate, active response to the disaster occurring in Bosnia. Stereotypes associating all Muslims with militant fundamentalists had created an anti-Islamic feeling in much of the West, which undercut the desire to help the Muslims of Bosnia. *New York Times* writer Thomas Friedman, on June 7, 1995, said, "I don't give two cents about Bosnia; not two cents. The people there brought on their own troubles."[47] Postmodernism, which "revels in relativism, the questioning of the possibility of facts, and the celebration of ambivalence," and multiculturalism, which needs to accept every position as right, made people hesitant to take sides and label the perpetrators of genocide as evil-doers.[48] The lack of a forceful, consistent policy by Western governments coupled with an apathetic attitude by their citizens proved to be a significant reason why the conflict dragged on as long as it did, resulting in such enormous devastation, when it could have been nipped in the bud by decisive international intervention.

STORY OF THE
BOSNIA PRAYER INITIATIVE

The invitation was simple: Who from among this company of forty-eight believers would be the first to step forward to start the process towards healing and forgiveness? Eyes looked around the room of this little house-turned-church in Tuzla, Bosnia-Hercegovina's second-largest city, to see who from the gathering would step forward. In the room were Croats, believers from a Muslim background, Serbs, Americans, Germans, one from Britain, and one from Finland—a variety to be sure, considering this city was in the middle of a war zone. However diverse, they all had one thing in common: they came together for prayer because they knew that only God could heal this land.

From the left side of the room, a handsome man in his fifties rose quietly, approached the podium, and began:

> I am Serb. I live here in Tuzla. I have lived here before and during the war. I never felt hatred against the Muslim/Croat side. My friends are still my friends. One neighbor had an unrighteous attitude because I was a guard in the military.

The Serbs/Chetniks [nationalist irregulars] have done criminal things. From war in places by the river Drina, there was killing and slaughtering. There was killing, robbery; concentrations camps by Banja Luka and other places. Persons, Muslims and Croats, were cleansed from Serb areas. I, from this pulpit, call on my brothers and sisters, the Croats and Muslims. I ask them to forgive the Serbs. Forgive all of what happened because all Serbs are not criminals. I believe they need to be forgiven, and I confess on behalf of the Serb nation that I am ready to forgive all Croats and Muslims — what they have done until now. I call all Serbs to come and agree with me and ask for a solution so we can all live as we did till now. Thank you.

John Robb returned to the podium. "Will you who are former Muslims and Croats, on behalf of your people, forgive the Serbs and what they have done?" The answer came from all over the room: "Yes." The Holy Spirit began to move in Tuzla just like he did in Mostar a few days earlier — prompting forgiveness and healing, setting the stage so that intercession for the land could begin.

THE BEGINNING

It was May 1995, and the Global Consultation on World Evangelization (GCOWE), an event sponsored by the AD2000 and Beyond Movement, was meeting in Seoul, Korea. John Robb, the director of World Vision's Unreached Peoples Program was facilitating the Unreached Peoples Track for the congress. During the conference, John reconnected with an old friend, Dr. Peter Kuzmic, president of the Evangelical Theological Seminary in Croatia. Dr. Kuzmic asked John when he was coming to Croatia to bring an unreached peoples seminar like the one he did previously in the former Yugoslavia. John immediately countered by suggesting that a special prayer initiative would be more appropriate given the horrors of what was happening in Bosnia.

A few weeks later, in July, with his heart still burdened because of the atrocities being committed in Bosnia, John and his wife met with others in order to pray. It was during this time of prayer that the idea for an in-country prayer initiative was rekindled. John immediately wrote to Dr. Kuzmic and made a proposal to bring an international team of prayer leaders and intercessors to Bosnia. Because of prior commitments, the only open window of opportunity was from August 16 until August 25, just a few short weeks away.

At this same time, Tommi Femrite, a prayer partner of John's, living in Colorado who is also the executive vice president for Intercessors International, began to sense a strong burden to begin to pray specifically for John. The Lord had stirred her heart to pray for protection, grace, and wisdom. After one particular time of prayer, Tommi was urged to send John a fax encouraging him to continue forward with what the Lord was placing on his heart.

John asked me (Jim) if I would like to take part in this prayer initiative to Bosnia. In addition to my former position at World Vision International (WVI) as a manager in the information technology group, I was also responsible for WVI's weekly chapel program. Because of special concern for Bosnia that we at WVI had since the conflict started, I had made sure our chapels periodically included "field updates" on the nation as well as extended times for intercession. In addition, because worship-leading in chapel was a joy of mine, John thought this asset might be useful on the international prayer team. However, while it was possible to get the time away, there was no funding available for my travel.

On August 7, 1995, John received final confirmation through a fax from Dr. Kuzmic inviting him and his team to meet with church leaders for prayer and reconciliation in the city of Mostar, a city that had been largely destroyed in the 1992–93 fighting. He also proposed that the team travel to Tuzla, Bosnia's second-largest city in the north, where, in addition to meeting with the Christians, prayer and ministry among Muslim refugees might take place. It was an almost impossible proposal because August 16 was only nine days away!

Some days earlier, John had called on the late Kjell Sjoberg, a distinguished Swedish prayer leader with whom he had served in a prayer initiative to Cambodia earlier in the year (see chap. 9). He hoped that Kjell might be willing to take part in the Bosnia prayer initiative as well. Kjell was recuperating from cancer and initially felt he could not come at that time. John then called Tommi Femrite from Colorado and Brian Mills, who is the coordinator for the European Prayer Link in the U.K., inviting them to be part of the team. As each of us sought hard after God's will, the Lord began to confirm his direction in all our hearts and to supply the funding needed for us to go.

The war in Bosnia was still raging, and simply to jump in like some sort of spiritual cavalry was not something any of us wanted to do. There would be sacrifice, danger, and most certainly heartaches and difficulties. As I sought the Lord for direction, he brought me to the point where I was certainly ready to go and be a part—if this was his will. However, I wanted to be certain that he wanted me to go.

It was clear that funding for the trip had to come from some unknown source, yet door after door suddenly closed on me as I tried a number of avenues in search of funding possibilities. Actually this excited me greatly, because if it was truly the Lord's will that I go, then the provision of resources would be a clear evidence of this.

With no other direction to turn, John and I arranged a meeting with the late Graeme Irvine, then president of WVI. At that meeting, Graeme made it clear: "You must go," he said. "Don't worry; we will find the funding from somewhere." My spirit leaped in confirmation, knowing that I had not only received funding from WVI's president, but the blessing of answered prayer as well.

Tommi Femrite had been on vacation and hadn't received John's invitation until five days before the planned departure date. Diligently she sought after God's direction and her husband's confirmation. As she did, the Lord seemed to be encouraging her with words such as these:

Precious child, come and crawl upon my lap and lay your
head upon my breast. Lean into my heart and hear it beat.

For it beats for the children. Their hearts are so wounded and the enemy would like to have them and others think of it as beyond repair. But I have a plan of redemption—a plan to restore, and a plan to bring healing. Impart hope to them, for their eyes are downcast and their hearts are heavy. But I have come that they might have hope and life and joy and peace. They will sing once again. For the martyrs are crying out and have sung the song of Moses and of the Lamb. Go, my child. Go. I have already provided for you. You will see my hand of grace and provision and protection through all of this. Stand strong. Stand firm.

Upon receiving these and other words of comfort, Tommi and her husband, Ralph, knew that she was to be a part of the team.

Brian Mills, author of *Preparing for Revival* and a veteran of a number of prayer initiatives, also realized that the Lord was calling him to participate. In the same short amount of time, he made the necessary arrangements. With persistence, John again called Kjell one last time. Kjell was the most experienced prayer leader on the team, having taken part in prayer initiatives in over eighty countries. He was also author of key works on prayer and was known to intercessors around the world. Kjell responded that he would rendezvous with John and the team in the city of Split, Croatia, the team's chosen entry point into the Balkans.

It was certainly remarkable that in such a short period of time a diverse group of international intercessors, most of whom did not know one another, was formed into an effective working team. John knew each one's unique gifts and abilities, but it was the Holy Spirit who molded this varied talent into the ministry team it needed to be.

FORMULATING THE MINISTRY

On Wednesday, August 16, John and I left Los Angeles International Airport aboard Lufthansa flight 451, bound for Frankfurt. We would then connect to Rome for the final leg to Split, Croatia. Tommi departed the same day and met us in Rome. Kjell departed from

Stockholm, arriving in Split a day earlier than the rest of us. In Rome's Leonardo da Vinci Airport, John and I met Tommi. After initial introductions, our conversation became quickly animated as we discussed the task ahead, including the latest news concerning Bosnia. The Croats were on the offensive outside of Dubrovnic trying to push the Serbs back to the north and east. This meant that we could expect military convoys on the first part of our journey south from Split. As the airport terminal began to fill with passengers for Croatia Air flight 381, we could see that there was an unusually high number of Croatian military people present, returning home to the front lines after having tasted a bit of life away from the war. The closeness of the war became even more striking when we boarded the plane and saw Croats reading the morning's main newspaper from Split. Not only were there maps and arrows indicating where the latest offensive was, but the double-paged center section of the paper was filled with obituaries containing pictures of those recently killed in the conflict.

As our plane entered its final approach to Split, the rugged beauty of the coastal mountains stretching right down to the sea was plainly visible. The picturesque red tile roofs of the homes clinging to the cliffs gave no indication that there was a war taking place. However, the presence of a UN helicopter on the tarmac and men bustling about in their army fatigues made it painfully obvious that there was indeed conflict in the land.

The Bellevue Hotel is situated on a square near the waterfront, at the end of a long promenade containing a variety of cafes and restaurants. This is where we first met Kjell Sjoberg, a tall, white-haired man in his sixties. His infectious smile gave everyone a clue that he certainly loved the Lord. After checking in and briefly putting our things away, we left the Bellevue and went down the boulevard Obala Hrvatskog Narodnog Preporoda for a walk in the warm and humid evening. Stopping for a drink in the midst of a sea of young people enjoying the warm, summer evening, we began to finalize plans for the prayer initiative ahead of us.

Kjell indicated that he felt the Lord wanted us to minister with an emphasis on reconciliation. Tommi, thinking back on the word the Lord gave her prior to her departure from Colorado, especially wanted to explore ministry opportunities to women and children. John agreed that prayer without reconciliation would not be fruitful, and added that warfare prayer would certainly be part and parcel of the experience ahead of us.

My thoughts went back to the days when my pastor and I walked the neighborhood surrounding our church in Orange, California, entreating the Master to move mightily among those in need of a touch from the Savior. I hoped to draw upon that experience during our time in Bosnia. As we continued in conversation, our corporate focus became more clear, and a sense of expectation of what God would do in the next few days began to lay hold of us.

OUR JOURNEY OF INTERCESSION BEGINS
FRIDAY, AUGUST 18, 1995

After a good night's sleep, we gathered for breakfast around Psalm 18, reflecting on the Lord's goodness and our recognition that he was our rock, our fortress, and our deliverer. Someone read from verse 32: "It is God who arms me with strength and makes my way perfect." We felt that God was telling us very clearly that the journey should proceed in his strength, not our own.

After breakfast John located a Peugeot station wagon, and we loaded our gear into the back of the vehicle that was to carry us over 1,115 kilometers during the next nine days. It took four sets of eyes to assist John in slowly navigating through the narrow streets of Split and onto the main coastal road south towards Bosnia. As we passed buses crammed with troops and British Leyland lorries filled with war supplies, we began to pray for peace:

> *Lord God, you are the author of peace. We pray that you will be glorified in this beautiful land and that you will raise up workers for the fields which are certainly to be white for harvest.*

As one prayed, the rest agreed responsively with "Yes, Lord," "Alleluia," and "Amen."

After almost 60 kilometers, we stopped for lunch at a small coastal town called Markaska. We focused on getting better acquainted as John and Kjell shared portions of their Cambodian prayer walk. We speculated about what some of the similarities and differences might be with what the Lord wanted us to do here in Bosnia. Tommi and I entered into the conversation in agreement with what God can do if his people come before him in prayer.

As we proceeded on our way, Kjell asked us, "Did you know that Paul preached in this area of the world? It says in Romans 15:18–19: 'I will not venture to speak of anything except what Christ has accomplished through me in leading the Gentiles to obey God by what I have said and done—by the power of signs and miracles, through the power of the Spirit. So from Jerusalem all the way around to Illyricum, I have fully proclaimed the gospel of Christ.' We are passing through present-day Illyricum." We all pondered this in our hearts, imagining the great apostle possibly trudging along the same road, preaching in the Adriatic towns through which we passed.

At Ploce, some 60 kilometers further south, we turned inland along the Neretva River and moved closer toward the border between Croatia and Bosnia. Our prayers for the area and its inhabitants continued until we arrived at the border crossing town of Metkovic, where our prayers turned into petitions for favor in passing the first of many security checkpoints. Passing from Croatia into Bosnia prompted prayers for peace as the war became more apparent due to the surrounding destruction of home after home. Instead of red-tiled homes nicely kept with summertime flowers blooming, we saw the burned-out hulks—shops and homes now overgrown and unkempt. At the town of Tasovcici, which was previously occupied by Serb families, almost everything had been destroyed, even the individual farmhouses up along the edge of the hills. Buildings and shops that remained standing along the side of the road looked as if they were limping along on broken legs.

We needed to cross the Neretva River near the town of Caplijna; however, the bridge over the river had been destroyed. To obtain a better look, we continued as far as we could go on the road to the bridge, got out of the Peugeot, and stood for minutes staring in disbelief. The roadway was completely buckled and the steel beams twisted like pretzels, providing no way across.

The alternate route over the river was a narrower, makeshift bridge located further up river. Once we located it, we crossed over and moved quickly up the rocky hills towards Mostar. After some period of time traveling along this windy road, we came upon a UN checkpoint where we were required to produce passports. At the checkpoint was a massive tank perched next to a bunker surrounded by razor wire and sandbags. Mostar was not far in the distance. A short time later we could see the war-torn city approximately 1,500 feet below on the valley floor as we rounded another curve in the road.

It was 4:30 P.M. when we entered Mostar and drove to one of the local hotels to place a call to the Agape Church. Traveling through Bosnia's third-largest city, we saw entire neighborhoods abandoned and utterly destroyed. Row after row of high-rise apartments and office buildings were completely gutted. We could only faintly recall such destruction from old World War II newsreels. Karmelo Kresonja, director of the Agape Humanitarian Agency and pastor of the Evangelical Church, gave us directions. As we proceeded those last couple of blocks to the church, the sky opened up and welcomed us to Mostar with the gift of an afternoon rain.

Agape Church is located on the ground floor of a twelve-story apartment building situated among other high-rise apartment buildings. The bottom floor windows of the church were covered with sandbags, and there were six bullet holes in the entry hallway put there by an irate Muslim man disturbed that his daughter had accepted Christ as her Savior. The worship services are held in two connecting rooms tightly packed with chairs and benches. Another room doubles as a conference room/small children's play area, and there is a church office, supply room, rest room, and small kitchen area. Pastor Karmelo Kresonja, looking a young thirty-one years old, came out and met us in front of the church, welcoming us warmly to Mostar and to his church. While introductions were taking place on the steps of the church, four more conference participants arrived from Rijeka, Croatia, a coastal community some 370 kilometers north of Split.

Among those from Rijeka were Pastor Milan Spoljaric and his wife Carolina, and Jenny and Cliff Luckhurst, missionaries from the UK, who are serving alongside Pastor Spoljaric.

The evening meeting was scheduled to start that night at 7:00 P.M., so it was suggested that we first get situated into the guest house operated by the church. This was previously a home on the second story above an automobile repair business. The front portion of the first floor containing the service bays was destroyed, with black soot still escaping the windows as if the destruction occurred yesterday. Because the guest house was located on a main road out of Mostar to the south, Croat and Muslim soldiers could be seen traveling in packed buses heading either to or from the areas of conflict.

Staying with us were Susan, Jasmina, and Jasmina's young son, Tibor. These two energetic Christian women often encouraged us by sharing about their own ministries among the lost in Bosnia. Susan was from Massachusetts and came to the Balkans to minister to Muslims, Croats, Serbs—any who were in need of the Lord. She often walked the five kilometers from the guest house to the Muslim side of the Neretva River carrying a little flour and sugar to newly found friends who were in need. Eventually, she would also lead them to the Lord. During some of the difficult periods when Mostar was under siege, Susan said that Jesus protected her as she walked on the Muslim side of the river, shells exploding on the sidewalk just minutes after she passed by.

Jasmina was from a Muslim background while her husband, Milac, was a Serb. The darkest time of her life was when her husband was in prison. She visited and brought him what little food she could find. She knew he also was disappointed and downcast.

When Milac was released, he felt he needed to go to Norway until the fighting stopped. Jasmina needed to contact her parents about this, but they were in Serbia and she did not have a telephone. Living in the same apartment complex were Nikola Skrinjaric and his wife, Sondra. Nikola, an evangelist and relief director from Zagreb, also worked with the Agape Humanitarian Agency.

Sondra began to meet often with Jasmina. She took her a Bible and began to open up the Word to her. Jasmina was confused at first because, as a Muslim, she knew about this person Jesus, but she was curious as to who Jesus Christ really was. With gentle persistence and loving kindness, Nikola and Sondra introduced Jasmina to the Savior.

Alone one night, Jasmina prayed, "I have only you, God." She reported that at that moment, she saw a light in her mind and recognized from what Nikola and Sondra had shared with her that it was Jesus Christ. Additional explanations from Nikola and Sondra reinforced the fact that Jesus was calling her, and her response was immediate. Since coming to Christ, Yasmina, along with her son, Tibor, have ministered effectively among many hurting Muslim women of Bosnia.

After a brief rest at the guest house, we all returned to Agape Church for the evening meeting. We gathered for a time of prayer beforehand, seeking the Lord's presence and asking him to have his way that evening. As the service began, welcomes and introductions were plentiful as we who were part of the international prayer team moved through the crowd and found some empty seats. Understandably, it seemed as if all eyes were on us. The chairs were small, as were the benches; however, they were just close enough to ensure that all 128 people who wanted to attend were able to do so. The single revolving ceiling fan was working hard to replace the room's tired, dank air with a fresh stream from a single open window.

Pastor Kresonja called the meeting to order in his native Serbo-Croatian language. As our names and countries were mentioned, we realized we were being introduced to the congregation and it was being explained why we were there. The visitors from Rijeka were also introduced. After a brief time of sharing, we were all invited to stand and enter into a time of worship in song. With words projected onto the side wall, a worship team consisting of two guitarists and a keyboardist began to lead us in several well-known songs of praise and worship. It was truly glorious! With hands lifted and hearts singing in one accord, song after song of praise and worship brought us into unity with the Lord. While we found it was easier to sing the familiar tunes in English, a real attempt to pronounce the Serbo-Croatian words was met with enthusiasm by all the foreigners.

At the conclusion of our worship time, John was introduced as the speaker for the evening. His objective for this meeting—the first of four meetings with the congregation in Mostar—was to lay a foundation for strategic prayer by communicating that God does have a redemptive strategy for all the peoples of the world. He started this thought by first describing the prayer team as one comprised of representatives from different peoples drawn together by a common burden of prayer for Bosnia.

Early on in his message, John came face-to-face with the ethnic complexities of the people in the room when, after continuing to refer to their country as "Bosnia," he was corrected by an older woman who added the word "Hercegovina." (Mostar is situated in the Hercegovina portion of the land referred to as Bosnia).

"The theme for our time of prayer together," continued John, "is from 2 Chronicles 7:14, where God promises: 'If my people who are called by my name, will humble themselves and pray and seek my face, and turn from their wicked ways, then I will hear from heaven and will forgive their sin and will heal their land.'" John emphasized that the key portion of this promise is where the Lord admonishes us to seek his face, which means prayer—intercessory prayer. With our meditation on this verse came an initial glimpse of hope—hope that the Lord God Almighty would indeed hear the prayers of his people and bring healing to a needy land.

"History belongs to whom?" John asked the congregation. "The politicians, the government leaders, the armed forces? No," he answered. "History belongs to the intercessors."

This quote from theologian Walter Wink turned out to be closer to a prophetic utterance than to an introductory remark for a message on intercession. Agape Church in Mostar—with a group of 128 believers— began to intercede in prayer, trusting that God could change the history of their tortured land. Simultaneously, they were joined by prayer warriors from around the world who are part of Intercessors International; the Spiritual Warfare Network; the AD2000 and Beyond Movement; World

Vision International; and the churches, friends, and families of the prayer team. In addition, throughout that month, a worldwide call to prayer involving many other Christians was taking place.

That first night, John shared that nations are comprised of people groups and that the Lord values each of the peoples on the earth. Revelation 7:9 affirms this: "After this I looked and there before me was a great multitude that no one could count, from every nation, tribe, people and language, standing before the throne and in front of the Lamb." All the peoples of the world—including all the peoples who were represented in this meeting and the peoples who were caught in conflict throughout Bosnia—are loved and valued equally by their Creator.

Toward the end of John's time of sharing, other out-of-town travelers arrived and were quickly assimilated into the group. There was Koprivnjak Antun, a former pastor and Roman Catholic priest who pioneered the establishment of the church in the Muslim section of Mostar, but who was now living in Zagreb; Reverend Stamko Jambrek, the secretary of the Evangelical Alliance of Croatia, and who also came from Zagreb; and Brian Mills from the U.K., a member of the international prayer team who had been picked up at the Split airport by Antun and Reverend Stamko.

As John closed his talk, we gathered into discussion groups of four to six people. Each group was then instructed to begin a dialogue on what they felt was God's redemptive purpose for each people group in Bosnia-Hercegovina, including some of the more positive aspects of this unique culture. Afterwards, we prayed for each people group—Serbs, Croats, and Muslims—and for the fulfillment of God's special purpose for each.

Later that night, we loaded into the Peugeot for the fifteen-minute drive back to the guest house, where a Serb woman named Vickitsa was graciously preparing a meal for us. Conversation over dinner with new friends was lively as our team listened intently to them describe how they survived the worst of the war; what conditions were like for them personally; how Mostar fared during the horrific weeks of shelling; and how Agape Church thrived in spite of all the difficulties. As fascinating as their stories were, travel fatigue soon began to overpower us, and we retreated for a much-needed evening rest.

SATURDAY, AUGUST 19, 1995

After breakfast and plenty of *kafka* [coffee], Pastor Kresonja asked our team to join his people in praying for the establishment of a new church being planted across the Neretva River in East Mostar, the Muslim portion of the city. As we were getting into the vehicles for our trip, Susan, the American also staying at the guest house, suggested we go to a place overlooking Mostar so prayer for the city could begin in earnest. Seven of us climbed into the Peugeot for the short ride up the winding road to a pull-out on the south side of town overlooking the city proper. The mountain just behind the one across from where we were standing was under Serb control and was also the source of periodic shelling of the city. As we gazed at the city below, the horrific carnage from savage fighting that had occurred between Muslim and Croat residents lay before us in the ruins of bombed-out buildings and destroyed bridges. Almost immediately, prayer began.

> *Lord, out of this destruction we pray for your presence to come mightily into this land.*

Another entreated the Lord to reign in majesty in this spiritually desolate land. We also pleaded with the Lord for reconciliation among the various ethnic groups, for the tiny minority of Christian believers in Mostar, and for peace in the land. I felt led to pray based on 2 Kings 6:

> *Lord, we recall in your Word where the servant of the prophet Elisha saw an army with horses and chariots surrounding the city of Dothan. Elisha prayed that his servant would see that those who are with him are more than those enemies surrounding the city. In answer to this prayer of Elisha's, you, O Lord, opened the eyes of the servant, and he saw the hills full of horses and chariots of fire all around them. May your chariots of righteousness surround this*

city, and may your children who live here sense your protection of them.

Lord, [another continued,] *surround Mostar with your presence so that your glory will be realized in this city, and that the name of Jesus will be lifted up.*

As we were praying, a vehicle pulled up. The driver excitedly yelled at us, and then as quickly as he appeared, he drove off again. Antun translated, saying that the driver indicated we shouldn't be standing out on this overlook because we were within the range of Serb snipers! With that word of encouragement, we quickly cleared out, heading on to Agape Church.

At the church, the international prayer team and other prayer initiative participants gathered for a briefing. Pastor Kresonja explained that East Mostar is the old city where the population is 100 percent Muslim. Mostar means "Stari Most," or "old bridge," after the quaint, centuries-old bridge that used to span the Neretva River until it was tragically destroyed by the Croats in 1993. Because the bridge in many ways symbolized the reconciliation process, including the need for rebuilding the fractured relationships between peoples, it was decided that we would include a time of prayer at the bridge. Pastor Kresonja cautioned that since we were a fairly large group of foreigners we would need to be circumspect in Muslim East Mostar. The day's prayer journey would include going through the UN/police security checkpoint, crossing over the Neretva River, and proceeding up to the church. Our mission was simply to go and pray quietly.

"We have a vision to plant churches in Mostar, Sarajevo, Konitz, Tuzla, and Bihac," Pastor Kresonja said as he concluded his briefing. "We begin as a humanitarian aid organization, and as our purpose is shared and confidence is gained, we can start one-on-one witnessing so that churches can be planted."

There was an air of excitement as we departed. Jenny Luckhurst, from Rijeka, visited each vehicle and indicated that she felt the Scripture verse for us that day was contained in Isaiah 16:3–5: "Give us counsel, render a decision. Make your shadow like night at high noon. Hide the fugitives, do not betray the refugees. Let the Moabite fugitives stay with you; be their shelter from the destroyer. The oppressor will come to an end, and destruction will cease; the aggressor will vanish from the land." We all reflected on this verse as we drove out of the church parking area.

Our caravan of three vehicles traveled down heavily damaged streets and past destroyed buildings. After a brief stop at the UN/police checkpoint, we continued another two kilometers up a hill, then pulled over and parked in an area containing both homes and small commercial buildings being reborn out of the rubble. We walked the short distance uphill and through an entryway where a newly painted grey double door was opened, revealing the church compound inside. Across the compound was what used to be a three-story home belonging originally to Alex Chantish, a well-known Serb writer of Christian stories. A marble plaque indicating a bit about Alex Chantish was posted next to what was originally the building's front entry door.

As we gathered in front of this building, Antun, one of our local escorts, began to share some of its history. Antun was formerly a Catholic priest. Subsequently, he became part of the ministry of Croatia's Evangelical Alliance and was sent to pastor a church housed in this building for two years. When the fighting in Mostar erupted, Antun and his family were the last from this church to evacuate East Mostar. At first the Serbs and then the Croats mercilessly began to bomb this section of Mostar during most of 1993. Because this building is situated somewhat strategically on the side of a hill overlooking much of the city, snipers used the third story to fire on those across the river who tried to remain during the Holocaust.

David Lively, then pastor of this newly reestablished church, continued with his part of the story: "I came from a church in Atlanta, Georgia, that adopted the Bosnian Muslims as an unreached people group. We wanted to reach them with the gospel. When I first arrived in Bosnia, I worked first in the relief camps and then coordinated the work assignments of the short-term missionaries arriving during the summer from our church in Atlanta."

David's passion for ministry among the Bosnian Muslims was stirring. While in Mostar, he soon met Pastor Kresonja, and a close association developed between them. Before long, it was decided that David would work to develop the East Mostar church as a plant from West Mostar's Agape Church.

A title search was conducted of the property, and it was determined that the Evangelical Alliance still held title to the property, so rebuilding could commence. David was able to develop relationships with the nearby Muslim people by offering them jobs cleaning up the property. In order to begin to share their Christian faith as soon as possible after they arrived in East Mostar, they invited representatives from Campus Crusade for Christ to show the *Jesus* film. David shared with us that his ministry emphasis is to focus on people who come from a mixed ethnic background because, from his experience, they seem to be more ready to accept Christ.

The building grounds were being maintained by a former officer in the Yugoslavian army by the name of Semier. He had been a POW during the conflict and had been moved back and forth between four different prisons. Part of the torture he had endured included being gassed with chlorine while being forced to stay with dead bodies in front of him for days.

In accounting for his coming to faith in Christ, Semier said, "It was as though I was 'pushed by a force,' reflecting on those dark days. As an army officer, I would tell my troops that they shouldn't be afraid because in the tradition of a true Muslim, God was with us."

He told us he had been in some horrifying situations, where the fighting would result in bodies being stacked "4 to 5 meters high," and often his only recourse was to call out to God to help him. When he left the army and was freed from prison, he came to Mostar, where he chanced across the group who was working to clean up this bombed-out former church. He rolled his sleeves up, was given some tools for clearing out the rubble, and quickly began to work. The grenades were still falling in and around Mostar, which kept tensions high and made work more difficult. However, as the front doors to the church were replaced, windows rehung, and work on the roof commenced, the small meeting room began to take shape, causing people living in the neighborhood to come closer.

Nikola Skrinjaric, the evangelist from Agape Church in West Mostar, started sharing with Semier and some of the other Muslims in the neighborhood concerning what he and his colleagues were doing and how they were doing it with God's help. Soon a German humanitarian organization supplied more roofing materials, including three workers to help. Also, visitors from the U.S.A., U.K., and Germany came by to assist with the building. As soon as the rubble was cleaned up and the meeting room completed, Friday 6:00 P.M. services began. Five people came to the first service. Then as others began to inquire about what was happening, they were invited to come. People from both Serb and Muslim backgrounds began to attend a weekly Bible study. Sometimes the church activities were held outside when the weather was good. As the work continued, no one from the surrounding community made any problems for the small church. Semier gave his life to Christ and continued to work and encourage others in the faith.

As David Lively and Semier concluded sharing, we all followed them into the completed meeting room, where we began to pray for the future of this ministry. As hearts began to intercede with the Almighty, Scripture itself became a basis of our intercession. Kjell Sjoberg was first to lead out:

> *The Father's prayer for the city is that it be rebuilt, the streets restored, and that this church also be rebuilt. In Ezekiel 36:33 the Lord indicates: "This is what the Sovereign LORD says: On the day I cleanse you from all your sins, I will resettle your towns, and the ruins will be rebuilt. The desolate land will be cultivated instead of lying desolate in the sight of all who pass through it. They will say, 'This land that was laid waste has become like the garden of Eden; the cities that were lying in ruins, desolate and destroyed, are now*

fortified and inhabited.' Then the nations around you that remain will know that I the LORD have rebuilt what was destroyed and have replanted what was desolate. I the LORD have spoken, and I will do it."

Another prayed for the church-planting ministry of Agape Church and for the special place it holds in the Father's heart. Brian Mills prayed according to Isaiah 58:12: "Your people will rebuild the ancient ruins and will raise up the age-old foundations; you will be called Repairer of Broken Walls, Restorer of Streets with Dwellings." Still another prayed for this church to be a place of ethnic unity.

I believed the Holy Spirit wanted me to share his encouragement from Isaiah 43:19–20: "See, I am doing a new thing! Now it springs up; do you not perceive it? I am making a way in the desert and streams in the wasteland."

Another from the group prayed from Isaiah 16: 1–5, emphasizing the desire that this church become a hiding place from the destroyer and a place to hide refugees: "Lord we pray that 'in love a throne will be established; in faithfulness a man will sit on it—one from the house of David—one who in judging seeks justice and speeds the cause of righteousness'" (v. 5). "Father," someone prayed from Isaiah 35, "may this church be like a highway of holiness, where your Word of truth springs up and is poured out over the land."

A prayer from Haggai 2:3–9 questioned, "'Who of you is left who saw this house in its former glory? How does it look to you now? Does it not seem to you like nothing? But now be strong, . . . declares the LORD. Be strong, . . . and work. For I am with you,' . . . And in this place I will grant peace,' declares the LORD Almighty."

Brian Mills spoke a final prayer from Job 42, indicating "that the latter will be greater than the former in peace, and that peace will finish the walls of this place."

At the conclusion of this marvelous time of prayer, we left the meeting room and walked throughout the property—stopping at the doorposts and entreating the Lord to bless all who enter; walking the four sides of the property to pray for protection; and inviting the Holy Spirit to come and raise up his house with his people so that the name of Jesus would be glorified from this place. It was certainly an exciting time and experience in prayer fellowship!

Proceeding out the gates of the church and walking along a narrow roadway, two distinct contrasting pictures were obvious. The telling story of destruction was everywhere; no buildings could be identified as having remained untouched. Yet piles of rubble and scaffolding towering near many of the buildings gave a feeling of hope as reconstruction had started.

As we neared one intersection, we passed a recently refurbished government building proudly flying the Bosnia flag that contained three fleurs-de-lis on each side of a diagonal line. These three fleurs-de-lis represent the three groups living in Bosnia: Muslim, Serb, and Croat. *Certainly,* I reflected as we passed by, *the newness of this refurbished building is creating a sense of hope and anticipation among hearts long burdened with pain and sorrow.*

The streets were quaint in nature, with small shops abutting each side of the cobblestone roadway. For some, it seemed to be business as usual, with abundant merchandise adorning their shop entryways and beckoning shoppers. For others, there was still a bombed-out shell of a building with the water left running and cascading onto the street. What's more, one did not have to travel far to see that the local parks had been employed as makeshift graveyards, an ever-present reminder of the horror of the war.

As we moved towards the Neretva River, what once must have been a beautiful riverside walk now seemed to lie wounded in various states of recuperation. We came to where the old bridge used to stand. It was destroyed in 1993 during the worst of the urban battle. While the old bridge's stone foundations were still visible on each of the riverbanks, there remained nothing more than a hastily constructed metal suspension footbridge. In comparison to the old bridge—an architectural wonder that had drawn visitors from around the world—this ugly utilitarian substitute was surely an embarrassment for the city, that once had so much pride centered on the centuries-old bridge.

We moved onto the footbridge, unobtrusively positioned ourselves some distance from one another, and began to offer prayers of peace and reconciliation for the city and the country.

Lord, [one prayed,] *instead of this bridge, please raise up believers who will be a new bridge of reconciliation between the various ethnic groups here in Mostar.*

[Another's heartfelt cry was,] *Lord, instead of an old bridge as a landmark for this city, may Jesus and his name be the future landmark for Mostar.*

After some twenty minutes of praying, which included prayers for those passing by, we crossed over to walk and pray quietly in another portion of the Muslim section on the west side that directly abuts the river. As we walked among the ruins of what had once been a very influential area of Mostar, we saw that a destroyed and abandoned five-star hotel, the best in all of Bosnia, was slowly being overtaken by weeds. An orphanage was significantly damaged: a café, destroyed; and a mosque, ruined beyond repair. The destruction was all encompassing.

After a nice lunch, during which the Lord decided to bring showers to Mostar, we headed back to the guest house for a brief period of rest before the evening service began. Kjell Sjoberg rose after a brief rest and headed outside to find a secluded place to pray and to focus on what he would be sharing in the evening's service. No doubt his reflection on the events of the day reinforced his desire to bring a message of reconciliation and peace among the peoples.

Pastor Kresonja began the evening service with a few words of welcome and then shared that as of the day before (August 17, 1995), Agape Church had begun its second year of ministry. He reminded the group of the Lord's faithfulness and recounted how they had begun their ministry two years earlier with a service of baptism in which eight individuals had been baptized into the fellowship of believers. He then invited the participants to stand and join together in a time of worship. The worship team, which had been increased by the addition of a talented young woman who played the violin, began to lead us in worship. We excitedly stood up, lifting our voices together to the Lord.

Pastor Kresonja led the group in a time of grateful prayer and then invited Kjell Sjoberg to come and share. Kjell spoke with his usual calm intensity, and Pastor Kresonja faithfully translated his words. Asserting that the hand of the Lord moves when his people confess their sins and become reconciled to one another, Kjell moved from story to story, describing how he had experienced the Lord's mighty work based on prayer and reconciliation. He told of situations in the Congo (formerly Zaire), Brazil, Spain, Cambodia, and Australia. Interspersed with Scripture, Kjell's forty-minute message established a solid foundation of encouragement that the Lord would indeed work among those who diligently seek his face as they were reconciled with one another. Kjell then led the group in prayer, entreating the Lord to stop the ethnic cleansing and bring peace to the land.

As Kjell closed his Bible and returned to his seat, it was obvious that the people had been moved by his message. Pastor Kresonja asked the worship team to come forward and lead in a song. During this song, the Holy Spirit continued to stir many who were already touched by Kjell's message.

John then went to the podium and announced, "God is not finished with us yet." Moving in obedience to the Holy Spirit, he continued: "There might be some here tonight who have something against another, something similar to those in the stories Kjell shared. Who would like to be a representative and speak words of reconciliation to others among us?"

The room stood still. Then, as many searched through their damaged hearts for the strength to respond, a woman from the rear of the room rose in answer to the request. "Thank you for your love and peace," she began. "I love each nation represented here and I pray for each by name. On behalf of the Serbian nation, forgive us of our wrong. Forgive us so that others will love you. Help each other receive my words and prayers on behalf of the Serbian nation." Thirteen other Serbs then stood in solidarity.

John looked at the faces in the crowd and addressed those who were Croat and Muslim. "Will you grant forgiveness?" he asked. In unison they responded, "Yes, we will forgive them." Then, as fifteen to twenty other Croats stood and extended forgiveness to Serbs and Muslims, a representative began, "Forgive us for sins done in this war that have hurt all nations. There is all power for forgiveness in his name. Heavenly Father, we glorify your name."

Before John needed to extend the invitation again, five former Muslim women stood, and one began to share: "Thank you for showing us the truth. I believe in the risen King. There is authority in the name of Jesus and in this name I proclaim freedom from all occult and demonic influences: curses, unforgiveness, pains. We repent of the sins we have caused as a Muslim nation. We give glory to Jesus in this. Amen."

"Are there others?" John asked, giving plenty of time for the Holy Spirit to work.

At this time, I felt that someone from America needed to repent of the sin of standing by and letting these atrocities happen. As I began to write a note to pass to John indicating this while at the same time listening to the confessions taking place, I suddenly broke down and began to weep from sorrow at how the U.S. had failed these people. While I was weeping, Tommi motioned to John and communicated to him that she felt I was the one who should confess on behalf of the U.S.

The next thing I realized, John was calling on me to stand and lead in prayer on behalf of those from the United States. As I started, all I could focus on was the gravity of it all—the deaths, the sorrow, the atrocities. All, it seemed, could have at some point been prevented if the U.S. and the international community had intervened. In broken sentences I began to pray: "We from the United States, Lord, are so sorry because our nation has stood by and done nothing to stop the killing. Lord, please, please forgive us."

59

Brian Mills then stood and, with a repentant heart, asked for forgiveness on behalf of Europe and the UN.

A man in the audience who was a former Croatian soldier stood from the back of the room and continued this time of repentance:

> Four years ago I was a soldier in the army on the Croatian side. I am thankful to God that I did not take a rifle and shoot others, even though I did make damage anyhow. In one way I hated all the other nations except for the Croats. I thought I was doing the right thing in being a soldier. Then I met Jesus Christ two years later and realized my mistake. I heard they killed my grandma and grandpa, and I, too, realized that I had brought pain and suffering to other nations as well. I am convinced of this, but I now have a different attitude—I am without hatred. I really believe God can use me among other soldiers. I would like to ask forgiveness for the pain I have caused all.

As he sat down, John looked out and saw a woman making her way to the podium. She humbly began to speak:

> My husband is a Serb. God has saved our marriage. God has used us to bless other nations. Whenever you are sent, you are to be a light for other nations. I pray to you, Lord, that you touch all those who are refugees in foreign nations. I also pray that those who are conquerors would receive your name. Bless them also in the name of Jesus Christ. Stop every nation from blaming and holding unforgiveness around the world. I thank you for this possibility, Lord. Cleanse us and set us free. Give us your power and glory. Amen.

John then shared with the group that each person needed to go to another from a different ethnic group and personally ask them for forgiveness. For some, this was a most difficult task. However, slowly at first, we all began to move around the room confessing, asking for forgiveness, and extending forgiveness. We hugged and wept together, asking the Lord to heal and to move in our lives.

As I moved around the room, a smile and a simple nod of acceptance told me that forgiveness was granted. For the next ten to fifteen minutes, the Holy Spirit moved mightily as hugs and tears flowed and forgiveness filled the room.

Pastor Kresonja then came to the podium and began to summarize the evening. "Here at our church we are at the cutting edge of the work of reconciliation and love for our neighbors around us," he said. "May the Lord allow us to continue in our work."

He drew the evening to a close in prayer, but before his dismissal, he reminded all that Sunday morning service began at 9:00 A.M. After a brief time of fellowship, we headed back to the guest house—somewhat weary, but blessed because of the Lord's goodness shown to us that evening.

Vickitsa had again generously prepared an enjoyable dinner of chicken, french fries, fresh tomato salad, and juice. It was past 9:30 P.M., and we were quite hungry. Following our meal, it wasn't too long until the eight of us living in the three-bedroom guest house headed off to our rooms for a much-needed night of rest.

Shortly after 4:00 A.M., I woke and began to talk with the Lord about my concern for our safety as we traveled to Tuzla the coming Monday morning. Klaus was a young German who had previously been the pastor for the Agape Church in Tuzla, but who now worked on the humanitarian assistance side of Agape, providing relief to the needy. He had traveled down from Tuzla two weeks earlier and mentioned to us that for 75 meters on the road, passing vehicles were subject to both visibility from the Serbs and periodic sniper fire. This would be the very road we would travel. I knew full well that there needed to be unity in our team, and this caused a genuine concern that my restlessness might bring disunity to the group.

"Lord," I pleaded, "please take my fear away and give me that peace which you have given to the others. You have uniquely called me to come here to Bosnia to minister, and I desire to do this with all my heart. Master, please give me your peace." With that, I dozed off for a few more minutes of sleep.

SUNDAY, AUGUST 20, 1995

After a hurried bite to eat, we gathered at Agape Church early so we could entreat the Lord in prayer concerning the morning service. We sought hard after him in those brief moments, asking humbly that he would bless all who would come with his presence.

Pastor Kresonja welcomed all to the service and invited Tommi and me to come and lead in worship. Pastor Kresonja remained as a translator; as we shared the words of songs in English, he would quickly translate. All immediately jumped to their feet, ready and willing to worship the Lord.

The first song was "Be Still and Know That I Am God," which was sung through in English twice. We then shared the words to "God Is So Good"—first in English, then in Swahili, which brought smiles to the faces of all due to the difficulty of pronunciation of some of the words. The Spanish verse was picked up quite easily.

After finishing with these three languages, we began to move on to the next song when someone from the audience mentioned that theirs was not included. We were red faced for not including their own language but joyful because of the ease at which people felt free to speak up. All joined in excitedly as Tommi and I led the group one more time in Serbo-Croatian.

Brian was invited to give the morning message. He thanked everyone for the opportunity to share and began by opening the Word to Isaiah 6:3: "And they [the angels who were in the presence of the Lord] were calling to one another: 'Holy, holy, holy is the LORD Almighty; the whole earth is full of his glory.'" Brian affirmed that God was at work in Bosnia-Hercegovina. He described several places around the world where the Lord was at work bringing reconciliation and peace. He gave personal testimonies concerning Ireland, reconciliation between Germans and Poles, and how a renewal movement was taking place in Belarus. Brian encouraged all present with John 13:34–35, admonishing us to love one another as Jesus commanded.

After Brian concluded his message, others stood to share their thoughts on the need for prayer and reconciliation. Vickitsa, who was our cook at the guest house, came forward to the podium to lead in prayer. With Pastor Kresonja translating she began:

Thank you, Lord, for this beautiful country. There are many ethnic groups, and lots of other groups of people here, and we are all your children. As your child, Lord, and a child of the Serbian nation, I pray, I beg, that you help those who are in darkness to come out from their darkness. Break the strongholds and set them free from darkness. Lord, I first ask Jesus to forgive the Serbian nation. Please forgive all. We cannot understand this darkness because it is too big. Have mercy over the Serbian nation; forgive; make this a land of reconciliation. Be glorified also in the Muslim people. I thank you that I can pray and you will hear my prayer. In the name of Jesus, I am thankful to you. Amen.

As Vickitsa returned to her seat, the Holy Spirit continued to move around the room and pierce the hearts of others, including an Australian who rose and prayed in English, saying, "Lord, you know how I, too, live in the divided nation of Australia. Forgive my nation for our century-old sin against the Aboriginal people. Bring divine reconciliation in the high places. Reconcile all people in Australia to God. Amen."

Pastor Kresonja drew the congregation together in prayer, asking the Lord to again help all to minister reconciliation wherever they can. With those remarks, he closed the meeting, inviting everyone to return at 7:00 P.M. for the evening service. We soon departed Agape, and after stopping at a typical Bosnian restaurant for lunch, we returned to the guest house so Kjell could pack his belongings in anticipation of leaving. Antun and Stamko were heading back to Zagreb and could drop Kjell off at the airport in Split. There were warm Christian hugs and words of love for Kjell, Antun, and Stamko as they headed off for their long journey. Kjell's contribution to the prayer team was a major one, and the rest of the team members felt it was a privilege that they could serve on the same team with him.

It was a beautiful Sunday afternoon in Mostar, and Brian asked Tommi and me if we wanted to come along for a walk in the beautiful day that the Lord had graced us with. We headed off uphill past a few children playing in the street, but soon we were engrossed in prayer as we walked. Brian started to pray what was on each of our hearts concerning what the Lord wanted us to do there in Bosnia.

> *Lord,* [Brian began,] *we sense that there is more you want us to do here in Mostar, more of what you want us to accomplish on this trip. Please let us know your perfect will for us here.*

Each of us led out with similar prayers in our own words. There was a sense that even though the weekend was without parallel in our lives, the issues surrounding us in Mostar were gigantic. We asked the Lord not to let us depart Bosnia without allowing us to fulfill his purpose in our lives. Our hearts were heavy, not from anything that had happened thus far on the trip, but because of the hopelessness that most of the inhabitants of Mostar felt. We wanted so much to be an encouragement to our newfound brothers and sisters. As we walked, we passed a fairly large house that had been destroyed by bombs. The building was totally demolished, and it lay mortally wounded in a neighborhood where others like it were just slightly damaged. Our hearts ached again and again when we came across such destruction.

As we walked, talked, and prayed, the route we chose led uphill to a place where there was an open area overlooking the city. We paused and reflected on the carnage below, caused by each of the three warring parties who have devastated this land with death and destruction. The word that came to our hearts was King David's when he saw Goliath taunting the armies of God: "Who is this uncircumcised Philistine that he should defy the armies of the living God?" (1 Sam. 17:26). It was as if the Scripture was also saying to us, "Who are those who inflict such atrocities on the innocents who live in the city below?" With that, we began to rebuke the powers of destruction operating through each of the three warring peoples.

Lord, [we prayed,] *in the name of Jesus, we come against the powers of evil working through the Bosnian Croats, Muslims, and Serbs to bring destruction in this land. We pray you will bring down the strongholds of evil that have worked through them to cause the innocent such pain and sorrow during this reign of death and destruction. In the name of Jesus, we break the stranglehold this evil power has on this land.*

In the spirit of David and as a prophetic action, we were moved to take stones representing each one of the warring parties, and during our rebuke, we tossed them down toward the devastation below.

As we were praying, I noticed that a woman across the road had come out of her apartment and was watching us. Not to cause a scene, I mentioned her presence to the others, and we naturally began to move on, walking and praying. The road ended, so we crossed over the opposite side and began to walk back down the hill. The woman was still standing outside her apartment, and as we approached her, I began to share with her how much we enjoyed the beauty of the hills surrounding Mostar. Because she spoke only Serbo-Croatian and we were without a translator, hand signals and voice intonations were the primary communication tools.

Looking upward to a UN outpost approximately 750 meters almost straight up on top of the mountain next to us, she motioned that it was the Chetniks who had destroyed the city, and that she had lost three of her relatives to the war. With that remembrance, she began to cry.

Tommi placed her hand on the woman's shoulder and shared how very sorry she was for her. The softness of Tommi's voice spoke louder than the words that were not being understood, and in this way, a special ministry of compassion began to unfold. The woman, whose name was Angelica, then invited the three of us into her little apartment for some kafka and showed us some pictures of relatives who had been killed in the war. We told her we were Christians and asked if we could pray for her.

Father, [Tommi began,] *we lift Angelica up to you. We pray that you would bless her hurts, touch her emptiness caused by the loss of those who are close to her. Heal her wounds, Lord God, as you minister peace to her life. Lord, love her. May she come to know you in a full and deep way.*

[Another continued,] *Father, your Word says that if one sojourns in a strange town and someone invites them in and shows them hospitality, that we are to leave our blessing in their home. Father God, we bless this home in Jesus' name with peace, with salvation that only Jesus Christ can bring, and with the love of Christ. We pray this in Jesus' name. Amen.*

At the conclusion of our prayer, Angelica responded with a question, "Evangelistas?"

We smiled and said together, "Yes, we are Evangelicals." We then pointed to our watches and said, "We must be going." In our best sign language, we asked the Lord's blessing again on her home and thanked her for the coffee. We then left the little apartment, walked down the concrete walkway to the street, and began to head back to the guest house.

Our steps were animated as we walked the one or two kilometers back in a mostly downhill direction, thanking the Lord as we went for giving us the gift of ministering to Angelica and being ministered to by her. As we hurried on, I sensed the Lord had used our visit with Angelica to give us a special blessing. I tried to share this impression with Tommi and Brian: "You know what I think the Lord is saying to us by giving us the gift of ministry to Angelica this afternoon? Remember when we walked up here, we said that the Lord wasn't finished with us yet, and we had agreed that there was more to do? In my spirit, I believe that our encounter with Angelica this afternoon is the Lord saying to us, 'What you are doing is what I want you to do. It is for this reason that I brought you on this trip. Just keep on keeping on. Continue to do what you are doing.' This is what I believe he wants us to do."

In gratefulness, we began to thank the Lord for his kindness towards us.

Lord God, [Brian began,] *thank you for today, for your grace and mercy, for the gift of meeting Angelica, and for allowing us to be with her and to pray with her. Father, bring salvation to her home and peace to her heart because of the loss of her relatives. Amen.*

[Tommi continued,] *Lord God, we thank you for bringing us here, for speaking to us so that we would come on this walk this afternoon. Thank you for the gift you gave us in meeting Angelica. Bless her, Lord, we pray. Amen.*

We arrived at the guest house seven or eight minutes after six o'clock. "Hurry, we are late for prayer before the evening service," John exhorted.

We all quickly changed our clothes so that within ten minutes we were all in the Peugeot backing out of the driveway for Agape Church.

The meeting before the service was to discuss some of the logistics surrounding our next morning's trip to Tuzla. We talked about the number of people and vehicles going, and where and when we would obtain petrol for the journey north. It was decided that we needed to fill up the Peugeot sometime after Sunday evening service so we could leave as early as possible in the morning.

Still concerned about the one portion of road visible to Serb snipers, I cautioned one last time, "I would like to make sure that whatever route we take when we get close to the Serb lines, that we take the best route." Pastor Kresonja assured us that no one was going to take any unnecessary risks.

Shortly before seven o'clock, the worship team came into the conference room where we were gathered for prayer, asking the Lord to bless this Sunday evening service and to anoint John as the speaker. We then went in to be with the others so that the service could begin.

Pastor Kresonja welcomed a full congregation to the meeting and commented on God's faithfulness to all during the last few days. He also asked the congregation to pray over us as we traveled up to Tuzla in the morning for the purpose of ministering healing and reconciliation there.

After leading in prayer, Pastor Kresonja invited the Agape worship team to lead us in a most uplifting time of praise and worship. Joining the worship team again was the young violinist. Her improvisation as we sang contributed richly to our worship.

John was introduced as our speaker for the evening and proceeded both to sum up our times together and to reinforce the power of intercessory prayer:

> *Slavabogu* [the Serbo-Croatian word for "Praise the Lord"]! We have had a marvelous time here with you over these last few evenings, and for that we are grateful to God. Tonight, I would like to begin with where we started on Friday evening, with 2 Chronicles 7:14: "If my people, who are called by my name, will humble themselves and pray and seek my face and turn from their wicked ways, then will I hear from heaven and will forgive their sin and will heal their land." We have shared that this verse is foundational to a life of prayer, is crucial for reconciliation and healing, and is most important in the work of missions. Through prayer—the most strategic weapon we have—the control of the enemy is weakened so that entire people groups can then more freely come to the Lord.

John exhorted us to live a life of praise and prayer, saying that it is prayer with praise that brings victory. When he had finished, Pastor Kresonja led the group in prayer and then closed the evening with the benediction.

After the service, we all said good-bye to many new friends and acquaintances we had made over the last three days in Mostar. I was then called into the church office because my wife, Brenda, was on the telephone. I tried to share in a few brief moments what we had seen and experienced, but in my tears and brokenness, I must have sounded all but unintelligible. After saying good-bye, we then got into the Peugeot and headed back to the guest house, where Vickitsa had again whipped up a tasty dinner. Not long after, we retired for the evening.

GOING THE DISTANCE IN PRAYER

MONDAY, AUGUST 21, 1995

We rose quite early, had some coffee and bread for breakfast, and loaded our gear and some extra water containers for the quick trip to Agape Church. At Agape, we first saw Klaus busy shifting boxes and bags around in the back of the red pickup truck that would carry most of the belongings for those of us in the two other vehicles that were part of the caravan to Tuzla. Dieter and Ljerka Eymann were a newlywed couple who had just returned from their honeymoon after having been married just two weeks before. Ljerka had previously been the secretary at Agape Church. She was the one who had been shot at by the Muslim man who attacked the church because his daughter had come to Christ. She and Dieter were traveling in a small Nissan, with another woman and her daughter as passengers.

In all, there were three vehicles traveling to Tuzla that day. Klaus and Pastor Kresonja would lead in the red pickup, followed by Ljerka driving the small Nissan. John would drive the Peugeot with Tommi, Brian, and myself. Before departing, those who came to see us off gathered with us and prayed over us.

We headed across to the east side of Mostar and on to the main road north to Sarajevo. We hadn't traveled far before we were stopped at a checkpoint controlled by Croat army soldiers. We needed to produce our passports. This was a Croat village named Potoci, located on the outskirts of Mostar. We could see plainly by the blackened, empty buildings that the destruction of this village was complete. As soon as we moved on, we began our intercessory prayers for healing in the land in general, and for Potoci specifically.

Lord, [someone began,] *bring healing to this land.*

[Someone else continued,] *Lord, for the lives that have been destroyed as represented by these buildings, we pray that you would bring peace to those who have been harmed in this village. Please touch and strengthen any who are still living in this area.*

Lord, [another said,] *please help them to forgive those who caused this destruction and not to harbor hate in their hearts.*

Continuing north, the road came alongside the Neretva River. As the canyon walls began to narrow, we soon came across bridges that had been destroyed and where vehicle remnants had fallen into the river below. A new road was cut into the mountainside and back down the canyon, joining the tarmac again. It created a temporary but difficult-to-travel bypass.

Some kilometers further upstream, the river widened into the lower portion of a lake, which, according to our map, was named Jablanicko Ezero. The scenery here was extremely beautiful, causing us to lift thankful hearts before our Creator:

Heavenly Father, this is such a beautiful land. We thank you for creating its beauty. Father, bring peace to this beautiful land. Bring your love, and bring reconciliation so this portion of your creation is not harmed or destroyed. Amen.

In addition to prayers and intercessions for the land, we often broke out in spontaneous songs of joy and adoration. Some of the popular praise songs we loved to sing together were "Lord, I Lift Your Name on High," "This Is the Day That the Lord Has Made," and "The Joy of the Lord Is My Strength." These songs lifted our hearts as we moved back and forth between the contrasting vistas of total destruction and unspoiled beauty. It also seemed to help us keep our focus on God.

Near the town of Tarcin there was a large UN roadblock that prevented us from continuing further. The road led directly into Sarajevo. At that time Sarajevo was under siege, and entry was not permitted. We were diverted onto a dirt road to the west and around Sarajevo. After a short distance along this road, we stopped, got out of our vehicles, stretched out our hands to the east toward Sarajevo some twenty miles in the distance, and began to pray.

> *Lord, we call on you to overthrow the principalities and powers that hold this city and its inhabitants captive,* [someone prayed].

> [Another added,] *Lord, raise up your standard in this city. Place your angels on the mountains that surround the city. Give UN, NATO, and other leaders unity of spirit in this land.*

> [Still another continued,] *Lord, place your way in the hearts of the people who still live in Sarajevo, and bring peace to their hearts and to all the ethnic groups in this country.*

After several minutes of prayer, we continued on. The dirt road at times got quite muddy, very steep, and hard to navigate due to sharp rocks and lurking potholes. Progress was also periodically slow due to large lorry transports carrying goods (and presumably war materials) along the same route.

As we then rounded one bend, we had to stop quickly because UN construction workers were scraping out portions of the road and doing some widening because of rain damage. As we waited for the scraper to move, we entered into prayer for these UN workers.

> *Father, for these who have come from different countries on behalf of peace, we pray that you would bless them and encourage them,* [someone prayed]. *Help them not to see their jobs as hopeless or useless, but rather as ones that contribute to the objective of peace.*

We continued through the towns of Kresovo and Kiseljak. At times we were less than two kilometers away from Serb gun emplacements. We soon descended into the town of Visoko, which itself was a short distance from Serb lines. As we entered the town, we saw a number of military men walking the streets in camouflaged uniforms with weapons slung over their shoulders. The shops and the city stores had sandbags and logs placed against their glass windows to limit damage during shellings. This lovely town was situated against the hillside, and when out from under the cloud of war, was surely among the most beautiful little subalpine communities in all of Europe.

We stopped, parked our vehicles, and headed into a small restaurant for lunch. A husband-and-wife team owned the restaurant and were very friendly and helpful.

After lunch, we returned to our vehicles, continued slowly through town, and passed under the main highway to Sarajevo as we headed uphill toward the town of Breza. The road was quite rocky, and John had to maneuver often to avoid being swallowed by large potholes. According to the map, the road did not exist. As the war had progressed throughout the country, it created areas of danger near the front, so new roads had to be cut around the front. As we entered the village of Breza, we passed a cemetery that contained mass graves with freshly turned dirt. It appeared that many from Breza had been among the casualties of more than four years of war.

From Breza, the road led us back up into the mountains and wooded areas. Scattered throughout the forests were open areas containing verdant green farmlands with pointed yellow haystacks standing ten to twelve feet in the air and surrounded by picket fences. Low-hanging clouds topped the mountains, giving evidence that we had increased our elevation. In this scenic rural area there was no sign of war at all.

We soon came to the town of Yarez where there were large factories idle, no doubt rendering many unemployed. Knowing we were passing through an important industrial section of Bosnia, we began to pray.

Heavenly Father, we can see that this industrial zone is the heart of this country, but at the moment it lies silent. We pray for your presence here.

Father God, [another continued,] *in Jesus' name, we pray that you would bring back industry to this area of Bosnia, and that in your time, you would raise up godly workers for these factories.*

Lord, plant your standard in this beautiful area. May these factories bring health and prosperity back to Bosnia in the name of Jesus Christ. Amen.

The grounds of one of the factories must have had 250 white UNPROFOR (United Nations Protection Force) vehicles on it. It was a regional staging center, with outposts surrounded by sandbags, razor wire, and manned by people standing guard with machine guns.

Also in Yarez, we saw many women and children walking along the streets. At a stoplight, Brian reached out the window and handed one of the children a piece of gum. No doubt many of these women had husbands and sons who were out on the front lines and involved in the conflict. As this became aware to us, we again continued our prayers.

Heavenly Father, [someone began,] *many of the men of Yarez have gone off to war. We therefore pray your protection around these women, that you would strengthen them, that you would encourage them, that you would love them, and that you would give them hope.*

Father, for those who have lost husbands — [another continued, but soon began to sob, causing others to weep as well at the sight of these who looked so grief stricken and lonely.] *Lord, for those who have lost husbands, please be their husband. Raise up a standard for Jesus in this town. May these people who are Muslim come to know you. Father, God, touch their lives we pray in Jesus' name.*

Leaving Yarez, we continued north along an even more quiet rural road than we had been traveling on thus far and came to a little town named Dabostica. After Dabostica, we continued into a town called Ribnica. It was here where we finally left the dirt road and rejoined the tarmac. As we were coming out of the mountains and waiting to go around another vehicle and get once again on smooth road, a number of boys came up to the car to say hello. We tried to chat with them since one knew English pretty well.

As we continued driving, we began to lift up these boys in prayer:

Father, for these children, touch their lives. May they grow up and not experience war, but experience peace in their homeland. Father God Almighty, we pray that these youngsters would come to know peace.

[Another one continued,] *May these boys grow up healthy and nourished. May they come to know you and to serve you, Lord. Plant your church near here so that they may grow up under your teaching, Lord. Amen.*

Just a short distance after Ribnica, we pulled off the tarmac for a break and to prepare for the fact that just ahead of us was the area where the Serb snipers would be within the closest range. We gathered together as a group and began to pray.

Lord God Almighty, [one began,] we pray for your protection as we begin this dangerous part of our journey. We entreat you to please blind the eyes of those who would seek to kill and destroy.

Lord, [another prayed,] we are in three vehicles, so we pray that you would protect each one. Go before us and also be our rear guard. Watch over us; send your angels to watch over us. In Jesus' name. Amen.

The actual area where the Serbs had their positions was located just before the town of Banovici, at Banovici cutoff No. 2. At this point we left the tarmac and went up into the hills via a dirt road. The route snaked up through the hills and through a wooded area that, for the most part, kept us out of sight. Periodically, however, there were open areas where we were plainly visible to those across the valley. "The joy of the Lord is our strength; the joy of the Lord is our strength," we sang together.

As we continued along the Banovici cutoff, we came across a couple of Pakistani UN peacekeepers sitting in their jeep watching out for snipers. We continued to pray:

> *Lord, thank you for being with us on this road. Continue to protect us as we journey in this area. Hold back violence from coming near us, we pray.*

Soon the dirt road came back to the tarmac, and we were able to continue on towards Tuzla. We had traveled for almost eight hours and had passed through twenty-five military checkpoints.

Our journey from Mostar to Tuzla left us weary as we checked into the Tuzla Hotel. Later, we discovered our rooms were located on the east side of the hotel, facing the Serb positions. There were dark-out curtains in each room so that if an alert came, the hotel could black out its lights quickly, not wanting to become an easy target for Serb gunners.

SALT AND LIGHT
TUESDAY, AUGUST 22, 1995

We awoke the next morning ready to do the work the Lord had prepared for us—to be salt and light in Tuzla, a town that is 96 percent Muslim, 2 percent Serb, and 2 percent Croat. Ironically, the name *Tuzla* means salt. We were told that the town is actually located on top of a salt mine. It's a major industrial area for Bosnia.

After breakfast, we drove to the Agape Humanitarian Agency and Church located less than a kilometer away. Pastor Nenad described some of the work that Agape was doing in Tuzla. He shared that he had come to Bosnia from Zagreb, Croatia, three weeks earlier, and as pastor, would continue the ministry that Klaus had started as the previous pastor. Klaus would do the work of the Agape Humanitarian Agency even though there were extremely limited funds. At the meeting was a man named Anti. Anti was with the Finnish Home Mission and attended Pastor Nenad's church. His responsibilities with the Finnish Home Mission were to assist people to repair and rebuild their destroyed homes. Anti soon became a part of our group and joined in with the day's activities.

As we discussed the options for the day, a plan started to come together. We felt that meeting with some of the nonevangelical church leaders was important so that we could include them in our prayer for peace and reconciliation. Therefore, we would first make a courtesy call on Father Peter Malanoric, an abbot of the Franciscan order and the leader of the Catholic Church in the city.

Our ride into central Tuzla took only a few minutes, so it wasn't long before we arrived at the very large Catholic church where Father Malanoric served. It was decided that Klaus, Tommi, and I would walk around and pray while Pastor Nenad, Brian, John, Pastor Kresonja, and Anti went inside to see if a meeting could be arranged. As the group went in, Klaus, Tommi, and I proceeded to walk around the church and pray for the meeting—for unity, peace, and for the development of a good relationship between Father Peter and Pastor Nenad.

Tommi, who had been on several international prayer walks, encouraged us to be as open as possible to the leading of the Holy Spirit and to pray according to his leading. We prayed in earnest for a favorable meeting, for binding the enemy who would want to disrupt any attempts at unity, and for other things we discerned as we continued our walk.

After a few minutes, the group came out and indicated that they were not able to see Father Peter at this time, but they had an appointment for two o'clock that afternoon.

Across from the Catholic church was a Muslim mosque. Out of curiosity, we decided to go see what was inside. Thirty children and five or six women were praying and weeping—obviously weeping because family members, possibly husbands and fathers, had been either killed or seriously injured. The grounds in front of the mosque contained graves— some very old and some very fresh. We left feeling the sadness of those who were mourning, not only because we knew their loss was great in terms of their families, but also because the Prince of Peace was unknown to them.

The drive to the Orthodox church took only a few minutes. It was a magnificent and imposing domed structure. Again, our purpose was to make a courtesy call on the Orthodox church leadership and pray with them for peace and reconciliation in the land.

The Orthodox priests had left Tuzla some time before, and the church was now in the hands of three lay leaders. We were greeted by two of the leaders—Jean, who was a teacher in the church, and Vitomere who assisted with the relief and development portion of the work of the church. The third lay leader was Professor Dr. Caslav Jevremovic, a professor in mining technology at Tuzla University. He was supposed to arrive at the church shortly, so we were invited in to wait. Jean and Vitomere showed us into a conference room where we got to know one another, sharing such things as where we were from and why we had come to Bosnia.

At one end of the long table were Tommi, Pastors Nenad and Kresonja, Anti, and Brian. At the other end of the table visiting with Vitomere, who was sitting in a larger chair against the wall, were John and I. The group visiting with Jean found that he was a man full of compassion, who wanted reconciliation between the Orthodox, the Catholics, and the Bosnian Muslims. As warm feelings began to develop between Jean and Pastor Nenad, it soon became apparent that Jean, a professor who knew many government officials, might be able to assist Nenad by introducing him to some of the Tuzla government officials.

Vitomere was a self-proclaimed atheist. He said he was Serb, raised Orthodox, but was married to a Croatian woman. As John and I were chatting with Vitomere, we shared portions of Scripture to encourage his faith. Somewhere in the middle of our conversation, Vitomere softened a bit and shared that the one thing that concerned him most was where he would end up eternally.

Jesus said, "In my Father's house are many rooms; if it were not so, I would have told you. I am going there to prepare a place for you," I responded to this confession. "Vitomere, you don't have to be troubled about your eternal security."

Vitomere continued to soften. As the conversation moved along, Tommi sensed from across the room that the Lord wanted her to share a word with Vitomere. She began to pray for him, and as someone brought in kafka, Tommi came over and joined us in the conversation while John went to share with Jean and the others.

Tommi immediately began to share with Vitomere what the Lord had impressed her with. She said that the Lord was very pleased with him and proud of him for the way he had protected and provided for his wife and son during the war. Vitomere began to get tears in his eyes. Tommi continued to share that while God was pleased it was time for him to allow the Lord to protect him and his family. While he had done the best he could do, that self-reliant strength he exhibited in protecting his family needed to be given over to the Lord, who, instead, wanted his tenderness of his heart to be released. Tommi then asked if she could pray for him, asking the Lord to make himself real to him. Vitomere agreed, and Tommi and I began to pray.

Vitomere began to pray with us, and before we knew it, the Lord gave the increase with one new child entering the Kingdom. The work Klaus had done previously in befriending and sharing the Lord with Vitomere had born fruit at last. With tears and hugs, Tommi and I realized that the Lord's presence and blessing was suddenly most real to Vitomere.

After making arrangements to meet with Professor Jevremovic the next morning, we walked across the street from the Orthodox church, through a park, and into the city center of Tuzla proper. Quaint shops, cobblestone streets, and tiled roofs—all proclaimed that at one time this was an extremely beautiful portion of the city.

Bullet and shell holes, however, revealed the current situation, as did windows covered with black plastic and rubble from past shellings. In the street where the cobblestones had been disturbed and broken sat several containers of fresh flowers. On a wall nearby were the names and pictures of more than seventy young people who had been killed in an instant at this very spot some ninety days earlier. We listened intently as our guides detailed what had happened on that warm May evening: More than five hundred young people had gathered in the Tuzla town center to have a drink and chat with their friends. Certainly their talk must have focused on the war raging around them and how useless the UN peacekeepers had been in keeping the Serbs from moving their forces and artillery in and around them. Without any warning, a single inbound shell exploded near the front of a café, robbing Tuzla of still more of its youthful future.

Three months later, while we stood looking at the destruction that remained, we began to pray for the families and friends of those who had perished. We asked the Lord Jesus to reveal himself to those impacted by this disaster, to reign supreme over this city, and to bring peace into the hearts of those who have known only hopelessness.

Pastors Nenad and Kresonja then suggested that we go and pray in Old Tuzla, a small village where Tuzla started many years ago. It was located seven to eight kilometers closer to the battlefront, which required going through a checkpoint controlled by both the UN and the Bosnian government militia. By having Anti's Finnish Home Mission vehicle as part of our caravan and because we were traveling under so many different passports, a survey for humanitarian work was all that was needed for us to pass. As we proceeded, prayers for protection, for pushing back the enemy, and for the Spirit of God to work began in earnest.

Old Tuzla was much like many of the other villages in Bosnia. It had a town square surrounded by little shops with second-floor living accommodations and red tile roofs. Spreading out from the town center were a variety of farm homes, both large and small. At the town square was a familiar monument to the "freedom fighters" who had fought in years gone by. Three men of military age were there talking, and based on their slurred speech and outlandish behavior, seemed to be pretty far along the way to inebriation. We walked slowly down a dirt road leading out from the town square. As the Spirit prompted us with his concern for the town and its inhabitants, we prayed quietly in groups of twos and threes. When someone received a sense of discernment, it was shared, and we united our prayers along that line. A hay cart being pulled by two cows and ridden by five young boys came by. Upon seeing the foreigners with cameras, they quickly posed, and pictures were taken.

> [After they had passed, one of our group prayed,] *Lord, these boys are so young and they live in such darkness. By your Spirit, please allow them to grow up and know Jesus Christ as Lord and Savior,* [said another].

A few hundred meters up the road we could see the minaret of the town's mosque. It was a strikingly white, two-story building with a red clay roof. As we approached closer, we could see that the exterior of the mosque was marked by holes from small-arms fire. The stone retaining wall was cracked by shells, and some of the tombstones in the cemetery were also damaged.

> *Lord,* [someone began to pray,] *come and reign supreme here in this place of spiritual need. Break down any strongholds of darkness, and raise up workers for your harvest to come and bring life, the life that only Jesus Christ can bring.*

As we returned to the town square, some felt we needed to walk around the central monument and pray quietly for Christ's light to shine in this town.

The 2:00 P.M. appointment with Father Peter back at the Catholic church was quickly approaching, so our trip back was somewhat faster than the drive out. During the meeting with Father Peter and his assistant, the team shared the prayer burden they had for Bosnia, how God had moved during the meetings in Mostar, and plans for the meeting with local believers that was scheduled for that evening. The Franciscan brothers told us about the war and about the many privations they and their congregations had suffered. They expressed their warm appreciation for the prayer effort and were especially grateful as Brian Mills closed their time together in prayer for the nation's peace and also for their ministry.

Meanwhile, outside, Klaus mentioned that the central marketplace located just down the street from the church was the center of a lot of illegal trafficking of wares. We proceeded through the market (only partially occupied because it was supposed to be closed on Tuesdays), silently petitioning the Prince of Truth to reign over that square and to protect the innocent who by necessity needed to shop among thieves. Walking farther along the street behind the church, we passed by a refugee center where many of the refugees coming into Tuzla from surrounding villages were placed until the government could find other housing for them. Heartfelt cries of intercession erupted for the poor and lost among them.

Throughout the planning for the trip to Tuzla, we hoped that there would be an opportunity to visit and in some way minister to some of the refugees who had come in from Srebrenica and other places. During the previous month, about seven thousand men from Srebrenica had been captured by Serb forces, and their location was still unknown. (We later discovered they would never return because they had been massacred and buried in mass graves.) Their families, mostly women and children, were waiting at the air base for word of their loved ones. Anti, our Finnish relief contact, indicated there was a possibility we could gain entry through the contacts he had, so he went ahead and inquired with the UN. He learned that there was an opportunity to go after our meeting with Father Peter. Time was a factor because the start of the evening's service at Agape was 5:00 P.M. (This was so that the people could return to their homes prior to the curfew that began each night just after dusk.)

At Anti's apartment/office on the sixth floor of a high-rise apartment, we met Dario, a twenty-two-year-old Bosnian Christian who worked with Anti at the Finnish Home Mission. Dario agreed to be our driver, so we climbed into his four-wheel drive vehicle. As we headed for the air base, Dario began to share his story with us. He was a former Muslim who had been drafted into the army four years earlier when he was eighteen years old. He had spent a lot of time on the front lines and had been wounded three times. There was still shrapnel in his body. His mother began to pray earnestly for her son and was astonished to find that he had become a Christian while still in the army. Then, in what he termed a miraculous development, for the war was still on, he was separated from the army and started to fellowship at Agape with his mother. Dario stuttered when he spoke, a condition that began to plague him just prior to his leaving the army.

The gateway to the air base was guarded by UN personnel, and there were many military and security forces about. Dario described the humanitarian purpose for which we had come, and the guards quickly allowed us through. The road passed by the foot of a tall, white guard tower that had been erected by the UN. Many of the other structures we saw were surrounded with razor wire and had guards posted. After moving along on the perimeter road for several hundred meters, Dario took us right out onto the runway of the air base and showed us what was nothing short of a phenomenal sight.

Off on each side of the runway, several yards into the dirt and mud, were hundreds of round UN white tents approximately twenty feet across and seven feet high. Located up and along the edge of the tarmac were lighting towers used to provide nighttime illumination, and stainless steel water tanks to provide potable drinking water. Five to seven city buses were parked on the edge of the tarmac for the purpose of resettling refugees off the air base in safer shelters in various other locations around Tuzla. This was necessary because just off the northeast end of the air base, there was a small hill from which Serb artillery had been shelling the air base periodically. They could begin shelling at any moment.

Seven thousand refugees, mostly women and their children coming from Srebrenica, had been brought to this spot during the last thirty days. Three thousand of the refugees had already been relocated to other centers, leaving the remaining four thousand near the runway portion of the air base. These were not habitual homeless people, but everyday Bosnian citizens who had been suddenly caught up in the turmoil of battle and deported from their homeland. Some had been prosperous, owning fine things and living in comfortable homes. Now they were alone, not knowing if their husbands, sons, or brothers were still alive. They had already witnessed appalling scenes: tortures, rapes, and killings. There seemed to be no answers to their incessant questions concerning the fate of their loved ones. What's more, they were well aware that although they were reasonably comfortable situated in the UN tents late in the summer, the tents would not keep out the oncoming cold Bosnia winter.

Dario stopped alongside the edge of the tarmac, and a crowd of about thirty women and children soon appeared. Tommi had brought some small soaps and shampoos, so we made our way through the crowd sharing them with those who had virtually nothing except for the clothes they were wearing. None of us were really ready for what we saw. There were so many who were so needy. A very outspoken woman who was extremely upset about the conditions described to John how she felt they were forgotten by the Bosnian government. Dario translated for John and Brian as they tried to comfort her. Another young woman who was holding her one-month-old child indicated that he was born on the day she arrived at the air base after fleeing Srebrenica. She did not know the fate of her husband. Such stories made us weep along with these stranded, suffering families. A twelve-year-old girl who spoke some English helped Tommi communicate with some of the other women.

Tommi met an older woman named Hildic. She was sixty-seven years old, and because of the events in Srebrenecia, she had no family. The UN had moved out all who used to reside in Hildic's tent, leaving her alone. A friend of Tommi's back in Colorado had given Tommi a gold bracelet to give to someone in need as a reminder that she was not alone and that someone back in the U.S.A. was praying for her to know God's love and protection. Tommi knew the recipient was to be Hildic. She gave the bracelet to her and told her that whenever she felt frightened or alone, to look at it and remember that God's presence would never leave her, and that Tommi and a woman named Carolyn were praying for her. Hildic's face filled with gratitude.

Also during this time, I met an elderly woman with a black shawl covering her head and shoes that were exceptionally shoddy. Only her toes were in them. Her name was Imina, and her face seemed worn not only with age but also from the terror she had witnessed. Her eyes were filled with hopelessness. She shared with me her concern that her feet would freeze when winter came. She was there with her daughter, Fatima, but was afraid her husband, her sons, and Fatima's husband had all been killed. I was so deeply moved by Imina's words coming through our translator, that another set of words from years gone by entered my mind, "*I was sad when I had no shoes until I saw a man who had no feet.*" Without thinking further, I bent down, taking off my own shoes and placing Imina's feet into them. She initially laughed due to their size, but after cinching them up, they seemed to fit and would afford considerably more protection than the ones she had. Imina was so grateful; she thanked and blessed me for my kindness. Some standing nearby asked Imina, Fatima, and me to stand for a photo. This disturbed me because this simple gesture was attracting too much attention. We then said good-bye, and I walked barefooted back to the car, weeping as I went.

> *O God*, [I sobbed,] *take care of Imina and Fatima. They have nothing, and they need you, Lord. We have so much, and these people have so little. Help me to understand what you are trying to show me here.*

As we started to leave, Tommi saw another older woman struggling with her bundles, trying to cross the mud patches and get to a waiting bus. She was frustrated, knowing that the bus held her only hope for leaving the airstrip. John went over and lifted her possessions, carrying them to the tarmac several meters away. She thanked him, crying as she mentioned that she had lost two family members in the fighting.

In tears, and somewhat emotionally spent, we returned to Dario's vehicle and traveled back into town. Dario drove quickly so we would arrive in time for the start of the evening's meeting at Agape Church. When we arrived, Pastor Nenad introduced us, and we greeted the little crowd of some forty believers. Klaus then grabbed his guitar and led us in a few Croatian praise songs that were catchy and fun to sing. Of course, worship can take place in any language and by people coming together from many backgrounds, but it seemed as if the worship that occurred in that place—surrounded by so much death and destruction—also made the presence of the Spirit of the Lord more tangible. As we lifted up praises to him, the Lord began to bless those at Agape Church.

Pastor Nenad said a few words of encouragement to the group that night and then introduced John as the evening's speaker. John went to the podium:

> What would you ask for if you could ask for anything? *Mir!* [The Croat word for "peace" was the united response from the audience.] We have been reviewing the words from 2 Chronicles 7:14 where the Scripture states, "If my people, who are called by my name, will humble themselves and pray and seek my face and turn from their wicked ways, then will I hear from heaven and will forgive their sin and will heal their land." But before healing for the land can come from the Lord, forgiveness is needed between those who live in it. In the book of Matthew, chapter 18, verses 15 through 19, it indicates, "If your brother sins against you, go and show him his fault, just between the two of you. If he listens to you, you have won your brother over. But if he will not listen, take one or two others along, so that every matter may be established by the testimony of two or three witnesses. If he refuses to listen to them, tell it to the church; and if he refuses to listen even to the church, treat him as you would a pagan or a tax collector. I tell you the truth, whatever you bind on earth will be bound in heaven, and whatever you loose on earth will be loosed in heaven. Again, I tell you that if two of you on earth agree about anything you ask for, it will be done for you by my Father in heaven."

John stressed that the Lord God Almighty was wanting to heal Bosnia of the war and hatred that gripped it. For peace to come, we as believers needed to identify with the sins of our people, confess them, and be reconciled to those of other ethnic groups. According to God's promise, he will hear from heaven and will heal the land.

The invitation was simple: Who from among this company of forty-eight believers would be the first to step forward? Eyes looked around the room that included Croats, believers from a Muslim background, Serbs, Americans, Germans, one from Britain, and another from Finland—an ethnic kaleidoscope who had come together that night. From the left side of the room, a handsome man in his fifties rose quietly, approached the podium, and began:

> "I am Serb," he said. "I live here in Tuzla. I have lived here before and during the war. I never felt hatred against the Muslim or the Croat side. My friends are still my friends. . . ."

As he began, Tommi thought at first that he didn't understand the invitation. He seemed to be justifying himself a bit. She sat and prayed quietly, "Lord, may all here tonight hear your message. Do this work in many hearts. Bring all of us to a place of confession of our sins, to a place of repentance without justification, and then to a place of forgiveness. It is only then, Lord, that reconciliation can be complete."

The man continued:

> One neighbor had an unrighteous attitude because I was a guard in the military. The Serbs/Chetniks have done criminal things. From war in places by the river Drina, there was killing and slaughtering. There was killing, robbery; concentrations camps by Banja Luka, and other places. Persons, Muslims and Croats, were cleansed from Serb areas. I from this pulpit call on my brothers and sisters, the Croats and Muslims. I ask them to forgive the Serbs. Forgive all of what happened because all Serbs are not criminals. I believe they need to be forgiven, and I confess on behalf of the Serb nation that I am ready to forgive all Croats and Muslims— what they have done until now. I call all Serbs to come and agree with me and ask for a solution so we can all live as we did till now. Thank you.

"Yes, Holy Spirit. Your message came through," Tommi sighed. "Thank you."

John returned to the podium. "Will you who are Muslim and Croat, on behalf of your people, forgive the Serbs and what they have done?"

The answer came from all over the room, "Yes." A woman then came forward to the podium to share:

> I was fifteen years in Croatia and have been to most places. For five months I was in like a camp, a prison with four walls. My husband was an officer in the army. We went to Macedonia where he was and he had to hide us and our two children for six months. We had no food. One night my husband came and said we had to pack things and I had to go to Tuzla. He remained behind. He couldn't come with us until now. On the 5th of March they all came here. On the 15th of May the war started again. I had the two children and no income or belongings. Sometimes he sent money by friends who would stop by. There was no toilet; water was also very low. My husband's comrades were killed in army. I had nothing, but other individuals helped me. Many nations are suffering. There was a famine in 1993 where we were starving. In the name of Muslims, I first forgive, and I call on other Muslims to forgive Serbs and Croats.

John then asked those who were Serbs and Croats if they would forgive the Muslims? The reply was swift and sure: "Yes."

Another woman approached the podium:

> I am Croatian. It is my nature to be a silent, closed person. I lost my husband in the war, but there was no one moment that I hated anyone. I never hated because people were naturally divided into good and evil. Bosnian people are very mixed. I like that—being different nationalities. It helps us to know about other religions—more rich. We lived all together and didn't want war. We used to live like we live now together, which is good. What is more hard, to forgive or ask for forgiveness? I think easier to forgive than to ask for forgiveness. The only thing that is important is that we can survive and not

kill each other. Any peace is better than war—no matter who rules. We need conditions we can live under. Who will be in charge? I don't care—only that my son and me have good conditions to live. For my son to have a nice childhood—so that grenades will stop and this war will stop. Thank you.

John again asked, "Will those who are from a Muslim background and those who are Serbs forgive the Croats?" The anticipated response was immediate, "Yes."

Another came forward to tell a bit of her story:

I am a person from mixed marriage. I was from Croatia but am mixed also. I gave birth to two sons. I remarried a Muslim recently, but who you are counts by the father. I always felt like a Croat when I was young. I am Croat and my sister was Serb. So we see different things in this area happening. My sister is Serb/Croatian, and my grandson Serb/Croat/Muslim/German. I hope he will grow up to be God's man, that he will praise God. If you will, please pray for my daughter-in-law, she needs to be a believer. I love this nation, and I am sure this will be a nation which believes in God. We would all be happy if we were less Croat/Muslim/Serb and more people of God. *Slavabogu.*

At the conclusion of these testimonies, John indicated that we needed to do one more thing before we prayed. We needed to move around the room, go up to others who were from different ethnic backgrounds, and ask each other for forgiveness.

"Then," said John, "According to Matthew 18, if we agree together about anything, we will ask God and he will give it to us."

We all started moving around the small room. We took each others' hands, asking for and extending forgiveness. Hugs were freely given and tears liberally shed as the Holy Spirit began to move among this small group of believers.

Those of us who were visitors also went around the room and asked for forgiveness, on behalf of America and the other countries represented, for sitting on the sideline and not intervening to stop the war. Forgiveness was granted wholeheartedly. I went up to a woman who was blind. Her husband had left her to look after her son in an apartment all by herself. I took her hand, and as my words requesting forgiveness were translated, she was quick to respond in her native Croatian language, saying, "You are forgiven."

After some time, John instructed us to break into small groups and pray for one another and for the country of Bosnia.

"The Lord's prayer urges us to pray, 'Thy will be done on earth as it is in heaven,'" John said. "It is God's will to bless Bosnia and bring peace. Let us pray to God like Jacob did, not letting go until we receive a blessing from God. Amen? Can God do it?"

The people answered with a resounding "Amen!" which sounded very much the same in a variety of languages and dialects. With that began a flurry of prayers ascending to God's throne as those who had found reconciliation and forgiveness began to intercede for one another and for their country which has been through so much pain.

As this time of prayer subsided, Brian Mills felt led to minister to those of mixed marriages. He asked all of those who were a product of such marriages or who were currently in a mixed marriage to stand. Approximately 35 to 40 percent of the people stood. He indicated that no longer should they consider themselves as being inferior since Scripture indicates that all believers in Christ have a high position. "Children of the King is who you are, like all who believe in the Lord God Almighty," he said. Brian prayed over those who were standing, blessing many with this sensitive act of encouragement. Pastor Nenad and his wife, Zorica, plus Klaus and his wife, Mary, were asked to come up so the prayer team could pray over them and their ministry.

Tommi was led to give a prophetic word to Dario, indicating that he would be great in the eyes of God and a leader for the sake of Christ. He had a calling on his life, and God wanted to bless him richly. Tommi later recalled how the Lord impressed her to pray over Dario specifically for his stuttering disorder and that as she and Brian prayed Dario's tongue was loosed and his stuttering stopped.

Pastor Nenad closed the meeting, and after a brief time of fellowship (everyone needed to hurry home before evening curfew), we headed back to the hotel. Later that night while reading in my room, I heard bombing and shelling in the mountains toward the eastern outskirts of the city. Our hotel was situated between the fighting and Tuzla proper, which prompted some anxious thoughts of what would happen if there was a major Serbian push towards the heart of the city.

They would have to pass by our hotel, I thought to myself as I got up and closed the room-darkening curtains. As I returned to turn out the light, air-raid sirens started blaring all over the city. Since my room faced east—the direction where the shelling would be coming from—I immediately raced to turn off the light and dove down on the floor between my bed and the wall opposite the windows. Another siren joined in, and then another. I heard people moving out in the hall and felt I needed to go out to see where the others were and also to determine what we needed to do. I put on my pants, grabbed my key, and went into the hall to see Tommi standing there talking with a man from another humanitarian agency.

"Do you know where your stations are?" asked the man.

"No one assigned us stations," replied Tommi. The thought of assigning stations or having a particular place to go in an emergency was comforting for the moment, but not having been told where, we felt a bit helpless.

"Everyone carries a radio," continued the man. "I will go in and have a listen, and if there is something happening requiring you to evacuate, I will come out and bang on your door." He began to walk away. "You will probably need to go down to the reception area and then be led to the basement by some of the hotel staff," he replied, walking backwards. "I'll let you know."

As he was talking, two young men walking with two women started down the hallway from the west end of the hotel corridor and turned into some rooms near the room of the man we just spoke to. One had a bottle in one hand and his other arm was around a woman friend.

Using broken English laced with profanity, he communicated that if this was the night that he was to die, he wanted to die in his bed. Tommi and I just looked at each other, wondering what he was talking about. We returned to our rooms where we urgently prayed for the safety of the inhabitants of the Tuzla Hotel and its environs until sleep finally took its toll.

WEDNESDAY, AUGUST 23, 1995

In the morning we had a quick bite and departed the hotel, driving to Agape Church where Pastor Nenad, Zorica, Pastor Kresonja, and Maria, Klaus' wife, gathered for a last photo opportunity and prayer before we headed over to the Orthodox church for an early meeting with Professor Dr. Caslav Jevremovic, with whom we had been unable to meet the day before. From there, the four of us plus Pastor Kresonja would be making the day-long journey back to Mostar by car.

As we pulled up to the Orthodox church, Vitomere was there with one of the women who had confessed publicly in the meeting the night before. Pastor Nenad had given Tommi a Serbian New Testament, and as she and Vitomere greeted each other, she gave it to him. He was very grateful, and for the next thirty minutes the two of them shared about the wonders of the new life in Christ that Vitomere was experiencing.

John, Brian, Pastor Nenad, and Pastor Kresonja went immediately in to their appointment with Dr. Jevremovic, while I listened intently to this woman as she continued to share her story. She used to live quite well in Tuzla. Her husband was a famous actor in the theater, and they often attended opening nights and parties reserved for the elite. Then the war came. Her husband went to the theater one day only to find that he was no longer one of Bosnia's top performers—simply because he was a Serb. He suddenly became an outcast and could find no work. The woman could find no work either, and soon they sold most of their possessions and moved into a smaller flat. She even sold her wedding ring in order to obtain money to buy food. She was Croatian and came to the Lord after being invited by a friend to attend Agape Evangelical Church. Her husband was not a Christian. He was arrested and placed in prison for being Serbian. Her son moved out of the area to avoid the war, which left her alone. She survived only on what others would give her. Life was tough, and she would cry out daily to the Lord, asking Him to intervene in her life and that of her husband.

One day while she was crying out to the Lord in this way, the phone rang. It was an officer from the prison indicating that she should come and take her husband home because he was being released. She hurried to prison to find him already gone. Returning home alone, she continued to pray until there was a knock on the door and her husband appeared, thin and gaunt from his prison experience. She was so happy.

The couple were together again, but there was still no work and no food. One day, while she was again in prayer, the phone rang, and it was a man from a Muslim tennis club. He had heard that this woman's husband was once a professional tennis player, and he had two people who wanted to take lessons. She fought back the tears as she told her husband, who hurried a bit apprehensively over to the tennis club to begin teaching the lessons.

How ironic! In the middle of a four-year-old war characterized by the worst ethnic cleansing since World War II, a Croatian Christian woman living in a 96 percent Muslim city surrounded by Serb forces prays about her and her Serbian husband's sorry living situation. He receives a call from a tennis club and ends up with a job teaching tennis to two Muslims. Isn't it truly amazing how the Lord works in answer to the prayers of His people!

While Tommi and I were talking to Vitomere and this woman, we were also praying that the meeting the others were having would be successful and help to bring unity between the Orthodox and Pastor Nenad from Agape. Professor Jevremovic and his assistant, Jovan, received John, Brian, Pastor Nenad, and Pastor Kresonja. When they entered the building, they were first shown some priceless icons rescued from other churches damaged by the war. John asked if they could pray for God's blessing on them and their church. The two men agreed, requesting that they stand before a particularly large icon in Orthodox fashion. The extemporaneous prayers of the evangelicals must have seemed odd to their Orthodox hosts, who are by tradition more formal in religious expression. However, Professor Jevremovic and his assistant appeared quite grateful that our team had come in love, showing concern for them and their church, and invoking the name of the Lord for peace and unity.

After warm good-byes and hugs to all, including Pastor Nenad, and with the clock moving just past 10:00 A.M., the five of us who had journeyed from Mostar two days earlier were headed south once again. The difference on the return trip was that instead of three vehicles traveling in convoy for safety purposes, we were all together in a lone Peugeot.

RECLAIMING THE LAND

The journey out of town took us again past the electric generating station, but instead of continuing straight ahead to the air base where the refugees were, we turned left and headed up the side of a hill from which we descended two days earlier. The roadway consisted of good tarmac, and while the potholes were fewer and farther between on this portion of the trip, Brian was "on station" in the front seat anyway to assist John in missing as many potholes as possible.

One of the first villages we passed through was Oskova which, although so small it did not even appear on our travel map, was a strikingly beautiful village. We noticed one thing almost immediately that was different from our trip up from Mostar. On the trip up, there had been a checkpoint at this location. Now it was gone.

Continuing on, we entered Banovici, a city that was 100 percent Muslim, and we drove slowly past the large bus terminal. War had also visited this town, as evidenced by the small arms pockmarks on the walls of buildings. A few kilometers out of town, we came to another place where there used to be a checkpoint, now also missing. This was the place where we had departed off the tarmac and drove through a cutout carved into the side of the mountain partially to shield vehicles from the Serb emplacements located across the valley. As the Peugeot sped as quickly as possible along the dirt road, our prayers for protection surged forth automatically.

Lord, we pray for your protection along this road, [one said,] *especially as we move along this portion.*

Jesus, go before us and protect us, and place your angels also at our rear guard, [someone else said]. *We pray that you will close the eyes of any Serb gunners who are in the area. Blind those who are across the valley.*

Partway through the cutout, we again passed the two Pakistani UN peacekeepers sitting in their jeep with binoculars focused on the hillside across the valley. They sat there like angel gatekeepers on a road fraught with danger. We would not know the extent of the danger until after we moved back onto the tarmac, some six to eight kilometers farther down the dirt road.

After we were safely back on the tarmac, Pastor Kresonja said, "I didn't want to worry you as we traveled on this section of the road, but do you remember the man who was standing in the garden back at the church this morning?" Before waiting for others to answer, he continued, "He is a bus driver, and while he was traveling up this same road just a few hours ago, his bus was shot up by the Serbs from across the valley."

"Was anyone hurt?" someone asked.

"No, but bullets passed just behind him as he drove by, and a few of the bus windows were shot out. He was extremely lucky," Pastor Kresonja observed.

Thank you, Lord, for watching over us, [someone responded in prayer]. *We are extremely grateful for your protection and for your mercy this day.*

Others continued to offer up prayers of thanksgiving to him who protected the bus driver earlier and who was watching over us on our journey.

As we continued through the town of Ribnica, our intercession continued for the town, its inhabitants, and for the women and children left alone because of the war. Outside of Ribnica, we headed off the tarmac again and along another dirt road that wound its way over and along another mountainous range. We stopped to take a picture of a tricolored sign that the UN forces had erected indicating that this was a sniper area. On the sign, a marker placed at either the red, yellow, or green points indicated the status of snipers ahead. We were again blessed that the sign registered in the safe green area.

The road continued, and again the countryside was as picturesque as any in Europe. There was no sign of a war taking place. Quaint farmhouses were nestled in open fields containing perfectly formed haystacks that were surrounded by picket fences. The scenery was indeed inspiring.

Entering the town of Yarez, with its vacant mills and factories, we again prayed for prosperity and for the presence of the Lord to be manifested. The checkpoint where we had stopped two days earlier had been removed. We again reflected on the way things had changed so suddenly.

The next village encountered was Breza, with its mass graves in what was probably a central park area. This portion of central Bosnia must have contributed greatly to the defense of the Bosnian nation, and it had paid a heavy price.

From Breza it is a short distance to route E 73, the main roadway from Sarajevo in the south to Zenica and Banja Luka in the north. Unfortunately, the road was again unusable, and in its place, dirt roads were seconded for necessary use. Our route took us just across E 73 to Visoko, where we stopped for lunch at the same place we had stopped on the way up from Mostar.

Eleven kilometers south of Visoko there was a main checkpoint as we entered a primarily Croatian section of Bosnia. Again, passports were presented, but there was virtually no delay in moving through the check-point. A short distance later, we entered Kiseljak, a town where the inhabitants are 99 percent Bosnian Croats. Our prayers continued to spill forth as we slowed to pass through this village, remembering those involved in the war and those left behind.

Some ten kilometers after Kresevo, John guided the Peugeot onto the tarmac of the main road from Sarajevo to Mostar. Our traveling speed increased as the tarmac became smoother in this area. It took no time at all to travel the fifty-one kilometers to Konjic, which is on the border of Bosnia and Hercegovina. From there, picturesque Lake Jablanicko Ezero continued for more than fifteen kilometers along the west side of the roadway south.

After the lake, the road followed the Neretva River and on into Mostar, some forty kilometers in the distance. As we traveled the windy road alongside the riverbanks, it cut through narrow gorges and moved back through several tunnels. Again, wherever bridges were destroyed, slow-going dirt road cutouts had to be negotiated along with truck convoys and UN equipment moving north.

Thirty minutes north of Mostar, near what used to be the utterly destroyed Croat village of Potoci, we were quite surprised to see a forty-five-truck convoy heading north. This convoy was not like the UN peacekeeping convoys we had been used to seeing. From the insignias on their vehicles, this was a unit of the Rapid Expeditionary Force comprised of French and British troops. Perhaps they were intended as reinforcements for those involved in and around Sarajevo. The amount of arms and supplies contained in those forty-five trucks must have been awesome indeed. Seeing this convoy added to our feeling that something was now happening in the country that we did not sense just two days before. On the Monday trip from Mostar, we were stopped at twenty-five checkpoints during the approximately eight-hour, 273-kilometer trip to Tuzla. Now, two days later, we saw evidence of NATO's new military resolve—and we were only stopped at six checkpoints during our entire drive south!

As we arrived at Agape Church, Pastor Kresonja's wife, Ivon, was there, as were a few others from the congregation. She had already heard about the marvelous time with the believers in Tuzla. Because we were going to head to the airport in Split early in the morning, we took a few moments and said our good-byes to all who were present. It was difficult for us to say farewell to Pastor Karmelo Kresonja, who had certainly been an inspiration to us all. The Lord was using him mightily for his Kingdom work in the country.

Back at the guest house, we were quick to finish packing and get to bed for some needed rest. In the stillness of the night, more than one of us wondered before the Lord at all he had accomplished in the last few days—along the entire route that stretched most of the length of Bosnia. The Lord ordained this trip; he used all who participated to bring intercession for the land's healing and reconciliation. He was also at work through the changing military environment. But what was in store for Bosnia in the weeks ahead?

HEADING HOME
THURSDAY, AUGUST, 24, 1995

The night passed quickly, and after gulping down some coffee and toast, we headed out in the trusty Peugeot for the Adriatic Coast and ultimately to our destination, the airport at Split, Croatia. Traveling out of Mostar to the south, we continued to pray for Bosnia until after we passed over the border into Croatia. From there it was only a short distance (10 kilometers or so) to the coast on a good road, minus the ubiquitous potholes—a real relief. As we moved onto the main north/south road along the Adriatic, UN and Croatian convoys were seen moving southwards to that part of the conflict occurring just north and east of Dubrovnic. The Bosnian Serb army was continuing their assault on this fabled ancient city, and the Croats were busy pushing them back.

We spent the last few hours as a team at the small coastal town of Podgora, a delightful seaside village. As we approached it, the blue-green beauty of the gentle sea beckoned us. We parked the Peugeot and walked along, then sat next to the sea while John and Brian plunged in for a swim before lunch. During lunch we reflected on our trip, on how the Lord had led us, and our conviction that he was about to do something powerful in Bosnia. We remarked at how he had put such a great prayer team together and how fortunate we had been to be part of it.

The airport at Split was extremely busy, with many armed forces personnel coming in because of the conflict. We saw French troops, American advisors, and others from the UN community. It was intriguing to watch some of the military planes land, quickly unload their troops and cargo, and quickly take off again. It was truly a busy day at the Split International Airport.

Our flight to Rome was uneventful, and we located a hotel for the night. After a night's rest along the coast in Italy, we awoke early for our flight to Frankfurt and then home to Los Angeles. We had said good-bye to Brian in Split, who flew directly to London, and to Tommi in Rome, who headed back to Colorado. Ministering with these newfound friends was certainly a highlight of the trip.

EPILOGUE

Arriving home, family and friends listened to our stories with interest, amazement, and in some cases, disbelief. I quickly wrote a three-page summary of the trip and distributed it to those who were interested; but what can you communicate in only three pages about the marvelous workings of God. Others, when they heard I was in Bosnia-Hercegovina, perked up their ears for a moment until they heard the term *prayer initiative,* and then their interest seemed to wane. Someone had even questioned before I left: "Why do you want to spend $2,000 to go all the way over to Bosnia and pray? Can't you pray for Bosnia from here?"

I quickly found out that prayer initiatives to Bosnia were not high on everyone's list of topics for meaningful conversation. And then the headlines broke again: "Louder Than Words," exclaimed a weekly news magazine headlining the article about a Serb mortar shell that had landed near a main market in Sarajevo, killing forty-three and wounding more than eighty. That was on August 28, just three days after we returned. Two days later NATO's largest combat operation in its history began, pounding Serb positions around Sarajevo, near Tuzla, and even in the south around Mostar.

After a couple of days of bombing runs on Serb-held emplacements, including those at the end of the runway at Tuzla where we had just been, there were negotiations, broken promises, and more NATO military responses.

The headlines again began to look like they used to: killings, warfare, death, and destruction until that became routine too.

"Lord," I prayed, "Continue to work your will in Bosnia-Hercegovina. Bless those we met on our trip, and keep them from harm."

The next thing I realized, there was a cease-fire. Then peace negotiations took place in Dayton, Ohio. Finally, I saw it: Slobodan Milosevic, Serbia's president; the late Franjo Tudjman, Croatia's president; and Bosnian President Alija Izetbegovic all standing together in seeming harmony after signing the peace agreement in Paris, France.

"Has peace really come?" I asked myself.

The newspapers explained that while the leaders did sign the accord, some of those they represented felt shortchanged, and thus many commentators felt the chances of a real peace were between slim and none. However, the shelling did not resume, the bloodbaths ceased, and the carnage was no more. Had death simply taken a vacation, only to resume after a sufficient rest?

During the first week of December, advance elements of the U.S. army quickly made preparations to receive up to twenty thousand troops to cross into Bosnia-Hercegovina from Hungary across the Sava River. In the meantime, the air base at Tuzla was repaired, and C-141 cargo planes began bringing in advanced equipment and supplies. Were peacekeepers really going to stand between the warring factions?

By mid-January, almost ten thousand American troops and as many others from a variety of NATO countries were patrolling the lines of demarcation separating the three combatant groups. Each side began to pull back, destroy bunkers, set prisoners free, and in general, abide by the peace agreements. In addition, accusations detailing where sites of mass executions took place began to be officially looked into by members of the International War Crimes Tribunal. Was this too good to be true?

"Taste and see that the LORD is good," the Scriptures say, for "His love endures forever" (Ps. 34:8; 136:1). The Lord brought about a breakthrough after four years of war and diplomatic stalemate. He did hear the prayers of his people crying out to him in their pain and sorrow. How did this peace come about, and what are its prospects for the future?

Prayer team overlooking the city of Mostar.

One of many war-damaged buildings in the city.

Park turned into cemetery in Muslim East Mostar.

Meeting with believers from all three ethnic groups.

Team members Brian Mills and Tommi Femrite with Angelica, a Croat resident of the city.

Sniper warning.

UN camp for refugees, mainly Bosnian Muslim women and children, who escaped from the massacres of their friends and relatives at Srebrenica and Zepa.

Jim Hill giving his shoes to Imina, a woman refugee from Srebrenica.

5

PEACE COMES TO BOSNIA:
EVIDENCES OF THE HAND OF GOD
AND PROSPECTS FOR THE FUTURE

Richard Holbrooke's much acclaimed book *To End a War* describes the intensive diplomatic and military efforts to end the conflict, especially from August to November 1995. One who reviewed the book said, "The author grants himself the starring role quite rightly. He is generous in his praise for many others, well-known and not well-known, who helped end the war."[1] The person to whom Holbrooke forgot to give credit was God. His role should be acknowledged because his was truly "the starring role"!

Western diplomatic efforts had generally been a dismal failure up until August. The UN embargo on arms, originally meant to pull the plug on the conflict, turned out to be the greatest help to the Serbs, who used their great advantage in this area to devastate their enemies. The Vance-Owen Plan and the Owen-Stoltenberg Plan of 1993 were both rejected by the Bosnian Serbs. Plan 3, as it was called, was coupled with a threat to use aerial attacks unless its formula for peace was accepted, but it had little credibility with the Serbs and also was rejected, as was yet another Western peace plan offered by the Contact Group that was refused by Milosovic. In spite of continuous Serb refusals of peace plans, their capture and humiliation of UN peacekeepers, ethnic cleansing, and even genocide, the UN and NATO did not enforce their threats to use military power.

In July 1995, the Serb army began shelling Srebrenica, followed by the hostage-taking of Dutch peacekeepers. In the days after July 10, "the biggest single mass murder in Europe since WWII occurred" as thousands of Muslims were rounded up and killed at the direction of General Mladic. More than seven thousand were killed in ambushes and mass executions.[2] Holbrooke writes that, in spite of the horror of what happened at Srebrenica and later at Zepa, there was "no more energy in the international system. Everywhere one turned there was a sense of confusion in the face of Bosnian Serb brutality."[3] Then on August 19, just as our international prayer team was arriving in Bosnia, three American peace negotiators died in a road accident on Mount Igman outside of Sarajevo. This was just the latest of a series of many depressing setbacks for Western attempts to end the war. Holbrooke recounts how during ten months as assistant secretary of state "most high-level meetings on Bosnia had a dispirited, inconclusive quality that often left . . . me depressed and frustrated. . . . There was little enthusiasm for any proposal of action, no matter what it was. The result was often inaction or half measures instead of a clear strategy."[4]

THE TIDE TURNS

It was in early August, when the international prayer initiative began to kick in, that the Serbs suffered their first military setback during the Croatian army's major offensive to recapture the Krajina. This was the Serb's first defeat in four years! In the aftermath of this action, the first sign appeared that the Serb alliance was weakening—the Croatian Serbs were abandoned by Serbian president Milosovic. In a communication sent to international prayer networks before departure to Bosnia, we asked intercessors to "pray for reconciliation, forgiveness, and the binding and overthrow of the evil one, who through wicked men was exploiting generations of bitterness and ethnic prejudice to bring this destruction. Pray for the latest peace initiatives by the United States, the European powers and the UN, and that the international community will act in a united, decisive manner in our effort to stop the carnage."

Inside the country we had met for intensive prayer with believers in Mostar and Tuzla, and along with them had come to the assurance that God had heard and would answer. We reported immediately afterwards: "In a conviction that 'history belongs to the intercessors' rather than to the politicians and generals, we came to the conviction during our times of united intercession, joined by many thousands around the world who were also praying, that God would indeed bring peace as a result of His people's agreement in prayer. What an awesome promise! A literal blank check He has given us in Matthew 18:18–19!"[5]

We believe that the special prayer initiative of August 19–26 inside Bosnia, supported by many thousands of prayer warriors around the world, was used by God to turn the tide — that is, to change the atmosphere inside the country and to create new possibilities for a diplomatic and military solution. Two days later, August 28, during his visit to Paris, Holbrooke writes, "My mind drifted back over the many failures of Western leadership over the last few years, and I hoped — prayed — that this time would be different." It is striking that the only time the word *prayed* is mentioned in his entire book is immediately following the prayer initiative! The "tumultuous events" of August 28–31 were what he describes as the crucial turning point.

Prompted by the Serb mortar attack on Sarajevo and the funeral of the American negotiators, the U.S. government finally decided to take a tougher stance. Holbrooke writes, "After all the years of minimal steps, the historic decision to 'hit them hard' had been made remarkably quickly. *What, therefore, had caused such a sudden and dramatic change of heart* after months in which there had been no NATO action, even in the response to

the horrors of Srebrenica and Zepa?"(italics added).[6] The many intercessors who prayed their hearts out could answer that question.

NATO began to bomb Serb military positions on August 30. That
same day Holbrooke and his negotiating team met with President
Milosovic and were astonished to be presented with a paper in which he
proposed an international peace conference where they could "settle
everything." Holbrooke writes, "For a moment I did not dare to believe it.
For sixteen months, the Contact Group had argued fruitlessly with
Milosovic over how to get the Bosnian Serbs to participate in negotiations
under the Contact Group plan." During their meeting, a softened
Milosovic also made it clear that he was distancing himself from his former allies, the Bosnian-Serb leaders Karadzic and Mladic, whom he now
said were "not my friends." Holbrooke describes his utter amazement that
"for the first time everything was on the table, including several issues
that had never been discussed as part of the peace process."[7]

In the days and weeks following this first diplomatic breakthrough,
the peace process picked up steam. With the NATO bombing and the
new willingness to negotiate that was shown by the Serbs, the siege
against Sarajevo was lifted in September. This was followed by a cease-
fire enacted in October and preparations for an international peace conference at Dayton, Ohio, in November. In another communication to
supporting intercessors, John wrote: "Continue to trust the Lord with the
Bosnian Christians that a peace agreement will be signed and implemented throughout the land. Pray that the present cease-fire will hold and
that ethnic cleansing will be stopped." Holbrooke later writes, "There
seemed to be *a certain air of destiny,* as if everyone working on the preparations for Dayton felt they might be part of a decisive moment in American
foreign policy" (italics added).[8]

During the Dayton peace conference, November 1–21, families on
the air base where the meetings were held lit "candles of peace" in their
windows, and thousands of others took part in peace vigils outside the
base. On one occasion, a "peace chain" was formed, almost stretching
around the entire base. Undoubtedly, many of these activists were praying

believers who were concerned that the goals of turning the cease-fire into a permanent peace and of agreeing on a multiethnic state required many further breakthroughs in negotiation—breakthroughs that many negotiators felt would be impossible. Holbrooke's account of the discouraging ups and downs gives further assurance that the hand of God ultimately made the Dayton Peace Accords possible.

On November 21, President Clinton announced with much relief: "After nearly four years of 250,000 people killed, two million refugees, atrocities that have appalled people all over the world, the people of Bosnia finally have a chance to turn from the horror of war to the promise of peace." The majority of its citizens, he said, wanted peace, and "today, thank God, the voices of those people have been heard."[9]

CURRENT STATUS AND PROSPECTS

In order to get a sense of what has been happening inside Bosnia since the Dayton Peace Accords were signed at the end of 1995, we have relied primarily on Dr. Peter Kuzmic. He continues to be involved there through Agape, the humanitarian agency, that he leads. He has also been participating with other Christian leaders in reconciliation efforts. In an interview with John Robb on July 11, 1998, he provided an update on what has been happening since the Accords and how the Bosnian Christians have been ministering to their people.

Robb: Please tell us about the role you and other Christian leaders have played in the ongoing reconciliation efforts in the country.

Kuzmic: Some American political leaders who are also committed Christians have been involved in meetings with us there. Their involvement has shown the importance of religion, not in violence . . . but of the potential for reconciliation, for peacemaking, for confidence-building, and so on, and as a result of that, a number of regional and local initiatives in Bosnia and elsewhere in the Balkans have been started.

Robb: How about the role of local Christian leaders?

Kuzmic: Roman Catholic Cardinal Puljic and his people have
          played a very positive role. The Orthodox hierarchs
          have not fully participated yet, but the Catholics
          have initiated a very important council for peace and
          reconciliation in Sarajevo, involving Nikolai Mrdja,
          the Orthodox bishop, as well as Muslims and the
          Jewish community. Evangelical Christians have
          served as interlocutors and facilitators—less in a
          structural way, more in a dynamic and interpersonal
          way—because evangelicals are the only nonnational
          religious group; they have believers from all groups.
          They have belief in the universality of the life of
          Christ and the internationality of the Christian faith
          versus ethnic-tribal religion. They are not in signifi-
          cant numbers but have played a significant role as
          the conscience of the other religious groups because
          they have exemplified that Christians can live
          together if they have the same religious foundation.

Robb: What are you trying to achieve?

Kuzmic: I believe that through evangelism, sensitive and com-
          passionate evangelism, we are providing the hope for
          the society and the light of the world that will pre-
          vent further decay and bring new quality into the
          social matrix that will build bridges rather than
          walls—but not evangelization that can be perceived
          as religious propaganda. Proclamation alone does
          not work. Holistic mission is what I mean, because
          proclamation alone can be counterproductive in situ-
          ations like this and it is perceived as senseless prose-
          lytizing. But I do believe that whoever is in Christ is
          a new creation and has a new identity that is bigger
          than the ethnic identity.

We have a Christological foundation for our ministry, and this is very important for providing spiritual capacity for the horizontal, the reconciliation effort. The horizontal level is always inspired by the vertical one. Our work for peace is inspired by Ephesians 2 and 2 Corinthians 5, the most important passages for us evangelicals. We have to work as peacemakers in the name of the one who is peace, who has torn down the wall, who has eliminated hostility.

We work against violence, expressing solidarity with the suffering, the weak, the victims, the refugees. Through Agape, God has enabled us to save thousands of lives. You gain credibility through that. You don't gain credibility through words alone or through an isolated spiritual action that is limited to the believing community. You don't preach against darkness from a distance, but bring a candle to dispel the darkness.

Robb: What about the role of prayer and spiritual warfare?

Kuzmic: Various churches in the former Yugoslavia, including the one I used to pastor, established a prayer network. We were praying against the powers of darkness, and some of the churches were even involved in a chain of prayer around the clock. There was a lot of this going on during the war. The book *Religion and the War in Bosnia* by Paul Mojzes describes the negative role of religion in the war. The resurrection of religious and ethnic methodologies are deeply linked with the way the demonic powers have arranged themselves. This is where they have drawn their strength and their hold. Religious mythology and ethnic mythology go hand in hand and must be understood. Robert Kaplan's book *Balkan Ghosts* will also show you a lot of demonic activity; also, *The Bridge Betrayed* by Michael Sells covers religious mythology. When you deal with spiritual warfare,

111

you need to read the spiritual history. Here is spiritual history with a vengeance!

Robb: What is the evidence of God's answering prayer since August 1995?

Kuzmic: The signing of the Dayton Peace Accords later that year, and many breakthroughs including the election of a moderate government for the Serb Republic. A number of new churches have been opened—for example, just recently at Jajce town where ethnic cleansing was practiced brutally. One of our young women from the seminary has just opened a new congregation.

Robb: What are some prayer concerns for Bosnia that others around the world can share?

Kuzmic: 1. *The wounds of war are still visible everywhere.* There is a great need for the healing of individuals, families, and whole communities. This will be difficult because there is still a lot of animosity around.

2. *For justice.* We need to be nonsentimental and biblical here. There is no peace without justice. The chief war criminals, especially Mladic and Karadzic, need to be made accountable at the International War Crimes Tribunal in the Hague. This is essential; otherwise, there will be a collective blaming of the whole ethnic group. Once the transfer of blame has occurred, people will be more easily dispositioned to forgive each other, so that not all Serbs will be demonized. This is an important component in this spiritual struggle against the powers of evil.

3. *For new Bosnian leadership.* There is a need for new leaders who are just and have a new vision for the nation. (He mentioned that some of his colleagues have had the opportunity to minister to Serb and Muslim political leaders.)

4. There is high unemployment and a need for economic reconstruction.

5. Pray for the return of refugees to their homes.

6. There is a need for NATO troops to remain for five years or even longer.

Organizations like Kuzmic's Agape and World Vision have been seeking to meet the needs mentioned in this interview. Agape, throughout much of the war and continuing into the present, has provided food, clothing, and basic necessities through several distribution centers in the country. As evangelical Christians, Agape's personnel believe there needs to be a spiritual component along with their relief effort. Nikola Skrinjaric, who oversees their relief operation, describes the importance of including evangelism in working with a refugee: "Unless you satisfy his spiritual hunger he would only be hungry again and ready to go back to war. . . . Let me ask you something, if someone invades your land, kills your children, rapes your wife, what would you need to be able to forgive? . . . Jesus is the only one who can heal such wounds. No setting up of partitions, no human effort can make your heart able to forgive. . . . If I really have a relationship with God, he will give me the power to forgive. He will give me the power to love those whom I have every reason in the world to hate."[10]

In spite of growing Islamization and hardening of the Bosnian Muslim population due to the atrocities they suffered at the hands of so-called Serb and Croat Christians, the relief workers of Agape have won considerable favor among them because of their loving service to the needy. The Muslim mayor of one city expressed his interest in their faith: "I am now very much interested in your Jesus because of what your organization has done to alleviate human suffering and bring the word of hope and life into this situation of despair and death. You are not the kind of Christians that fit the mental image that we have of Christians, because you have not come for territorial gain or with a political agenda or ethnic propaganda. Instead, you have loved us without pushing your religion down our throats."[11] This same mayor gave Agape the free use of a central building for food distribution and said, "Feel free to preach your message.

You have been a little reluctant to do so thus far." Says Kuzmic in response, "If Bosnians see tangible acts of compassion in the name of Jesus Christ, then they will be able to hear the gospel in the right way. . . . Above all, we need to be compassionate evangelizers, bringing the good news of Jesus Christ into the bloody situations as the only living and lasting hope for Bosnia and all people."[12]

Such compassionate evangelization has resulted in significant growth for the Evangelical churches. Before the war, there were only a few dozen Evangelical believers in all of Bosnia-Herzegovina. Today there are hundreds in seven established churches, and pioneering efforts are underway that should result in twelve more. As a result, Kuzmic joyfully affirms, "Bosnia, the least evangelized country in Europe, is evangelized now!"[13] He refers to the hundreds of thousands of pieces of Christian literature distributed, new churches planted, the gospel being preached on radio, and the establishment of the country's first Bible school in Mostar, which is turning out trained workers to develop new ministries throughout the nation.[14]

World Vision has devoted itself to the reconstruction of war-damaged homes, over 60 percent of which were destroyed or damaged during the war. As of August 1998, through World Vision's efforts more than three thousand apartments and houses, plus many schools and some health clinics, had been reconstructed. In addition, loans and business training had been extended to hundreds, and perhaps most importantly, many thousands of primary school children and hundreds of teachers had gone through trauma-healing workshops. World Vision has also conducted reconciliation and conflict resolution training workshops for community leaders and has sought to build trust through its church relations program. Thank God for Agape, World Vision, and all those who are helping to rebuild this fractured nation. They need our ongoing prayers.

6

LESSONS LEARNED FROM
THE BOSNIA INITIATIVE

Here is a summary of some of the salient lessons we learned from the experience of coordinating and participating in the Bosnia prayer effort. Similar lessons can be deduced from the stories of the other nations that follow in chapters 8–10. We believe these lessons will be of use in other such efforts elsewhere.

1. God can turn things around through united prayer and spiritual warfare! Our experience in Bosnia gives hope that other human conflicts around the world can be healed if God's people will avail themselves of the immensely powerful resource they have been given in intercessory prayer. The impossible situation of more than four years of war with no political or military solution in sight was changed suddenly through the prevailing prayer of thousands of believers who joined their hearts and faith in this special initiative.

2. It was an international and interdenominational effort. The one-week initiative inside Bosnia was part of a monthlong special prayer focus on Bosnia by people around the world, both Christians and non-Christians.

Our team of five came from three countries. We were supported by many prayer networks in touch with the AD2000 Prayer Track as well as our World Vision colleagues. Clearly, we were an extension of the international Body of Christ standing in solidarity with our Bosnian brothers and sisters in their suffering.

3. There is value in having an international, intercultural, and male/female team. The unique perspectives, experiences, and gifts that each team member brought enriched the whole team due to the beautiful synergy the Spirit of God created among us. Jim Hill, as a worship leader and encourager, brought songs inspired by the Spirit. Kjell Sjoberg spoke with prophetic insight and boldness. Tommi Femrite employed her gifts as a sensitive prophetess and intercessor. Brian Mills used his abilities in reconciliation ministry and teaching, and John Robb served as team leader and overall coordinator. We had never worked together before, but in spite of being thrown together at short notice for a week of taxing, potentially life-threatening ministry, the Spirit made us one almost immediately. Though we came from diverse backgrounds, we shared a joint burden in prayer and mission that drew us together and made us a functional team.

4. Such prayer efforts must be originated by the leading of the Lord. Prayer initiatives and journeys need to be undertaken in dependence on God and with his direction. We all shared the profound sense that we were to undertake this effort. We also had the strong assurance of his guidance step-by-step throughout the whole journey.

5. Appreciate the importance of loving, bold confrontation of sin and the need for reconciliation. Prophetic ministry includes speaking words that are uncomfortable. God used the direct exhortations of our team to lance the boil of ethnic hatred and prejudice and move local believers into a stance of identificational repentance for their peoples.

6. United, faith-filled prayer is essential. After representatives of each ethnic group identified with and confessed the sins of their people against the other two ethnic groups, they could pray with unity for the healing of their land according to the conditions of 2 Chronicles 7:14. Out of these times of heartfelt reconciliation followed by intense intercession, God gave us a deep assurance that he would answer soon, even within weeks.

7. Pray holistically. As we drove through burned-out communities, we prayed for their peace, healing, and restoration. We also prayed individually for the adults and children we encountered according to whatever the Spirit birthed in our hearts. (Team members also prayed for John's driving, providing a lot of unsolicited backseat advice too!)

8. Pray transconfessionally. We sought out Roman Catholic and Orthodox leaders in order to include the whole of Christ's church and draw them into the prayer effort. We tried to be sensitive to their particular expression of prayer, such as their desire to pray in front of icons, even though it was foreign to our own tradition of faith.

9. Emphasize praise and worship. We experienced that there is nothing like corporate praise and the declaration of God's goodness and glory to change the atmosphere in a locality. The praise of God releases faith as it did for Jehoshaphat and the embattled people of Judah. All our team members and the local brothers and sisters gave ourselves to uninhibited, wholehearted worship. With our mouths we declared God's high praises, which, according to some interpretations of Psalm 149, he uses to bind the powers that are hostile to his reign.

10. Be willing to take risks. Both physically and psychologically, we sought to identify with the local people who were having to risk their lives in war-torn conditions. We drove a rental car that the rental company refused to insure, and we traveled within range of Serb guns to meet with believers in the northern city of Tuzla. A terrifying dream assaulted John the night before, which included firebombed cars being destroyed with grenade launchers by angry terrorists. Jim also was disturbed by early-morning feelings of foreboding. A bus traveling a few hours ahead of us had been shot by Serb snipers. We did not enter into these risks presumptuously but with the calm confidence that we were there on an assignment from God and that many around the world were praying for us. God gave us peace that we were in the center of his will and that he would take care of us no matter what happened.

11. Gather and disseminate information to supporting intercessors. For this initiative we did not have as much time as we would have liked to delve into the culture, the present and historical context, the situation in the churches, and other issues. This kind of research is critically important because in the realm of prayer, you get what you specifically ask for. Normally, we devote several weeks to the documentary study of books, magazines, and interviewing people "in the know" who can provide us with relevant information. From these findings we extract key prayer concerns to distribute to international prayer networks. We look for several overarching concerns as well as manifestations of the controlling spiritual powers and make them the main focus of the prayer initiative. Then thousands of home-based intercessors agree with us on these specific matters according to Matthew 18:18–19. This is a powerful world-changing approach!

12. Expect God's illumination step-by-step. Intercessors need to be good listeners. We need to listen to God speaking to us through his Word, through the other members of the team, and also through the local people. As we listen and pray, we can count on God to put his finger on the main issues that are hindering his shalom from coming upon a society. In Bosnia, it was the need for reconciliation and identificational repentance. In Cambodia, it was a spirit of murder, death, and bloodshed connected with the nation's past.

13. Submit to the authority of local church and parachurch leaders. Visiting prayer teams need to realize that they are there to support spiritual leaders who have been given the responsibility for that local territory. We are to stand with them in taking their land back from the evil one. We as outsiders cannot do this for them but need to stand in solidarity with them. We believe this is why some prayer journeys have failed to see much impact—they have been undertaken independently from the local church leadership. We have found that after a period of teaching, exhortation, and modeling in intercession and spiritual warfare our team needs to step back and let the local leaders take the initiative. They must assert their spiritual authority together to deal with the issues that are revealed. We have seen the wisdom of this policy not just in Bosnia but also in many other places. God has used the experience to equip local leaders to continue taking this kind of action long after the initiative is over.

14. Engage for the long term. Generally, we can't expect to see deep transformation happen overnight. Persevering intercession is needed over months and sometimes years. Occasional information updates sent out to intercessors including the answers to prayer are helpful in holding their interest and stirring their continued involvement.

15. God may desire the team to learn from a specific prophetic act or series of prophetic acts like those included in this book. These acts may seem out of the ordinary at the time, but they are important components that the Lord uses to focus the prayer efforts, unite the team, and clarify or identify what specifically is at issue.

16. Use the relationships gained during the prayer journey, and discern whether the Lord would invite a follow-on ministry. Tommi was invited to return to Bosnia the next summer and host a women's conference where she reinforced the work of the prayer initiative. Jim and John remain encouragers/supporters of Pastor Kresonja and have been involved in two subsequent summer youth camps. International intercessors are not "one-time" or "in-and-out" people. Relationships that develop are continually nurtured since the Lord might have more to do.

17. Take time to discern what happened and document it. At the conclusion of the trip, make sure there is an effort to document the specifics of what took place. Try and capture the sights and sounds of the moment and obtain sign-off from other team members to ensure an accurate account is compiled. Share the results with other international intercessors for their encouragement and edification.

18. During the prayer visit, recognize that you are in a different culture and go with the flow. People who participate in international prayer initiatives ordinarily do not stay at five-star hotels and operate on their own schedule. Many times, accommodations may be shared, which may mean that there will be several people standing in line before a single bathroom. The food is different; you don't understand the language; the climate is unfamiliar;

you have jet lag; there is often no set schedule; you get assigned by the leader to do something you wished he chose someone else to do; and people pray in a different way than what you are used to. Go with the flow and be an encourager. Remember, each team member was selected by the leader because of a specific gift or ability he or she has. Therefore, you should do your best to be about your ministry.

7

CONFLAGRATION IN KOSOVO

Serbian Lieutenant-General Dusan Samardzie, commander of the Third Army, told a new intake of young officers:

> *This is a turning point for Yugoslavia, when we need to show the world our military ability and might. Kosovo-Metohija's integrity has been threatened by Albanian secessionists, with assistance from abroad. Our ancestry and posterity would never forgive us if we surrendered the cradle of Serb culture to someone else.[1]*

During the earlier Bosnia crisis, Secretary of State Warren Christopher expressed the other side of this most difficult coin when he spoke of his concern for the regional instability of the Balkans: "Bold tyrants and fearful minorities are watching to see whether 'ethnic cleansing' is a policy the world will tolerate. If we hope to promote the spread of freedom or if we hope to encourage the emergence of peaceful multiethnic democracies, our answer must be a resounding NO!"[2] In the case of Kosovo, Serbia's second-largest province, recent events have demonstrated that the word *no* has not come without a huge price: 78 days of war; 1 million refugees forced out of their homes and their country, with many others internally displaced; 5,000 Yugoslav troops and police dead; 1,200 Serbian civilians dead; countless Kosovars murdered; 35,000 NATO sorties flown; 20,000 bombs dropped; 40 bridges destroyed; more than 100 Yugoslav planes destroyed along with 120 tanks. In terms of raw dollars, this conflict totaled $40 billion in cost to Serbia, $2.2 billion in cost to the U.S., more than $2 billion in cost to NATO, and several billion dollars of infrastructure, both public and private, destroyed.[3]

However, more importantly for the future, there has been significant damage to the relationship between the two primary ethnic groups that occupy this contested piece of ground—Serbs, numbering some 180,000, living alongside the Kosovar Albanians, who have a population of some two million.[4] This rivalry is further complicated by the recent outburst of extreme emotions for and against the "super powers"—NATO and the U.S.—and towards Russia as well as other European nations individually. The ongoing cycle of hatred and destruction has peaked once again. Blood has been spilled on the ground in Kosovo—Serbia's traditional birthplace and the location of its spiritual roots—widening the discord and hatred that has gripped the area for years.

The recent strife shouldn't be surprising, however, because social trauma and war have been at the heart of the region surrounding Kosovo since its beginning, and this "cultural norm" has—with the help of the angel of darkness, even Satan himself—continued to this day. George Otis, in his book *The Twilight Labyrinth*, quotes well-known trauma expert Kai Erikson to highlight trauma's social dimension in order to give a broader look at how trauma impacts society: "'The fabric of community,' [Erikson] insists, 'can be injured in much the same way as the tissues of mind and body.' The sudden loss of familiar and nurturing institutions, for example, can destroy a community's sense of identity. At the same time, 'traumatic wounds inflicted on individuals can . . . combine to create a mood, an ethos—a group culture almost—that is different from (and more than) the sum of the private wounds that make it up.' Either way, trauma changes the collective."[5]

While the history of this region is both extensive and extremely complicated, it reveals the generations of trauma that lie at its core. Therefore, it is critical that our assessment of the Kosovo situation begin with a fairly substantial historical focus, including early beginnings; the medieval period; the Ottoman period; the two world wars and Tito; the emergence of nationalism after Tito; Slobodan Milosovic; the road to war in Kosovo; and finally a question for pondering: Is peace really present? Factors giving rise to conflict situations and ways Satan and his powers are manifested also will be identified. We conclude the chapter with a survey of recent prayer efforts in Kosovo and the surrounding region.

A HISTORICAL PERSPECTIVE

EARLY BEGINNINGS

The real ongoing debate that spans the depth and breadth of Albanian and Serb society is: Who was there first? As the author of confusion, Satan's influence can be observed in the conflict among historians who disagree on who was in the region first, adding additional heat to nationalistic bonfires that already burn out of control in the region. During the sixth and seventh centuries A.D., Slavs from central Europe arrived in the Balkans where Albanians of Illyrian origin had already lived since pre-Roman times. One factor that may have turned the southward movement of Slavs from a trickle to a flood was the arrival, in the northwestern part of the Balkans, of an especially warlike Turkic tribe, the Avars. They subjugated or coopted some Slavic tribes but drove many others away. It was at this point, according to Constantine Porphyrogenitus, that the Croats arrived from Central Europe to deal with the Avar threat. This they did, bringing with them their neighbors, the Serbs. Both populations then settled in the territories abandoned by the Avars: the Croats in modern Croatia and western Bosnia, and the Serbs in the Rascia area on the northwestern side of Kosovo, and in the region of modern Montenegro.[6] The peoples of southern Illyria, however—including modern Albania—averted assimilation and preserved their native tongue. In the course of several centuries, under the impact of Roman, Byzantine, and Slavic cultures, the tribes of southern Illyria underwent a transformation from the old Illyrian population to a new Albanian one. As a consequence, from the eighth to the eleventh century, the name *Illyria* gradually gave way to the name first mentioned in the second century A.D. by the geographer Ptolemy of Alexandria. He referred to the Albanoi tribe that inhabited what is now central Albania.[7]

THE MEDIEVAL PERIOD

Medieval Kosovo is often referred to in general terms as the "cradle of the Serbs," as if it had been a Serb heartland from the outset; but the reality is quite different. Just over eight hundred years separates the arrival of the Serbs in the Balkans in the seventh century from the final Ottoman conquest in the 1450s. Of those eight centuries, Kosovo was Serb-ruled for only the last two and a half, which is less than one-third of the entire period.[8]

The author of the mind-set that this area is the cradle of the Serbs was King Stefan Dusan (1331–51). He originated the conquest by the Serbs of the Albanian-speaking lands and set up the patriarchal throne at the Pec monastery in 1346.[9] Subsequently, churches and monasteries were scattered throughout the region, especially in the Western half—an area known to Serbs as *Metohija*, a Byzantine Greek word for monastic estates, which reflects the fact that many Orthodox monasteries were granted rich endowments here by medieval Serb rulers.[10] Monasteries and churches were decorated with beautiful mosaics, frescos, and tapestries depicting the heart of Serbian history and folklore. Over the years these have become a source of pride, pointing to Kosovo as a spiritual home for the Serbs. This was made clear in the first thirty minutes of a two-and-one-half hour interview with current Serbian president, Slobodan Milosevic, with *Newsweek* magazine's Lally Weymouth on December 8, 1998. Responding to questions on the importance of Kosovo to the Serbs, Milosevic affirmed twice that its importance is based in part on the number of Serb churches and monuments located there.[11]

A mind-set indeed, but where do such shared mental patterns originate? George Otis refers us to Howard Bloom's book *The Lucifer Principle* where Bloom asks the question, "What propels the cultural tides of human beings?" In response, Bloom elaborates on a concept of the *meme*, "a cluster of ideas that leaps from mind to mind, changing the way entire societies think and act."[12] Otis continues to explain the term: "Memes, like all ideas, start off small. Occupying nothing more that the private mental spaces of individual artists, philosophers or politicians, they jump and shout until they finally manage to seize the imaginations of their hosts. . . . What sets the transforming meme apart from the ordinary idea is its ability to transcend the confines of the single mind and infect the consciousness of millions."[13] The result of this is that, in the broadest sense, cultures begin to represent our collective thoughts and fantasies about life and death. However, as Otis points out, "Demonic agents have often advanced memes through the skillful exploitation of traumatic events like war (the Russian revolution), pestilence (smallpox in India), and natural disaster (Pele worship in Hawaii)."[14]

In addition to Kosovo's being regarded as the cradle of the Serbs, there is a much more ominous rallying cry for the Serbs relating to the coveted ground of Kosovo: a small piece of ground outside of Pristina known as *Kosovo Polje,* or the "Kosovo Field." It was here, according to an all-important yet incorrect popular myth, that on St. Vitus day, 28 June 1389, the Turks destroyed the medieval Serbian Empire and that the defeated Serbs were immediately placed under Ottoman rule. According to Noel Malcolm, in his book *Kosovo: A Short History,* Serbian statehood actually did survive for another seventy years "with only a limited degree of Ottoman interference."[15] Also, it was not the battle on Kosovo Field that allowed the overall Ottoman conquest of the Balkans, but an earlier Turkish victory at the river Marcia in Bulgaria in 1371. Author Miranda Vickers agrees with the importance of this preceding battle: "The battle of

Marica made the disintegration of the rest of Serbia easier; the central government, such as it was, lost the bulk of its forces in the battle."[16]

It was the battle of Kosovo Field, however, that became encased in that elaborate web of heroic folklore, myth, and legend "which helped keep alive the spark of Serbian national consciousness for more than five centuries of Ottoman rule. The conflict between Christianity and Islam emerged as a major theme in Serbian folk poetry, and the Kosovo legend enhanced the ideology of Serbian rebellion against foreign rule."[17] Authors Alex N. Dragnich and Slavko Todorovich, in their book *The Saga of Kosovo*, elaborate further:

> To the Serbs, Kosovo is that heartbreaking medieval embroidery made in 1402, in the stillness of the Serbian monastery Ljubostinja, with the needle of the pious Serbian princess Euphemia. She sketched her Requiem in gold thread on a pall to cover the severed head of Prince Lazar (the Serb prince who lost at the battle of Kosovo Field): 'In courage and piety did you go out to do battle against the snake Murad . . . your heart could not bear to see the hosts of Ismail rule Christian lands. You were determined that if you failed you would leave this crumbling fortress of earthly power and, red in your own blood, be one with the hosts of the heavenly King.'[18]

As a result, one ethnic group believes one set of myths and legends, and the other group believes something else. Myths such as this are imaginary memes that become part of the public psyche, and as such can "also provide a dwelling place, a psychic habitat of sorts, for personified supernatural forces. Since these fantasy realms are not confined to a single mind, they can exist over many generations, or until such time as they are replaced by competing memes (such as the Gospel)."[19] However, if there is no spiritual awakening, the strongholds formed by negative memes can (and often do) "prepare a society for collective possession by demonic spirits. A frequent hallmark of this condition, which can last for brief or extended periods, is extraordinary violence—a fact that should come as no surprise since one of the devil's titles is Apollyon, or "Destroyer" (see Revelation 9:11). Our spiritual adversary, as author Michael Green reminds us, 'is a killer by instinct and appetite.'"[20]

Scriptures speak loudly of this, and we have seen evidence of how Satan has worked hard behind the scenes in Kosovo: "The god of this age has blinded the minds of unbelievers, so that they cannot see the light of the gospel of the glory of Christ, who is the image of God" (2 Cor. 4:4). People have been blinded due to the confusion that is wrought by such myths and folklore, which abound and which are craftily woven by Satan's "deceitful spirits" (1 Tim. 4:1, RSV).

OTTOMAN RULE

The Turkish Empire lasted from 1371 to 1912, during which time the Ottomans imposed their system of government and culture on those they ruled. However, while the Slavs were looked down on by the Turks and forced to pay high and multiple taxes, the worst thing the Ottomans did to the Slavs was to keep them from any political or economic development. As one writer put it, "Serbs were cut off from contact with the main developments of the rest of Europe. Their customs became embalmed in a deep, inward-turning, excessively proud nationalism, ready for Satan to exploit in terms of divisiveness and ethnic one-upmanship. Trade routes no longer passed through Serbia; economic improvement was discouraged through a lack of incentives and crippling taxation."[21] As a result, imbedded in the Serb collective memory that exists to this day is this period of "bitter Turkish overlordship, during which time the Serbian nobility became extinct and Serbians became a nation of peasants led by a small cadre of clergy and merchants."[22]

After 1816, Serbia, although it remained a province of Turkey, became independent. (However, documentation of this independence indicates that it occurred at the treaty of Berlin in 1878.)[23] With this, many of the Ottoman reforms in the Kosovo region impacted Serbia, such that the best years were the 1860s to the early 1870s. During this time period, rail lines were built, the telegraph was installed, and roads were cut through to the Adriatic. However, several significant regional conflicts occurred during the subsequent years that kept long-term peace from entering the region: the Russo-Ottoman war of 1877–78, wherein Serb independence was recognized; Austria's forced occupation of Bosnia-Hercegovina; and the Albanians' demand for autonomy.

Several years later, the first Balkan war of 1912—pitting Montenegro, Bulgaria, Serbia, and Greece against the Ottoman Empire, with Albania on the side of the empire—was fought with several components being repeated today. Of the Serbs in this first Balkan war, Vickers observes, "The realization that Kosovo might finally be liberated after more than five centuries fired their imaginations and emotions, and the Serbian army was unstoppable."[24]

With this war came the atrocities for which the region is now famous. According to a Serbian officer at that time, "The horrors actually began as soon as we crossed into Kosovo. Entire Albanian villages had been turned into pillars of fire, dwellings, possessions accumulated by fathers and grandfathers were going up in flames, the picture was repeated the whole way to Skopje. . . . For two days before my arrival in Skopje the inhabitants had woken up to the sight of heaps of Albanian corpses with severed heads."[25] Such atrocities attract more atrocities, and the enemy gains momentum because he "prowls around like a roaring lion, looking for someone to devour" (1 Pet. 5:8).

As a result of the second Balkan war, lasting two months in 1912, the alliance of Greece, Serbia, and Montenegro responded to attacks from Bulgaria. The result of this brief but significant skirmish was that the Serbs gained full control over both Macedonia and Kosovo. Thus, according to Mojzes: "At the outset of World War I, Serbia had already emerged as the predominant Slavic state in the Balkans, poised to lead other Slavic states to independence. The tragedy was that the finally independent united states of southern Slavs was perceived differently by the Serbs, who saw themselves as agents of liberation, and the other Slavic peoples, who envisioned a different process of unification."[26]

THE WORLD WARS AND TITO

World War I broke out when, on June 28, 1914, Archduke Franz Ferdinand was assassinated in Sarajevo by a Bosnian Serb radical who sought to use violence as a methodology to unify Serbs living both within and outside of Serbia. Uncoincidentally, this was on the anniversary of the 1389 Battle for Kosovo, a date already permanently etched in the minds of all in the region. The result was that Austria, and soon after Germany, declared war on Serbia. Austro-Hungary, Russia, France, Belgium, Montenegro, and Britain were all drawn quickly into the conflict. Some significant results of World War I on the region were: the Austrian Republic was proclaimed, as was the Republic of Turkey; an independent Hungary was formed; and the Montenegrin National Assembly proclaimed its union with Serbia. In addition, part of the Serb-populated Hungarian territory was ceded to Serbia, and Czechoslovakia, Poland, and Bulgaria all became independent states. On December 1, 1918, even though there were no official borders except for those of Serbia, came the birth of the Kingdom of Serbs, Croats, and Slovenes, more commonly known as Yugoslavia.[27]

The Kosovars were initially treated like any other Yugoslav citizens. It did not take long, though, for promises of rights for ordinary Kosovar citizens to be quickly forgotten. These promises were dear to the hearts of the population, since they included schooling with books and media publications in the local language. In response to repeated complaints by the Albanians, a statement drawn up by the Yugoslav delegation to the League of Nations in 1929 plainly said: "Our position has always been that in our southern regions, which have been integral parts of our state or were annexed to our kingdom before January 1, 1919, there are no national minorities. That position is still our last word on the question of the recognition of minorities in Southern Serbia."[28] This stubborn, chauvinistic attitude together with the influence of the spirit of deception continued to fuel the fires of nationalism and disunity between the Kosovars and the Serbs. It represented a level of unresolved social injustice that continued to fester over generations.

Whether it is the Crusades, the Holocaust, troubles in Northern Ireland, or other situations where there has been social injustice that has yet to be resolved, the enemy considers this "home turf." George Otis explains further: "[Spiritual bondage] is most likely to emerge in situations in which moral injuries have been left untreated by repentance and restitution. In such an unhealthy environment, bitterness moves like a raging virus, invading the inner sanctuaries of human identity and reason. If unchecked, it will go on to shrivel the souls of individuals, communities and even entire generations,"[29] as we see today in the Balkans.

In the late 1930s, Mussolini had eyes for Albania and began to move quickly down that road. With the fall of Albania's government in February 1939, Italy invaded with thirty thousand troops. In 1940, the Italian army launched an attack on Greece in order to recover the lost province of Cameria in northwestern Greece, which had a sizable Albanian population. Six months later, the Axis powers launched its *Blitzkreig* against Yugoslavia. Italy, fully in charge of Albania, then became the co-conqueror of Kosovo.[30]

From a regional context, World War II (1941–45) was not only a war of liberation but was simultaneously a civil war in which the Serbs were pitted against the Croats and the Muslims, who were, in many instances, allied with the Nazis. According to Mojzes, "An agonizing war engulfed the country, one in which it is claimed that over a million people were killed. At least half of them were casualties which Yugoslavs inflicted upon each other."[31] A result of all of this horror and tragedy was a vacuum in government created as King Peter II Karadjorgevic was in exile in London. However, on the ground in Yugoslavia was Josip Broz Tito, leader of the Partisans, who were "in effect, the revolutionary military arm of the Yugoslav Communist Party (CPY)" and fought against the fascists in alliance with the Soviets during World War II.[32] In his review of Aleksa Djilas's book *The Contested Country: Yugoslav Unity and Communist Revolution, 1919–1953*, author Istvan Deak identifies CPY's threefold basis of creating a united Yugoslav political consciousness as: "ethnic and linguistic similarities and common traditions, the wartime 'national liberation struggle,' and the 'building of socialism.'"[33] However, as successful as these objectives were, they were objectives only if they did not supercede the Communist dictator himself. According to author Aleksa Djilas:

> Communist repression was sufficient to overcome sepa-
> ratism and nationalist extremism. But the Communists failed
> to achieve lasting results in propagating Yugoslav unity. The
> memory of the Partisan struggle, "the building of socialism,"
> workers' self-management, the cult of Tito, even Tito's non-
> aligned foreign policy—all these were propagated at some
> time by Yugoslav Communists as common rallying points for
> all national groups. But the groups remained unconvinced.
> And because under communism the spirit of critical, rational
> inquiry could not develop, the nations of Yugoslavia failed to
> free themselves from pseudoromantic images of themselves
> and negative stereotypes of each other. The dominant form
> of political consciousness beneath the veneer of Yugoslav
> Marxism remained mythologizing ethnocentrism that could
> envisage full rights only for members of one's own group.[34]

The Kosovars viewed Tito as a man who reversed the previous objec-
tionable policies towards Albanians in Yugoslavia and enabled some
reforms; namely, the use of the Albanian language and a level of autonomy,
which by the 1970s "had come close to attaining equal status with the other
federal units of the Yugoslav state."[35] While these were demonstrations of
positive policies toward Kosovo, others were in place that would ensure
that Kosovo would continue to remain primarily undeveloped. For example, because of the economic politics of Belgrade, Kosovo was considered
too vulnerable a site for the construction of major industrial projects. As a
result, while Kosovo contains over half of Yugoslavia's coal reserves and
sizable chrome, lead, zinc, and other deposits, it was relegated to be a sup-
plier of raw materials to the wealthier parts of Yugoslavia.[36]

Tito worked hard to keep Yugoslavia together, responding in part to
pressures that required linguistic and cultural reforms. However, these

efforts were not totally successful, as author Robert Howse explains: "I now believe that the main reason all these seemingly pluralistic policies failed to create a sense of commitment for Yugoslavia as a multicultural state is that they never ceased to be conceived of in collectivist terms; that is, they were viewed as collective rights or privileges brokered by ethnic elites, not as rights of the individual to free self-development in his or her own linguistic and cultural context."[37]

THE EMERGENCE OF NATIONALISM AFTER TITO

In May 1980, Tito died. Afterwards, the process of transition toward a multiparty democracy caught Yugoslavia "with an extremely weak central authority, disintegrated political and administrative institutions, and no serious political party with a Yugoslav platform. For this reason, the inherited Yugoslav political institutions and administrative state appeared incapable of maintaining unity in the absence of a strong central authority. It was the system of socialist self-management that generated such ethnic polarization of South Slavs."[38]

While there was no successor, Tito did manage to establish his replacement in the form of a collective leadership comprising a rotating eight-member state presidency, with elected members representing equally the six Republics and the two autonomous provinces: Kosovo and Vojvodina. However, this was impossible with "such an incompetent *nomenklatura*, i.e. groups of leaders at the federal, republican and provincial level who retained their high positions due not to any real ability but to their unshakable loyalty to Tito."[39] As such, another leadership vacuum ensued, brought on in part by the international community in general and the West in particular. "Failing to revisit the major nation-state and international order paradigms (regionally associated with strong state nationalism) in order to provide revised principles and decisiveness, the international community reacted instead with compromises and indecisiveness and by dividing and aligning along the ethnic lines of Yugoslavia. As a result, the ethnic cleavages of Yugoslavia became the ethnic cleavages of the world."[40]

For Kosovo, Malcolm indicates that it was a cockroach found in the soup of one of the students at the University of Pristina that started the initial protests. Soon, other students who were equally tired of conditions at the university joined in the protest, so that there were at least five hundred demonstrating in the streets chanting "Food!" and "Conditions!"[41] As police moved in, several students were killed, and the demonstrations were put down.

This took place with significant losses for the Albanian Kosovars; for it was that year that the Serbs changed the republican constitution to repeal many of Kosovo's and Vojvodina's powers.[42] However, more than power restrictions were to be inflicted on the Kosovars by the Serbian government; soon-to-be president Slobodan Milosevic was busy preparing a future for himself and for Greater Serbia.

SLOBODAN MILOSOVIC

Born in Serbia in 1941, Slobodan Milosovic became a lawyer in 1964. Married to a "Marxist ideologue," he became an executive in a state-owned company and then head of a major bank. It was not until 1984 that Milosovic came into politics. During the riots in Kosovo, Milosovic came out strongly on the side of the Serbs. In a fateful meeting with the Serbs in Kosovo, he promised assistance and gave sympathy to their plight. This meeting "led to a great change in Milosovic's political personality. A Serbian journalist stated that 'after that night, suddenly there was a psychological change in him. All at once, he discovered he had this power over people.'"[43] On May 8, 1989, Milosovic assumed the position of president of Serbia.

According to author Anna Hursarska, Milosovic saw inflaming Serb nationalism in the Kosovo situation as a way to personal power. "He dissolved the local parliament in July 1998, and Belgrade embarked on a wave of mass purges of 'disloyal' Albanians. According to Muhamet Hamiti of the Kosovo Information Center, more than 130,000 ethnic Albanians, or Kosovars, have been dismissed from jobs in government, the police, media, schools, and hospitals since 1989."[44] As a result, it became clear that Milosovic had four main goals: to establish complete control of Serbia; to reestablish Serbian control over Vojvodina and Kosovo; to eliminate the 1974 constitution; and to establish a unified country under Serbia, with a semifree market and a semidemocratic Communist party.[45] He did not waste any time in working on his agenda, stirring nationalistic feelings by denouncing Kosovar demonstrations and declaring that it and Vojvodina belonged to Serbia.

His timing was perfect: for on June 28, 1989, at the six-hundredth anniversary celebration of what the Serbs perceive is the very cause of all their difficulties—their loss at the Battle of Kosovo Polje—Milosovic gave a stirring speech that offered no hope for the majority of Albanians who lived in the surrounding community. His words were addressed to the Serbs present and revealed a significant sense of foreboding: "'The moment has come when, standing on the fields of Kosovo, we can say openly and clearly—no longer!' The clear implication was that the Serbs had won a significant victory in Kosovo today and that it would not be the last one. He ominously [and prophetically] concluded: 'Today, six centuries later, we are again fighting battles, they are not armed battles although such things cannot yet be excluded.'"[46]

Richard Holbrooke, U.S. negotiator for peace in Bosnia, says of Milosovic's speech in 1989: "When I asked Milosovic in 1995 about this famous speech, he heatedly denied that it was racist, and charged Ambassador Zimmermann with organizing a Western diplomatic boycott of the speech and the Western press with distorting it."[47]

In July 1990, faced with rising anti-Serb feelings and demonstrations throughout Yugoslavia, Milosovic "staged a referendum, asking Serbian voters to endorse constitutional changes that would virtually eliminate any vestige of provincial autonomy."[48] Kosovo declared itself a republic, with Dr. Ibrahim Rugova, a poet and literary critic, as president operating out of Stuttgart, thus playing into Milosovic's hands. Now Milosovic could dismiss the provincial government and assume full control of the province's government and media.

Milosovic's hunger for power; promotion of tyranny and injustice; instigation to rioting and committing murder through his army and police; condoning rape and genocide; and being a divisive and unjust ruler/tyrant was an "outward manifestation of a whole field of powers contending for influence. 'For we are contending not against flesh and blood'—though we most certainly joined the battle at precisely that point—'but against the principalities, against the powers,' against the spirituality of institutions, against the ideologies and metaphors and legitimations that prop them up, against the greed and covetousness that give them life, against the individual egocentricities that the Powers so easily hook, against the idolatry that pits short-term gain against the long-term good of the whole—all of which is manifested only in concrete institutions, systems, structures, and persons."[49]

THE ROAD TO THE CURRENT WAR

Behind Kosovo's lead, Slovenia spearheaded the drive to sovereignty and international independence, with the United States recognizing it as a country in 1991. Croatia declared independence on the same day. The debacle in Bosnia-Hercegovina was a much more complicated matter, where premature recognition of independence by the U.S. occurred in April 1992, yet the war was declared over by the Dayton Peace Accord in November 1995. However, it was Serbia's war of territorial expansion against Bosnia-Hercegovina that impacted Kosovo the most. Noel Malcolm describes this impact using two terms as follows:

> The rhetoric of Serbian nationalism now concentrated on the Islamic "threat"; speeches made by extremist leaders such as Radovan Karadzic referred to the "demographic aggression" (i.e. high birthrate) of the Bosnian Muslims in terms identical with those used about the Albanians, and the Serbian media often alluded to the threat of an "Islamic crescent" extending from Bosnia through the Slav Muslim territory of the Sandzaak to the predominantly Muslim Albanians of Kosovo. . . . In practical terms the Bosnian war had another serious effect on Kosovo, in the form of the international economic sanctions which were eventually

imposed on Serbia and Montenegro. This led to the closing of the Kosovo-Macedonian border to most forms of direct trade, and it also further depressed the ramshackle Serbian economy.[50]

While the rest of Yugoslavia chose war, Kosovo president Ibrahim Rugova chose passive resistance even in everyday situations peppered with the confrontation of the Serbian police, who were, at times, caught up in their own rhetoric against the citizens of Kosovo. He believed that "since there were so few Serbs in Kosovo [barely 10 percent of a population of 1.8 million], and as that proportion was steadily falling, independence was bound to come in the end. So he argued for passive resistance, and rejected calls from Croatia and Bosnia to begin an uprising against the Serbs."[51] However, at Dayton in 1995, the Kosovars were not part of the peace settlement package, which brought quick disillusionment and a violent political confrontation between Rugova and other government leaders. Rugova managed to maintain his presidency of Kosovo, but it was clear that the policy of passive resistance would not continue.

Interestingly enough, Milosovic had an auspicious ally standing close by in the form of the Orthodox Church, which was well groomed to play its part. Under Milosovic, the national newspaper *Politika* praised the Serbian Orthodox Church "for its service to the Serbian people and even declared that Orthodoxy was 'the spiritual basis for and the most essential component of the national identity of Serbs.'"[52] The Orthodox Church went on a propaganda attack. For the church, the "Albanian population explosion (in Kosovo) and the exodus of Serbs was labeled as genocide of Serbs." With this there were appeals regarding "alleged rapes, murders, expulsions, and the destruction of Serbian cultural monuments and sacred sites—in other words 'ethnic cleansing' of Serbs—by Albanians."[53] Of late, however, the Orthodox Church has come out against Milosovic. In June 1999, at the conclusion of the bombing, Patriarch Pavle said, "If the only way to create a greater Serbia is by crime, then I do not accept that, and let that Serbia disappear." Bishop Artemije, the most senior representative of the church in Kosovo, was even more pointed in his criticism. "'We are both aware, as God knows, how much evil has been done in the course of the last year and especially in the last three months,' Artemije said. 'The great part of the guilt lies with Milosovic.'"[54]

Active resistance against the Serbs made its first public appearance at a funeral of an Albanian killed in a gunfight with Serbian police in 1997. Three armed men in camouflage uniforms and black *balaklavas* arrived and said, "We are the Kosovo Liberation Army [UCK], the true representatives of the Kosovo struggle," they declared to enthusiastic shouts from a crowd of fifteen thousand.[55] While this was the first confirmation that there was organized active resistance, in May 1993 in the city of Glogovac, the KLA killed two Serb police officers and wounded five more.[56] This was only the beginning of various strikes by the KLA against Serb police and municipal leaders in Kosovo in response to their harsh treatment of the Kosovars in everyday life. Chris Hedges, *The New York Times*' Balkan Bureau chief from 1995 to 1998, gives an example of this everyday oppression:

> On several occasions, I saw two or three beefy Serb police officers . . . walloping young ethnic Albanians with their clubs in the center of Pristina. I once watched a cop shove a young boy of about ten, who held a small wooden tray of individual cigarettes for sale, onto the sidewalk. The cop laughed as the frightened child scrambled to rescue the cigarettes from the mud puddles. One of their favorite pastimes was to set up roadblocks and collect money from a long line of cars for invented traffic violations. Drivers that did not have money or did not pay had their documents seized.[57]

These hit-and-run tactics continued until February 1998, when Serbian President Milosovic ordered a lethal sweep against the strongest of the KLA rebel areas in western Kosovo, killing more than eighty Kosovars, including thirty women, children, and older men. This was a shock to the Kosovars and furthered their anger, resulting in still more attacks. Milosovic responded against the rebel fighters with units of the Yugoslav army's elite sixty-second and seventy-third Airborne Brigades. With this, Serb reservists were called up, boosting the total Serb strength in Kosovo to almost forty thousand, including helicopters and artillery.[58] This buildup and the ensuing struggle radically began to impact the civilian population as Serb police and military began to burn and loot homes and make refugees out of "suspected" KLA sympathizers. The world began to take notice, and its leaders began to make threats against Milosovic. U.S. Secretary of State Madeline Albright said in an interview on Jim Lehrer's *NewsHour* television show, "We believe this is his [Milosovic's] ethnic cleansing and it must stop. Serb actions have transformed the fighting into what is clearly an internal armed conflict, and Belgrade, itself, has internationalized the conflict by taking it to Kosovo's borders." Tony Blair, prime minister of the U.K., included his viewpoint in the same interview: "The only circumstances in which we will ensure that President Milosovic responds to diplomatic pressure is if that is backed up by the threat, the credible threat, of the use of military force."[59] However, the world was not quick to respond. As a result, from August 1998 until after the NATO cease-fire on June 11, 1999, Serb forces brought continued terror into the lives of the Albanian Kosovars, causing them to flee their homes into the surrounding snow-covered mountains with only what they could carry on their backs. Failure to flee often resulted in mass executions, which would soon be uncovered for the world to see.

For those unable to seek refuge in the forests, Milosovic ordered their forced removal from the province. With no place left for them to go, they ended up in hastily-constructed refugee camps in Albania and Macedonia. With families torn apart, men often separated and murdered, and children orphaned with no one to care for them, the situation was horrific—a travesty of justice with no solution in sight.

NATO leadership decided that a bombing campaign was the only solution, so on April 24, 1994, they began to bomb Serb forces in the field as well as their control centers in the heart of downtown Belgrade; after all, they must have reasoned, bombing the Serbs had worked in Bosnia four years earlier. However, Milosovic did not capitulate so easily, and the destruction continued for seventy-eight days.

The weekend of June 12–13, 1999, brought news reports of rapture for some and anguish for others as NATO and Russian peacekeepers entered Kosovo just as the Serb army was departing. As expected, there was immense jubilation among the more than eight hundred thousand refugees in the camps of Albania and Macedonia, as well as among the Albanian Kosovars who remained behind in Kosovo. However, in the capital city of Pristina, where the transition of power took place for all the world to see via international media, hatred and fear again raised their ugly heads. Two Serbs challenged NATO directly with weapons and were killed with return fire. Another Serb policeman refused to lay down his weapon and was dispatched immediately. On a road outside of Pristina, two foreign journalists from the German weekly *Der Stearn* were ambushed and killed. After all, if the international media had not called attention to the holocaust taking place in Kosovo, NATO would not have showered Serbia with bombs, and Serbs would not have to depart their beloved Kosovo.

As many Serbs departed Pristina heading north, rocks and sticks were thrown at them by the crowds who lined the streets. Hatred filled the air like the stench of the newly found mass graves that NATO uncovered. For those Serbs who chose to remain behind in Kosovo, there is fear that the KLA will return the wrong that the Serb police and paramilitary inflicted on the majority population during the last two and a half years. During the night of July 23, 1999, near the town of Lipljan, fourteen Serbs were massacred while they harvested their crops at night. The killings provoked outrage among the Serb population of Kosovo who were expecting NATO to defend them. As a result of violence such as this, there has, of this writing, been an exodus of approximately three-quarters of the province's prewar population of two hundred thousand Serbs, about a tenth of the total population.[60]

When NATO firmed up an agreement and halted their bombing campaign, there was a brief moment of elation, and the world breathed easier. However, as formalized military conflict came to an end, two questions not wanting to be asked were on the forefront of most everyone's mind: What will be the role of the KLA? And what about a sovereign state for Kosovo? In terms of the KLA, Chris Hedges observes: "The [NATO] plan would gradually cede local police control to the KLA, which would probably comprise most of the force. But Serbia would keep troops in the province and handle security along the borders—especially the border with Albania, where the KLA has set up logistics bases and smuggling routes for weapons and fighters. The plan also calls for a phased disarming of the KLA."[61] However, Hedges is also quick to end his essay on a more disparaging note: "In Kosovo, the stationing of international troops may prevent all-out fighting and provide the breathing space to negotiate a workable solution. But given the deep rifts between the sides, the latter is hardly likely. In the end, it will come to this: Led by the KLA, Kosovo will separate from Serbia, whether by negotiations or by violence."[62]

Milosovic, while under the requirement to abide by the signed peace agreement, has his own obvious thoughts on the subject of an independent Kosovo. In his 1998 interview with *Newsweek*'s Lally Weymouth, he makes his opinion on a separate Kosovo quite clear: "Kosovo is a region of Serbia first of all, which was always a part of Serbia. Always in history through the centuries." When Weymouth sought clarification by asking, "Was always or will always be?" Milosovic responded, "Was always and of course will always be a part of Serbia. Why should it be different in the future if it was not in the past?"[63]

In spite of these rough spots, the process toward the establishment of peace and the rebuilding of Kosovo has begun. As in Bosnia, we are convinced that united prayer by God's people has made a difference.

PRAYER AT WORK IN AND FOR KOSOVO

The generation of conflict, death, and destruction in the Balkans "represents the moving biological ground over which the past is transferred into the present. To ensure that his interests are preserved along this continuum, the enemy cultivates elaborate deceptions involving lineages and ancestors. Using these powerful elements of tradition, he is able to recycle ancient enchantments."[64] To combat these ancient enhancements, prayer for Kosovo and Albania must be significant and it must be continual, even as it was during the worst of the recent conflict.

Undoubtedly, prayer for Kosovo first began with those in proximity who had an awareness of the issues involved. There are only seven Evangelical churches in Kosovo, and in neighboring Albania there are 160 that have surfaced since 1991. Still, the believers attending these churches, either in the midst of strife or those who were significantly impacted by the expulsion of Kosovar refugees into Albania, were among the first to bend their knees. *Religion Today* reported that "Albanian Christians have been praying for Kosovo since last year [1998]." Acts of love and mercy accompanied their praying. From the time the refugees began to appear by the thousands in Albania, it was said "from the north to the south, from the east to the west. . . . There is no town in Albania where there is a church and that church is not doing anything" to assist the refugees.[65]

Prayer and other forms of Christian service were also made more difficult because of the politics involved. "'We are certainly committed to the Kosovo-Albanian churches,' says Simo K., one of the Pentecostal leaders in Serbia. 'The registered churches in Kosovo belong to our denomination. But to push for the registration of the new churches, we need some sort of a guarantee from the Albanian brothers that they will steer clear of nationalistic politics in the future, or the Serbian authorities will conclude that we support the "Albanian rebels."'"[66] However, even with the difficulties, the Serb Christians have been able to reach out during the bombing campaigns. According to *Religion Today*, "Several churches in Belgrade receive outside aid to purchase and ship food, medicine, and other goods. Four Evangelical churches help distribute the aid in Kosovo. The ministries managed to distribute 34,000 pounds of food, seven and a half tons of clothes, and 900 beds from February to mid-March."[67]

Pentecostal American missionaries Ted and Lori Bultsma were ministering in Novi Sad, Serbia, until their pastor told them it was not safe to remain. They returned to the States on April 3, 1999. Writing about their ordeal and how prayer intensified the moment bombs began to drop, Lori Bultsma indicates, "My, how the prayers in my life have changed. I was pretty serious about prayer before, but now it feels like the prayers are coming out of my gut instead of my head or heart."[68]

In Kosovo itself, there were some two to four hundred Evangelical Christians before the refugee exodus. The churches had a difficult time coming together in the past "but became unified while working together to distribute aid," said Linda Keys of World Relief.[69] Chris Mundis, director of the Assemblies of God, Europe, tells of a meeting he had in January 1999 with nine pastors and lay workers from Pristina. "'They have a real sense that hope is only in the Lord,' he said. The congregations are 'doing the work of the church' by providing humanitarian aid to about 500 families and evangelizing regularly, including showing the *Jesus* film. . . . The group talked and prayed together all afternoon."[70]

Keeping tabs on church leaders who were inside Kosovo was also difficult. Dr. Peter Kuzmic, president of Evangelical Theological Seminary in Osijek, Croatia, gave *Religion Today* an update on the status of the church in Kosovo during the midst of the conflict: "'There are seven Evangelical churches in the province and only one pastor is known to have escaped,' Kuzmic said. 'There is no international presence there and we can't get our people in, . . . 'These are outstanding Christian leaders and they are unaccounted for. They must be in hiding.'"[71] However, at the succession of hostilities, each missing pastor was accounted for—a true answer to the prayers of believers around the world.

In Albania, the churches have been gathering for prayer in addition to practically aiding Kosovo refugees. "Most churches have put down all their agendas and programs and are focusing totally on the refugee work," said Eugen Begu, general secretary of the Albania Evangelical Alliance. To the Albanian Christians, the Muslim-dominated enclave is a mission field. Begu reported: "We have never had the opportunity to go to them. Now the Lord is using this situation to bring them to us. Our goal is not to take advantage of this situation and go hit their heads with the gospel. We recognize that we can show the gospel by serving them, caring for them, listening to them, and living the gospel in front of their eyes."[72]

Pleas for prayer support from the Balkans have been regular and emphatic. "Your prayers are such strong moral support, please don't cease praying," requested Reverend Lazar Stojsic, president of the Serbian Evangelical Alliance.[73] As part of its call for a day of prayer and fasting on Sunday, May 16, 1999, Eugen Begu indicated that "Albanian Christians are seeking God's guidance for wisdom to be the people of God in their continuing response to the needs of Kosovar refugees during this time of crisis and have asked churches worldwide to join them in prayer."[74] Peter Kuzmic called the world to prayer for the missing Kosovar pastors spoken of earlier. The CBN network included E-mail letters from pastors, missionary workers, and other Christians pleading for international prayer from their homes and churches in Albania, Serbia, and Macedonia.[75]

World Vision's prayer focus has been directed toward this crisis since before the bombs fell. In September 1998, John Robb E-mailed international networks of prayer warriors on behalf of UN and NATO authorities who were "holding critical consultations to determine whether to intervene in this troubled province." "In the name of Jesus," Robb told other prayer warriors, "let us resist the destructive powers of darkness who want to foment greater and greater hatred and carnage." Robb sent out more prayer advisories in late 1998 and early 1999, and as the conflict increased, other Christian groups, especially those with a media focus, began to pick up and carry requests for prayer. An example of this is in *Religion Today* magazine, with a January 1999 article entitled "Pray for Kosovo, Christians Plead."[76]

However, it really wasn't until the bombs were about to fall or were falling that most Christian organizations brought the Kosovo conflict to the head of their prayer lists. This was, in part, due to the fact that the atrocities were better understood when there was film footage documentation on nightly television; especially as lives were being lost, Kosovo became a headline event. Not only were the various news organizations making information readily available, but so were the relief agencies that were assisting the refugees. According to the *Washington Post*, the latest count indicates there are twenty-eight relief agencies assisting the effort in Albania and Macedonia.[77] A quick look at these reveals that eleven are Christian charities, most of which have some sort of call to prayer in their published material.

Again, as the crisis escalated, so did the information and requests for prayer. There have been web sites and articles from denominations, individual churches, and various Christian organizations, including the media. *Religion Today* has had a number of articles calling readers to prayer; the Christian Broadcasting Network (CBN) carried E-mail prayer requests from church leaders ministering in the Balkans; Saint Andrews Church in Chorleywood, U.K., carried a "Prophecy on Kosovo" from Mark Stibbe; the Mennonite Central Committee has listed seven prayer items for member churches to consider; the Presbyterians called for prayer for the ministry of Decani Monastery in Kosovo, which had been hit by a bomb; the Baptists have asked for prayer on behalf of their ministry with the refugees in Albania; Focus on the Family has called for prayer with information from missionaries Ted and Lori Bultsma, and *The Capitol Hill Prayer Alert*, a nonprofit organization that has many senators and representatives as its members, has called on Congress to "itself take a day to dispense with its regular duties to hold a Solemn Assembly for its own members."[78]

The importance of continuing prayer—for the refugees; that the KLA will not cause trouble; that the Serbs can return to Kosovo peaceably; that there is enough food for all; that shelter will become available prior to the fast-approaching winter—cannot be overstated. The world has observed the atrocities, and many have come before God Almighty to intercede on behalf of the oppressed. However, there is another important piece of this puzzle that has not, as yet, been entered into the equation at any significant level, if at all. This important "next step" for Kosovo involves prayer combined with the following Holy Spirit-led activities:

- Christians from the various ethnic groups coming together and asking forgiveness of one another—"identifying" with each other, taking on each other's burdens, and confessing their sins one to another.

- Prayer against the cycle of bondage that has been present for generation after generation due to unhistoric and unreliable myths regarding the development of their culture.
- Prayer against the "legend" of Kosovo Polje and the grip it has on the Serbs.
- On-site intercessors skilled at researching the devil's history of oppression with discernment and giftedness in order to plan out a strategy of resistance and take authority against antihuman powers for the long-term deliverance and healing of Kosovo.

There is a good reason why this has yet to take place in Kosovo:

- Lessons were not applied from the Bosnia experience.
- Entry was denied to international prayer leaders trying to come into Kosovo before and during hostilities.
- As the hostilities increased, most Christian nongovernmental organizations were focused on what they do best, providing relief and rehabilitation, rather than facilitating on-site prayer teams.

While overtures were made to come to Kosovo before NATO commenced its bombing under the auspices of one of the Christian relief and development organizations, the overture was not positively received. However, now that there is the availability of entry into Kosovo, local Christian leaders and internationals with a passion for prayer should come together to facilitate reconciliatory prayer throughout the Balkan region, not only in Kosovo. Additionally, according to the May 31, 1991, newsletter from Drs. Mark and Betsy Neuenschwander's International Health Services Foundation, such spiritual warfare activities as "spiritual mapping and identificational repentance must be done to establish a beachhead" in Kosovo.[79] This is the most important "next step" for Kosovo—without it, the conflict will simmer on and probably heat up once again.

The sense that Christians are in warfare in Kosovo is beginning to take hold. Sonja Nowack, a member of the Albanian Evangelical Alliance's (VU) Prayer Commission, reported that spiritual warfare was evident in the successful attempts of non-Christian relief organizations to take over some of the camps. However, even in this, "refugees later expressed that as a result of [others] running the camps, they saw that the Christians really cared for them."[80] The Neuenschwanders reported that they were "dealing with forces of hopelessness, confusion, high unemployment, and division and strife." They called for Christians everywhere to "pray for the right Christian leaders to become involved in prayer with us . . . [and] pray with us against the demonic prince of the Balkans which includes the forces of hatred, bitterness, death, destruction, religion, pride, ethnicity, and segregation."[81]

In June 1999, a Balkan Peace Consultation took place in Greece. The discussion of peace through reconciliation was at the forefront. In addition, there will be a Hope for the Balkans conference in June 2000, where peace and reconciliation will again be the focus. The various evangelical alliances also planned to meet again in September 1999 for further consultation "to encourage reconciliation."[82]

It is the Lord to whom both Serb and Albanian Kosovars must come if forgiveness and reconciliation are to prevail in the Balkans. God's people around the world and inside Kosovo need to pray heartily for those who can give leadership to this process of bringing all parties together in the name of the Prince of Peace. Unless strong leaders arise and facilitate real repentance and forgiveness between the ethnic groups, the historically and demonically driven cycle of revenge and bloodletting will continue to torment Kosovo, Bosnia, and the whole region.

An elderly Kosovar woman is helped over difficult mountain forests as she and her family flee advancing Serbs and head for Albania. (Credit: John Schenk/World Vision)

This is the sight where the first massacre of 54 Kosovars took place in February 1998. (Credit: Hilary MacKenzie/World Vision)

After hiding in the nearby forests for three months, a boy named Liridon returns home only to find devastation and ruin. (Credit: Rod Curtis/World Vision.)

Tragedy and desperation mark a Kosovar family as they flee terror by crossing over into Albania. (Credit: Rod Curtis/World Vision)

As NATO "K-FOR" troops seek to enforce an uneasy peace in Kosovo, family members return to their burnt-out home in the village of Bukosh. (Credit: Kevin Cook/World Vision)

A broken skull, rib cage, and boots are exposed in one partially covered grave in Kosovo. (Credit: Kevin Cook/World Vision)

8

HEALING THE WOUNDS OF THE DESTROYER IN CAMBODIA

Ruby blood that sprinkles the towns and the plains
Of Kampuchea, our Homeland
Splendid blood of workers and peasants,
Splendid blood of revolutionary men and women soldiers!
This blood changes into implacable hatred and resolved war,
April 17, under the flag of the Revolution.
Freedom from slavery.
FROM "GLORIOUS APRIL 17!"
A NATIONAL HYMN OF THE KHMER ROUGE

We are the humble Cambodian race. We live, we love, we work each day.
We have a history of genocidal problems that we can hardly face.
We are the survivors of Pol Pot's gloom.
We toiled, we starved, we died each day.
We suffered agonies,
Hoping some day we'd be rescued from our doom. . . .
Do not forget us when we go away.
We fear, we shout, we cry each day.
Your task may be in vain
Because dark clouds may come again our way.
TAKEN FROM "KHMER CONSCIENCE"

PREPARATIONS FOR A PRAYER OFFENSIVE

It was during my (John's) first visit to Cambodia during February 1994 that the idea for a special prayer initiative emerged. World Vision Cambodia had arranged for me to conduct an Unreached Peoples Seminar for local Christian workers concerned to focus mission efforts on the majority Khmer people as well as on the minority groups that were still fairly untouched by the gospel of Jesus Christ. While we were meeting in the Anglican church premises in Phnom Penh, pastor, evangelist, and hymn writer Barnabus Mam told me that the churches were embroiled in a "spiritual battle." He explained that the powers of darkness were very strong in the land and were continuing to manifest their influence through the Khmer Rouge guerillas, who often made sorties from their jungle redoubts along the Thai border to attack farming villages, UN workers, and Vietnamese residents. The nation was kept in constant destabilization and was not able to move ahead in its development.

I was shocked to hear his characterization of the Khmer Rouge as "demon worshipers" since I had always assumed they were Marxists. He and others at the seminar agreed that they were involved in the placation of spirits and that their strongholds at Pailin and elsewhere were associated with worship of the spirits and so were spiritually protected. In addition, to make themselves invulnerable in battle, Khmer Rouge leaders were known to wear amulets around their waists made from the bodies of human fetuses. Due to the protection of the demonic realm, the government forces could never prevail against the Khmer Rouge, even fifteen years after they had been driven from power into the remote western borderlands.

During this same time, the church in Cambodia was rent with division. There was competition and misunderstanding among church leaders, making it hard for them to cooperate in extending the gospel to the unreached peoples and to participate meaningfully as one body in nation building. Barnabus went on to ask for special prayer for Cambodia. Would it be possible for prayer networks outside the country to pray for this situation? We also discussed the possibility of my bringing an international team of gifted intercessors to support them in a coordinated effort backed by external prayer networks to authoritatively pray on-site against the destructive powers and for God's transformation.

Subsequently Barnabus Mam, along with Chhon Kong of Cambodia Christian Services and with support from our World Vision staff, began planning a special prayer initiative for March 1995. In November 1994, as part of the preparatory process, we sent out several key prayer concerns to the international prayer networks connected to the AD2000 Prayer Track led by Peter and Doris Wagner. The first request was to "pray for the overthrow and dissolution of the Khmer Rouge guerilla/terrorists." Two months later, a February 7 *New York Times* headline proclaimed that the Khmer Rouge chain of command was dissolving! The article reported that thousands of rank-and-file guerillas were defecting, some going over to the government forces. We were electrified to see the very words we had used in prayer to God being broadcast by a well-known newspaper.

RESEARCHING THE ROOTS OF DESTRUCTION

In the months before my second visit to Cambodia with the prayer team, I began to research the historical and cultural roots of the war, genocide, and suffering that seemed to plague this tiny country of Indochina. This is most important since current human conflicts often have deep underlying antecedents buried in the society's past. What I discovered from library sleuthing and interviews with former missionaries and a Cambodian immigrant convinced me that Barnabus and the Cambodian seminar participants were right—there were spiritual forces that had been welcomed into the land centuries before, and they were still claiming their right to dominate and destroy it.

It was during the ninth century that the door was opened to the destructive forces that have ravaged this unfortunate land for so much of its history. An early ruler, Jayavarman II, established the cult of the god-king, known as *devaraja*. Employing the services of a Brahman priest at his coronation on Mount Kulen, this ruler dedicated himself and the land that was to become Angkor and later Cambodia to Shiva (or Siva), Hindu god of fertility and destruction. In so doing he made himself an earthly incarnation of the god and set up the *linga*—a stone idol depicting the male sex organ of Shiva—in a temple at the center of his kingdom.[1] From that time on, the rulers of Cambodia, assisted by Indian Brahmans, sought protection in devotion to Shiva. Researcher George Otis Jr. observes: "So began the royal patronage of Siva which continued through the reenactment of the ceremony by each successive ruler until Prince Norodom Sihanouk was ousted in 1970."[2]

Another power welcomed by the early Cambodians was Naga, the five-headed (or sometimes seven-headed) serpent god that, according to legend, ruled over the waters and the soil and from whom the Khmer people are descended. In one temple at Angkor, the serpent spirit was said to have appeared nightly as a beautiful woman to unite with the king. If the king failed to keep his tryst with Naga, disaster and death would follow.[3] Local Christian leaders told me that Naga is today called "the guardian spirit of the Cambodian people." Two local development facilitators write: "Naga, the seven-headed serpent who showed favor to the Buddha, has been the real prince of Cambodia. His ubiquitous symbol adorns public places, both civic and religious, and the country's architecture and other art. The Naga's primary ancient stronghold has been the fabled Angkor . . . one of the seven wonders of the world, hidden in the jungles of northwest Cambodia."[4]

The resemblance of Shiva ("the destroyer") and Naga (represented as a many-headed snake) to Satan (the biblical character known as "the serpent") is striking. Devotion to such a spiritual being often tragically involved the land's rulers in sacrificing their own people for the worship of the one whom Jesus described as a murderer—one who wants to rob, kill, and destroy. During our subsequent visit in March and while on a tour of Angkor, the former center of the Khmer empire, we were shown a massive grave site where a later king—fearful that the awesome stone temple and monuments he had just completed for his god would be discovered by his enemies—executed all the builders who had toiled for many years. One wonders how many thousands of men and women were destroyed through slave labor in the process of building the seventy-two major stone-and-brick temples and monuments of Angkor, which cover seventy-five square miles of territory. One building, Angkor Wat, is the largest religious structure in the world.

This profligacy in taking human life continued on through the centuries according to David Chandler, a leading scholar of Cambodian history, who writes: "The transmission of Siva's potency via the overlord and his ritual acts to the people and the soil was an important source of cohesiveness in Cambodian society. It has also been a source of continuity. As late as 1877 human sacrifices to a consort of Siva were conducted at Ba Phnom at the beginning of the agricultural year. Like those described in 5th century Chinese sources, these had the objective of transmitting fertility to the region, and . . . were sponsored by the local officials."[5]

Opening and keeping open the door to Shiva and Naga had its price. After the decline of Angkor in the fifteenth century and without the protection of mountain ranges to prevent attack from the east and west, Cambodia was devastated in a recurring cycle of civil wars and invasions from hostile neighbors on both sides. The Khmer Rouge and their horrific reign were just the latest example of a destructive pattern flowing through history. Seanglim Bit, in his book *The Warrior Heritage*, discusses the extreme psychological and social damage to the national psyche that the legacy of war and aggression have caused, starting from the militaristic god-kings and carried on through their successors. Bit observes that because of the bloodshed and brutal episodes in the past a warrior model, in which the warrior is "the representation of strength and honor" and in which aggression has been used to serve the interests of those in power, has come to dominate the culture.[6] He mentions the "volcano effect," which at times has exploded in pogroms against minorities and the Cambodian folktales that memorialize for them and their children this kind of sudden, arbitrary violence. Under the Khmer Rouge leadership, it approached paranoia: they even exterminated their own cadres as their efforts to remake the country failed.[7]

A fearful preoccupation with the spirit world and the endless need to protect oneself and one's family from its dangers was confirmed by many I consulted. One former missionary said it is "the thing that really governs people." Another compared Cambodian religious practice to an onion, with Hindu and Buddhist leaves on the outside and a core of animism at the center. One scholar agrees: "It can be argued that the requirements of the spirit world in Cambodia, together with the moral precepts centered on activities in the village Buddhist temple, form the organizing force of rural social life."[8] It is no wonder that the Cambodian Christian leaders with whom I met in 1994 described the battle for their land in spiritual terms.

THE KHMER ROUGE HORROR

It is understandable given this background that the Khmer Rouge could take over the nation and plunge it into one of the most awful episodes in human history. Yathay Pin grieves, "The tragedy of Cambodia has not yet run its course, nor will it for generations. Millions have died, a culture has vanished."[9] *Kampuchea Today* reflects: "Kampuchea [Cambodia] was reduced to ashes. The whole Kampuchean people became slaves and convicts under death sentence. The whole social and material infrastructure was destroyed. In no time at all, everything that was built by the Kampuchean people during the last thousand years was torn to pieces."[10]

When the Khmer Rouge regime of Democratic Kampuchea ended after four years in 1979, the world was able to glimpse how really satanic their impact had been:

1. An estimated 1.5 to 3 million deaths were caused, some through outright executions and beatings but mostly through excessive forced labor, starvation, and disease. There were also widespread purges of Khmer Rouge cadres as mentioned earlier.[11]
2. They destroyed the system of social relations, especially by breaking up the extended family—and even nuclear families, separating kids from their parents—to create work units for their collectivized economic schemes.

3. Religion was suppressed, whether Buddhism, Islam, or Christianity; temples and churches were destroyed, and monks and pastors killed as Khmer Rouge ideology became the sole acceptable way of thinking.

4. The culture was almost eradicated with the death of those with special skills, such as dancers, artists, craftsmen, weavers, etc.; the loss of most literary works from the national library; the effacing of archaeological sites; and the destruction of musical instruments along with "uncountable artifacts bearing witness to Cambodian culture and civilization."[12]

5. Agriculture was devastated by the loss of many different strains of rice since farmers were only allowed to plant one kind and water flow patterns were disrupted by disastrous irrigation projects.[13]

6. The dispersion of hundreds of thousands of Cambodia's citizens who fled as refugees to nineteen other countries (150,000 to the U.S.A.), most never to return. Many of these continue to suffer posttraumatic stress and nagging fear due to the experience of warfare and harsh treatment, as well as recurrent physical pain known as "Pol Pot syndrome."[14]

7. Millions of land mines were left behind, nearly ten million, or as one UN Children's Fund worker puts it: there are two mines in the ground for every Cambodian child. They continue to kill six hundred Cambodians and maim more than two hundred per month—many of them children because half the population is under fifteen years of age.[15]

THE PRAYER INITIATIVE AND ITS IMPACT

In March 1995, more than fifty national Christian workers from a variety of church backgrounds and locations throughout the country gathered in Phnom Penh for a three-day conference to pray for the nation, the church, and the unreached peoples; it was entitled "Praying for Cambodia and Its Peoples." It was organized by Cambodia Christian Services, an umbrella organization including both church and parachurch groups in the country. It was my privilege to lead an international team of eleven from seven countries to speak at the conference and to provide support for the local leaders in their effort to come against the spiritual darkness oppressing the land. We were in turn supported by intercessors in many countries who prayed with specific information supplied ahead of time. This makes for a potent combination, as we have seen in Bosnia and other places as well.

The most senior member of our team and also the most experienced in spiritual warfare ministry was the late Kjell Sjoberg—a tall, dignified Swede who had led similar teams to more than eighty countries. The Lord used his marvelous discernment and prophetic boldness in a wonderful way during the initiative. I will quote from his trip report as well as mine as I describe those amazing days with the Cambodian brothers and sisters, as well as the intense time of prayer for the nation and the later sense of breakthrough experienced at Angkor.

The first remarkable development, no doubt in answer to the prayers of so many around the world, was the invitation extended by the nation's military command to Barnabus Mam and some of the other pastors to conduct a Christian funeral for a believing general who had died a few days before the conference in an air crash. Here is how Kjell Sjoberg recounts it:

> Cambodia is a Buddhist country, and there never has been an official state funeral held according to Christian customs. The funeral took place the same day as we started our prayer conference. At four o'clock in the morning, the pastors . . . were asked to solemnize a Christian funeral for the general. They were given 40 minutes in the official program. The highest military leaders with all the generals were present, ministers in the government and members of the royal family. The pastors were able to give the Gospel and a Christian message to 300 of the leaders of the country. In the end 267 New Testaments with the Psalms were distributed to the leaders who eagerly received them. Everyone wanted a Bible and the Bibles were not enough, so the pastors asked Christians who were present to give their own Bibles to the officers. They had never had such an opportunity."[16]

This was a glorious interruption to the conference, and all of us were in prayer for the funeral that first day. After the conference got going in earnest at the end of the first day, Dr. Joe Ozawa, a psychologist and pastor on our team, ministered powerfully to the Christian workers in the area of inner healing, laying on of hands and praying for them individually. Sjoberg recounted:

> "At the river of life were trees for the healing of the nations" (Rev. 22:2). Cambodia needs a divine healing ministry flowing from the river of life. They need personal love letters from their Father in heaven. Such letters were delivered by Joe Ozawa in our team. He took much time to minister to individuals . . . They received when Joe said: "The Lord will remove the heart of stone from you and give you a heart of flesh." Joe gave a message to the fatherless. When he asked in the end of a meeting, 80% were fatherless. We met young men who had lost all their relatives.[17]

This set the stage for the most significant time in our meeting together. During the night, the Lord was speaking to Kjell Sjoberg about the situation and about the people attending the conference. The next day he strode to the podium, opened his mouth, and to my recollection, gave the shortest presentation—only one sentence. That sentence, however, stunned and pierced the hearts of all, especially the Cambodians. It was: "Some of you have blood on your hands!" For a time there was such silence you could have heard the proverbial pin rebound from the concrete floor. But what came next was like the breaking of a dike—weeping, wailing, and torrents of tears. One by one, pastors and evangelists confessed that during the "killing fields" time, they themselves had killed others with their own hands. At that time they had not yet come to Christ and since then had been keeping their crimes secret for fear of retaliation upon themselves and their families. However, suppressing the truth had taken its toll, hindering the unity of the church and making them distrustful of one another. Kjell, prompted by the Holy Spirit, had seen that this needed to be confessed for the release to happen and for us to go forward into spiritual warfare together. As he was fond of saying, "The lower we go in repentance, the higher we go in spiritual warfare." In his newsletter he later recounted:

> "In that day the Lord will punish Leviathan the fleeing serpent. With his fierce and great and mighty sword, even Leviathan the twisted serpent; he will kill the dragon who lives in the sea" (Isa. 27:1). On which day will the Lord punish the serpent who lives in the sea? The day when the bloodguilt is uncovered. "And the earth will reveal her bloodshed and will no longer cover her slain" (Isa. 26:21). Killing and bloodguilt is the national sin of Cambodia. I was convinced that the only way for us to have authority to deal with the Naga serpent spirit in Cambodia was if the people confessed their part in the bloodguilt. Without a breakthrough in repentance we would not have authority to go to the stronghold of Angkor Wat."[18]

Because of the unique, even overwhelming, way the Spirit of God had broken in upon us, we changed course. A room was provided for individuals, numbering about one-third of those present, to go and confess their sins long buried and now crying out to be vented. There were three who had served as Khmer Rouge soldiers, one as an executioner who had killed hundreds, perhaps a thousand. He had also gone into Vietnam and killed hundreds more, mainly women and children. Others had allowed many villagers to starve by taking their food for the Khmer Rouge. Some women had carried out abortions as midwives. One woman had buried a newborn baby alive. Another had killed her alienated husband through witchcraft. As they wept, the interpreter also wept—he had been imprisoned in one of the camps and seen thousands die with his own eyes. These were heinous crimes, but what amazed us all was the grace of God, that the Lord could forgive and restore people who had done such things!

Based on the confession and repentance for the sin of murder and the bloodguilt, we now felt emboldened to pray aggressively for the healing and deliverance of the land from idolatry and the dominion of darkness. Under the leadership of the pastors, we broke into four teams to pray at various sites in and around the capital that had historical and spiritual significance. We were careful to be low-key and quiet, as is our normal practice, so as not to provoke unwanted attention. One team, led by Barnabus Mam, went south to Ba Phnom, the site where Jayavarman II first established Shiva worship and the cult of the god-king. Here is Kjell Sjoberg's version of what happened:

> Ba Phnom is a mountain that Satan has used in the same way he tempted Jesus on a mountain: "All these kingdoms of the world will I give you if you fall down and worship me." Jesus refused to worship Satan, but the kings of the Khmer kingdom accepted the deal from Satan to get power of other kingdoms. . . .We traveled for three hours and had to cross the Mekong River by ferry and arrived at a village near the mountain. We asked a young mother if she knew the ancient place where humans had been sacrificed to Shiva. She answered: "There are no old people left in our village. The old people knew about our history, they have been killed, but we do not know anything." A man on a motorcycle stopped and he knew the place. He took us to a place with a small religious temple. Here Siva the Destroyer had been worshiped. . . .What we saw was a place of destruction. Near the wall was a huge, broken pot filled with human bones. We were told that this ancient place had been used by the Red Khmer [Khmer Rouge] as a place of killing. Just near where we stood, a mass grave had been found, where Pol Pot had killed 2,000 people. Pastor Barnabus Mam had been in a prison camp at the foot of the mountain. His sister had been killed in the area. *What we saw were demonic patterns of destruction from the foundation of the nation repeated through its history* (italics added).[19]

The team I participated in conducted a Communion service at Choeng Ek, a major killing ground outside Phnom Penh where approximately nine thousand were executed, mostly civil servants, intellectuals, and some Khmer Rouge cadres killed in purges. A sign explaining what happened there attributed it to people who, though human in appearance, had the "hearts of demons." Even now, twenty years later, bits of bone and clothing are still visible sticking up through the barren ground. I could almost hear the cries of these nameless victims as we prayed with our Cambodian brothers and sisters for healing, reconciliation, and transformation of the society.

At the end of the conference, seven pastors joined with our eleven for the flight to Siem Reap. From there a short bus journey took us to the fabled Angkor Wat, the largest religious structure in the world and part of a vast complex of temples and monuments that served as the center of the Khmer empire from the ninth to the fifteenth centuries. Angkor continues to be the spiritual and cultural heart of the nation. It is still an active place of worship; even King Sihanouk, I was surprised to discover, still worships there annually, retaining Brahman advisors for the celebration of ancient rituals dating from the original god-kings.

Kjell Sjoberg, characteristically blunt yet discerning, was not taken in by the imposingly beautiful, ancient edifices. Standing atop one of the stone bulwarks, he led us in a prophetic reading and proclamation of God's word of judgment on all such man-made religious systems that spring from Babylon. "Fallen, fallen is *Angkor Wat* (Babylon) the great whore she who has made all the nations drink of the wine of the passion of her immorality" (Rev. 14:8). Most all of the temples were surrounded by serpent motifs dedicated to Naga. In the temple of the sacred sword, Kjell used Deuteronomy 32:33–43, which starts with the words, "Their wine is the venom of serpents, the deadly poison of cobras" (v. 33), but the Lord says, "When I sharpen my flashing sword and my hand grasps it in judgment, I will take vengeance on my adversaries" (v. 41).

At Angkor Wat our team broke into two as the Cambodian leaders led us through the maze of buildings covering a couple hundred acres. The exquisitely carved stone frieze that extends around the central portion of the temple portrays battle scenes in which the god-kings vanquished their enemies with unspeakable atrocities. Barnabus Mam was overcome with weeping as he saw the very same tortures and killing methods that had been used by the Khmer Rouge as they dispatched their victims. *This was to us another indication that the same spirit of destruction and death that had possessed the original rulers had been manifest in the murderous clique that tormented the land in the late 1970s.* Here is how Kjell Sjoberg described the place:

> I believe that Angkor Wat, the national monument and pride of Cambodia, was another gate of hell on earth. It is pictured on the flag of Cambodia and on the currency notes. It is the biggest religious building on earth. It is a stronghold of death. It was the capital for the kings who ruled in the Khmer kingdom over Cambodia, Vietnam, Laos and Thailand—in Indochina. The present kingdom of Thailand has its roots in Angkor Wat and many of the temples of Thailand are just copies of Angkor Wat. The reliefs picture the thirty-two levels of hell along one side wall of Angkor Wat. On the other side of the temple are one battle after another showing how people are being killed, beheaded and tortured. All the methods of torture pictured on the walls of Angkor Wat in the 12th century were used by Pol Pot when he tortured and murdered one million people in Cambodia. . . . Angkor Wat gave the demonic patterns of hell that have been repeated in our lifetime.[20]

In this "wonder of the world," the place of centuries of ignorant worship of false gods, we quietly prayed and sang praises to the one who alone deserves the worship of humankind—"for He alone is worthy . . . Christ the Lord." Some of us climbed the central tower where a large statue to Buddha now stands. Just behind it was a dark shaft that drops close to one hundred feet down into the earth, giving credence to Sjoberg's sense that this was a "gate of hell." We wondered what purpose it had served and whether people had been sacrificed and disposed of here in ancient ritual. Barnabus boldly jumped out over the mouth of the pit as I was cautioning everyone to stand back in case someone would fall in. He shouted out that he and the other leaders were closing the gate to the underworld, and we all agreed in prayer for the opening up of the gates here and throughout Cambodia to the "King of glory . . . the LORD strong and mighty, the LORD mighty in battle" (Ps. 24:8).

Our last prayer action took place on Mount Bakheng overlooking Angkor Wat. It was a high place structured much like a Mayan temple where kings worshiped Shiva and became his incarnations, renewing the original covenants made with this false god. Ezekiel 36 was an important Scripture throughout the prayer initiative. Inspired by verse 25—"I will sprinkle clean water on you, and you will be clean; I will cleanse you from all your impurities and from your idols"—we carried out the following actions, which Sjoberg describes: "We laid out the whole map of Cambodia on the ground. All of us carried a bottle of drinking water with us because of the heat. When we prayed and blessed Cambodia, we poured out water over the map. The children who were standing around us also stretched out their hands over the map."[21]

In a number of places where we prayed it was the local children who were the witnesses, and in this last instance they actually felt prompted to join in with us, laying their hands on the outstretched map of their country as we prayed for the peace and renewal of the nation. It was as if the Lord were saying, "I want this new generation to be free from the ravages of war and the destructive deception of idolatry."

One in our team had brought a cobra skin from India. Afterwards, as a further prophetic action, the seven Cambodian pastors placed their feet on the skin and together renounced and broke all covenants that had been made with Shiva and Naga by their forefathers. Sjoberg explains: "Our spiritual battle was against the seven-headed Naga serpent, who was respected as the founder of the nation. Jesus told his disciples: 'I have given you authority to tread upon serpents and scorpions, and over all the power of the enemy, and nothing shall injure you' (Luke 10:19, NASB) . . . Our time in Angkor Wat ended with singing, rejoicing and dancing on the cobra skin. We believe that we came to change the history of the nation of Cambodia by prayer."[22]

Thus ended our on-site prayer initiative. Other prayer teams also came and went from Cambodia carrying out similar efforts in various places as the Lord led them. Most importantly, the Cambodian brothers and sisters who had been part of the conference and expedition to Angkor continued to apply the promise of Joshua 1:3, "I will give you every place where you set your foot," by taking territory in the spiritual realm throughout the country as they carried out their ministries. What has been the result? How has the Lord answered?

DISSOLUTION OF THE KHMER ROUGE AND
A CALL FOR FORGIVENESS

First, the Khmer Rouge continued to dissolve as an effective political and military force to the point of extinction. One month later, the government reported that they had been reduced to a mere nuisance because they had become so weak. Though it was difficult to dislodge them completely from their jungle hideaway, the government claimed that seven thousand had defected, leaving only about two thousand fighters.[23] While I was in India in June 1997, local news articles reported that rival factions had developed among the Khmer Rouge, and they were "disintegrating." Pol Pot and two hundred of his comrades were being attacked by Ta Mok, a one-legged Khmer Rouge general known as "the butcher" because of his brutality.[24] Subsequently, Pol Pot was tried by his own colleagues just before his death—the ultimate disgrace and abandonment for this genocidal tyrant. Ta Mok, the last major leader, was captured in March 1999 and remanded to the capital for trial.

At the same time, God has been transforming the lives of some former Khmer Rouge killers, as witnessed in the conference earlier. One of the leaders, who ran the infamous Tuol Seng torture camp from 1975 to 1979, later became a Christian as a refugee, went on to plant churches in the refugee camps, and he is now pastor of the Golden West Cambodian Christian Church in Los Angeles. Recently he gave himself up to the authorities back in his native land to stand trial and to identify others who have remained in hiding. Duch, as he is called, explained his reasons: "It is OK; they can have my body. Jesus has my soul. It is important that this history be understood. I want to tell you everything clearly."[25]

Barnabus Mam reported recently on the way Duch's case and another mentioned below are influencing the church and nation:

Regarding the case of Duch, the former chief security officer of Tuol Seng prison, church key leaders and expats were

165

working together to produce a bilingual statement on "Forgiveness of Those Guilty of Atrocity." It will be circulated within the church in the city and in the provinces so that the church will teach her members on forgiveness, healing and reconciliation. Last year CBN and Kampuchea for Christ produced "One Thousand Years in the Killing Field," a true video story of Rev. Setan Aaron Lee and his wife, who were badly treated by the Khmer Rouge local authority and yet decided to forgive them, especially when Setan was preaching at a church in Khao I Dang camp, Thailand, and saw a Khmer Rouge executioner. This video was broadcast on Easter evening over the best-received TV channel in Cambodia.[26]

HEALING AND CHURCH UNITY

Secondly, in the months after the prayer initiative, there was a healing of much of the earlier disunity among church leaders, enabling them to come together with church leaders from elsewhere in the region to focus on reconciliation in late October 1995. This was facilitated by Reg Reimer of World Evangelical Fellowship. Confessions of deep bitterness and racism burst forth from Cambodian, Vietnamese, Laotian, and Thai participants. The Cambodian leaders have since worked together in four cooperative councils to impact their nation for Christ. For the most part this had not been possible in the past, but now the number of churches has grown substantially, no doubt related to this increased unity. Barnabus Mam wrote in June 1999 of the continuing impact of the prayer initiative:

> I have seen impact through the united efforts in the nation over the past few years. The church leaders in each city and province are coming together and meet together in the pastors' fellowship each month. Top leaders of the four evangelical councils [Evangelical Fellowship of Cambodia (EFC), Cambodian Christian Federation (CCF), Cambodian Christian Evangelical Alliance (CCEA), Cambodian Baptist Federation (CBF)] often meet with one another to plan and make strategy to reach and disciple the whole nation for

Christ. The church grew from about 50 churches in 1992 to over 1,000 churches by 1999. Despite difficulty, 21 Jesus film teams are actively showing the *Jesus* film every night in towns and remote villages in Cambodia with positive response. Some VIPs and families have come to know the Lord as the result of Gospel radio broadcast and executive question-and-answer on Christian life lunch fellowship. . . . Church planting movement is everywhere. In addition to a thousand Khmer churches, at least a church is planted among each of the following ethnic groups: the Chinese, the Vietnamese, the Laotian, the Thai, the Jarai, the Krung, the Tompuan, the Kravet, the Mnong in Cambodia.[27]

To add to what Barnabus reports, colleagues of ours in World Vision Cambodia during the months after the initiative told me of "spontaneous conversions" that had occurred in the villages as a result of dreams and visions of Christ given to the villagers. Before the initiative, one of our team had sent me the undated vision received by American preacher Jill Austin, which seems quite prophetic now. She claimed the Lord had spoken to her with the phrase *killing fields* as she was getting dressed one morning. Later, in the midst of a meeting, he said that "the cry of the martyr's blood cries out to me from the ground." She recounted the experience: "Then the Lord told me that He was going to give the Cambodians a building . . . a huge warehouse. . . . Inside it was full of the glory of the Lord and He told me that a huge net was going to pull in multitudes and multitudes of new believers. The martyred saints were walking around, and their prayers and the prayers of the living were moving like a heavy mist over the whole nation of Cambodia. The Lord said a great visitation of revival was coming."[28]

SOCIAL AND POLITICAL PRAYERS

Thirdly, there has been social and political impact according to Barnabus, who wrote as an inside observer:

The ruling parties stopped arresting the opposition party members. They can talk openly in the national assembly.

Politicians who were exiled are now welcome back to live and work in Cambodia. The government has done something to close down red light districts, to collect illegal weapons to destroy them, to arrest more and more blackmailers and kidnappers. People can travel free of trouble throughout Cambodia because there is no more Khmer Rouge strongholds. In Phnom Penh, people can even travel at night. A number of good and free hospitals have been established in Phnom Penh and Siem Reap. Many roads in Phnom Penh are being repaired and rebuilt. April 13–15, 1999, is the first Khmer New Year days to be ever celebrated with no bloodshed and violent acts. Thank God that there was not much bloodshed and killing during 1997 coup and 1998 election as there was supposed to.

CONTINUED GROWTH

Lastly, it is very encouraging to hear how the prayer movement continues to grow. This is the best sign that God's transforming hand is still at work to bring forth even more positive changes in the nation. Barnabus mentioned a whole series of prayer activities that he and others have carried on since 1995: a national day of prayer with the collection and circulation of prayer requests throughout the nation; spiritual warfare seminars; weekly and monthly prayer and fasting meetings; a twenty-four-hour prayer chain; and teams sent out to do prayer walking in various towns. No wonder God is answering and renewing this land. According to the Lord's gracious promises, we believe even better things are still to come! Glory to him for it all!

John Robb
with bird sellers
in the shadow
of Naga, the
serpent god.

Piles of skulls at Choeng Ek, one of the infamous "killing fields" of the Khmer Rouge.

Team members Kjell Sjoberg and Joe Ozawa ministering to local Christian workers.

Angkor Wat, one of the "wonders of the world."

Team praying with Cambodian pastors at Angkor Wat.

Pastor Barnabas Mam weeping over the atrocities carved in stone at Angkor Wat.

Final prayer action on Mount Bakheng where local pastors renounced the influence of Shiva and Naga and prayed with our team for renewal and healing for the nation.

International prayer team from seven countries.

9

HOPE AND HEALING FOR RWANDA

There are no devils in hell. . . . They are all in Rwanda.
TIME MAGAZINE, 16 MAY 1994

*The sweetly sickening odor of decomposing bodies hung over many
parts of Rwanda in July 1994: on Nyanza ridge, overlooking the
capital, Kigali, where skulls and bones, torn clothing, and scraps of
paper were scattered among the bushes; at Nyamata, where bodies
lay twisted and heaped on benches and the floor of a church; at
Nyarubuye in eastern Rwanda, where the cadaver of a little girl,
otherwise intact, had been flattened by passing vehicles to the
thinness of cardboard in front of the church steps; on the shores of
idyllic Lake Kivu in western Rwanda, where pieces of human bodies
had been thrown down the steep hillside; and at Nyakizu in
southern Rwanda, where the sun-bleached fragments of bone in the
sand of the schoolyard and, on a nearby hill, a small red sweater
held together the rib cage of a decapitated child.*
HUMAN RIGHTS WATCH REPORT

*All over the world the Church is called to cast out demons, not only
out of individuals but also nations. God wants the Church to rule, to
bind principalities and powers with authority, and to determine the
politics of nations.*
INGULF SCHMIDT

My (John's) normal office routine was interrupted by an urgent fax from Kigali, Rwanda. It was January 15, 1997, and though I had many pressing things on my mind, my attention was arrested by the memo's subject: "Urgent Prayer Ministry Needed in Rwanda." The message was from Tekle Selassie, an Ethiopian former World Vision colleague, then serving with another organization carrying out reconciliation efforts in the war and genocide-shattered country.

Like a Macedonian call that I could not ignore, his fax mentioned his talks with local church leaders and their feeling that the need to organize a special prayer initiative was of paramount importance to the rebuilding of the church and nation. He asked me to contact Antoine Rutayisire, nationally respected leader of the African Evangelistic Enterprise (AEE), who had already implemented several prayer and fasting activities, to discuss the possibility of an internationally supported prayer initiative facilitated by World Vision and his new organization, Rouner Center for Missions and Ministry. Gratefully, there had been other prayer efforts by the Anglicans, Presbyterians, and others but no internationally coordinated focus combined with the visit of an international team of prayer warriors to support local church leaders in strategic-level intercession and spiritual warfare for the nation.

Tekle later told me that during his second visit to Rwanda he had received a premonition of further serious violence and destruction: as he was praying, he saw a large, clenched hand hanging in the clouds as if ready to strike again. At that time, the refugees from the war, many of them Hutus who had taken part in the 1994 genocide, were in the midst of returning. There was enormous potential for revenge and counterattack between them and the Tutsis, the smaller rival ethnic group that had been the focus of the earlier government's attempt to wipe them out as a people. There was every reason to believe that my Ethiopian friend's vision might be a warning from the Lord.

Like many others around the world in 1994 who saw the news reports on the developing killing spree in Rwanda, I had been aghast at what happened, feeling powerless to do anything to stop what was going on during that awful pogrom. What would make a peaceful, largely agrarian nation with one of the highest percentages of nominal Christians in Africa suddenly erupt into one of the most intense and startling genocides in the history of humanity? What would cause one ethnic group, the Hutus, to rise up against their Tutsi neighbors—even their Tutsi friends and relatives—with machetes, guns, and grenades to slaughter up to 800,000 of them in less than three months? Then U.S. ambassador to Rwanda, David Rawson, in response to such questions, bluntly yet perceptively answered: "We underestimated the power of evil. The devil is a roaring lion. Evil here in Rwanda is not some little matter like a headache. Our prayer [life] must be more than, 'Lord, cure my migraine.'"[1]

Subsequent talks with church leaders in Rwanda confirmed how right Rawson was in his simple assessment. There was something about the devil and something about the lack of prayer that figured into what happened there. This is a theme we will come back to later, but first we need to look at some of the human factors because, as we have already seen in the Balkans and in Cambodia, Satan and the spiritual powers allied with him exploit human fallenness and use willing human agents to accomplish their heinous agenda against people—those loved by and made in the image of the Creator.

HUMAN FACTORS SET THE STAGE FOR VIOLENCE

Rwandan Augustin Karakezi, in a 1996 interview, explained that the genocide that began in April 1994 was "the culmination of a long history of violence and discrimination. . . . It was well prepared and had been in the making for many years."[2] He mentioned how extremist political parties, the government, and the army organized it, taking control of the media to manipulate the people. Others agree. "What distinguished its corrupt rulers from other Third World autocrats wasn't their lust for power but their ability to manipulate age-old tensions and transform their largely uneducated population into a nation of murderers."[3] "The ruling faction of the country's elite manipulated the existing 'ethnic' raw material into an attempt at political survival." Manipulation by political leaders that played upon both the illiteracy of the majority and their docile tradition of "systematic, centralized and unconditional obedience to authority"[4] proved to be a powerful combination that the spiritual powers obviously used to instigate the anti-Tutsi campaign. Authorities also used the media to dehumanize the Tutsi as "cockroaches" and "rats." Killings of them were euphemistically referred to as "collective work"; chopping up men, as "bush clearing"; and eliminating women and children, as "pulling out the roots of the bad weeds.[5]

Another human factor was clearly the overcrowding caused by the nation's rapidly expanding population, making land more scarce, thereby providing an extra reason to exterminate neighbors—greed for their land and other property. Gerard Prunier observed: "The decision to kill was of course made by politicians, for political reasons. But at least part of the reason why it was carried out so thoroughly by the ordinary rank and file peasants . . . was the feeling that there were too many people on too little land, and that with a reduction in their numbers, there would be more for the survivors."[6]

There were also more distant historical causes dating from the colonial occupation of the country by the Germans and Belgians who had used a divide-and-conquer policy to turn Hutus and Tutsis against each other thereby to strengthen their own grip upon the territory.[7] They also sowed destructive notions of racial superiority into the minds of the two people. Indeed, there had been no trace of violence between Tutis and Hutus before the coming of the Europeans.[8] The colonialists became enamored with the Tutsis, thinking they were better looking, more intelligent, and more highly cultured than the Hutus. When combined with policies favoring the one group over the other, this attitude both inflated the Tutsi ethnic ego and crushed the Hutus' feelings, giving them "an aggressively resentful inferiority complex." In so doing the colonial masters left a "social bomb" that would someday explode, causing incalculable damage in later generations.[9]

Here again we see the evidence of false patterns of thinking and prejudices that the enemy of humankind sows in people's minds in order to pit one group against another for the destruction of both—first psychologically and ultimately physically. In analyzing the roots of the later genocide, Gerard Prunier commented on the "colonial cultural mythology of Rwanda": "Tutsi and Hutu have killed each other more to upbraid a certain vision they have of themselves, of the others, and of their place in the world than because of material interests. This is what makes the killing so relentless. Material interests can always be negotiated; ideas cannot, and they often tend to be pursued to their logical conclusions, however terrible."[10]

Modern-day Europeans and Americans also share the blame for what happened in Rwanda. Before and during the carnage that erupted, Western governments focused on their own national self-interests, including extricating their own citizens and peacekeepers, rather than on taking practical, decisive actions to avert the humanitarian catastrophe that was unfolding. According to a Human Rights Watch report:

> Policymakers in France, Belgium, and the United States and at the United Nations all knew of the preparations for massive slaughter and failed to take the steps needed to prevent it. Aware from the start that Tutsi were being targeted for elimination, the leading foreign actors refused to acknowledge the genocide. To have stopped the leaders and the zealots would have required military force; in the early stages, a relatively small force. Not only did international leaders reject this course, but they also declined for weeks to use their political and moral authority to challenge the legitimacy of the genocidal government. They refused to declare that a government guilty of exterminating its citizens would never receive international assistance. They did nothing to silence the radio that broadcast calls for slaughter. Such simple measures would have sapped the strength of the authorities bent on mass murder and encouraged Rwandan opposition to the extermination campaign.[11]

Complicit in this omission, likely because of the distraction of covering the concurrent O. J. Simpson murder trial, the world's media was largely silent until after the genocide had run its course. A recent ABC news program contrasted the copious news coverage the twelve thousand white victims killed in Kosovo's atrocities have received with the relative lack of media attention given to the slaughter of eight hundred thousand black Rwandans and suggested that racism is partially to blame.[12] This may be more evidence of the influence of the "prince of the power of the air"—to distract those who could have given voice to the unheeded cries of Rwanda's killing fields so that his work of destruction could run its full course.

The church is also implicated. In the late 1920s, while the nation was still under Belgian administration, mass conversions took place. By 1932, the church had become Rwanda's most important social institution. However, motives for conversion in many cases were other than spiritual. It was often to gain social and political advantage, and consequently, Christian values did not penetrate deeply into people's lifestyles and attitudes.[13]

"Another factor in the tribal strife, at least among the Christians involved, was a superficial faith. The people were not discipled to have the courage of their convictions in the time of trial."[14] Even during the great East African revivals of the 1930s, which began in Rwanda, moral failings like drunkenness and immorality were addressed, but the church and its leaders largely ignored the larger social justice problems of the nation because many of them had developed a cozy, comfortable relationship with the authorities, which undercut their prophetic role. Antoine Rutayisire explains how this occurred: "We must indeed blame the church for what happened in that they saw it coming and did nothing about it. . . . The church married the government, a marriage that was proposed in 1942 when the king supposedly became a Christian and was baptized. Regretfully, all his subjects then became Christian as well, and took baptism."[15]

Antoine later told me during an interview in April 1997 that before the genocide up to 90 percent of the people were merely nominal Christians due to the failure of the church to do the work of discipling these multitudes. In his opinion, only 10 percent were "real Christians," that is, committed to the lordship of Jesus Christ over their lives. He and others I spoke with said it was the nominal or cultural "Christians" who did the killing, not the minority of true believers. Carl Lawrence, an author who interviewed many in the aftermath of the genocide, agreed that he had heard "no verifiable cases of believers in Jesus Christ killing other believers."[16] On the contrary, there were many cases of believers who risked, even laid down their lives, to protect and rescue those who were being threatened. Our team also heard similar accounts while we were in the country. These brothers and sisters in Christ "have written one of the most inspiring chapters in the history of the Christian movement in Africa."[17]

SATAN'S FORCES AT WORK

These are some of the many human factors figuring into the evil events that played out in April to June 1994. But behind these actors of flesh and blood can be seen the machinations of the principalities and powers. Only people in the grip of demonically dehumanizing influences could have cut down men, women, children, even little babies, as if they were so much jungle bush needing to be cleared. Even animals don't treat each other so cruelly! What are some of the supernatural factors that bear out such an interpretation? During the same interview with Antoine Rutayisire, we discussed preparations for the upcoming prayer initiative, and because of my suspicion about the role of spiritual darkness in what had happened, I asked him to provide some insight into this dimension. He began a fascinating yet disturbing exposé of the deep syncretism (intermingling of religious beliefs) practiced by nominal Christians in Rwanda. This provided valuable prayer ammunition to our team and to networks of intercessors around the world who joined in the initiative.[18]

"Syncretism is a big problem in Rwanda," he explained. "Most of the people have taken part in traditional religious practices because of their fear of the spirits. Western missionaries simply negated the existence of these spirits and didn't teach them how to deal with them." Antoine then mentioned a local song that goes something like this: "We take the Eucharist and then go home to drink from the pot of the spirits." Binego is the most powerful spirit in the Rwandan pantheon. Antoine had gone through the initiation ceremony as a child and so knows all about this spirit-being. Binego is a spirit of bloodthirstiness, and his praise song goes roughly like this: "I am the slaughterer, son of the angry one. The one who washes his hands in blood. I am the spy, son of the warrior. I spy to attack, to loot and enrich myself. I killed the bride, and the dowry had to be paid back; the farmer and his fields could not be harvested; the old woman, child, . . ." It continues with a whole range of different kinds of people in society who were to be slaughtered in obedience to this god.

Another spirit, called Nyabingi, is a female being. She is very cruel. Some people are possessed and taken to her priestess. She dominates the territory of the northern part of the country where people live under the fear of her. They sometimes give their daughters to live with sorcerers in her service or take other gifts to them.

Ryangombe is the father of Binego. Faustin Uzabakiliho, another Rwandan I interviewed during the same period, thinks that in the popular belief, Ryangombe is the owner of all the land. In the Kubandwa cult, people construct small houses for Ryangombe in their homes and dedicate their children to him as well as to their ancestors' spirits.[19] The kings used to worship him, and they received power, economic blessing, and many children as a result. It is assumed that in later years the presidents also carried on this tradition, but secretly.

Antoine believes that it is perhaps because of this traditional, intimate link between the human and spiritual powers that there has been a special satanic attack on the political leadership of the nation. No one who has reigned in the country has died of old age. The last three presidents have been killed, so they are praying for the protection of the present one. In old times, it was taboo to have two kings living at the same time. When the father appointed his son to succeed him, he had to drink poison. Otherwise, it was considered to bring bad luck upon the nation. Certain other secrets of the kingship the leaders were sworn never to reveal. A document with such information divulged by one of them was translated but lost during the genocide.

Faustin Uzabakiliho summed up the situation in this way: "The real issue in Rwanda is not ethnic identity, though it has been used by the devil as a shield. The problem is more linked with the very sinfulness of human nature. The Rwandan turmoil was caused by the powers of this dark world, the spiritual forces in the heavenly realms. That's what we have got to fight against. It is rather a spiritual warfare as described by Paul in Ephesians 6."[20]

RATIONALE FOR THE PRAYER INITIATIVE

The prophet Isaiah said that God had posted "watchmen" on the walls of Jerusalem whose mission was to "never be silent day or night," to give themselves and the Lord "no rest" till he made their city a "praise of the earth" (Isa. 62:6–7). This, Antoine told me during our interview, was the theme of all their efforts. AEE wanted to mobilize people to pray throughout the country, believing this was the only way to fight the darkness. They started this effort in 1994 and began teaching on prayer in various regions. Now they wanted to get the Christian leaders and intercessors together in the capital for this special prayer initiative: "We want to establish a prayer chain for the whole country. People start to get active in intercession, then go back to sleep. We need to wake up the church so they will stay awake." He maintained that he and other leaders wanted to see Ezekiel's vision of the resurrection of dry bones happen in the nation. As he spoke, the bones of thousands of those who had been murdered still lay unburied throughout much of the land, left as a solemn reminder of the nation's holocaust.

He thought that spiritual warfare "could be the beginning of a journey" for Rwanda. They needed guidance on how to do it however: "Spiritual warfare is especially important and has not been taught. The Christians are totally ignorant about it. There has even been resistance from Evangelicals about praying. They express a feeling of hopelessness:

'Why waste time praying for political leaders, for sinners? What good will it do?' Recently, during the April 1–7 'mourning week' in memory of the 1994 genocide, we carried out a prayer march. The purpose was to go and symbolically cleanse the roads, but there was a very small response," he complained.

"In addition," he went on, "there is a minimal knowledge of Scripture on the part of the believers and an ongoing clash is happening between the new and older leaders of the church. The Roman Catholics are losing members to the Protestants and are very angry about it." He also reflected on the deep sense of hopelessness so many felt due to the loss of such large numbers of their countrymen in such a brutal fashion. "There is also a lot of discouragement and cynicism, together with a real casualness towards the things of the church, because the church did very little to prevent the genocide."

He felt Christians needed to love and pray for the government, but by and large the church did not care. A few months earlier, the government itself had taken the initiative to organize a day of prayer and thanksgiving; there is an active prayer group in the parliament; and the speaker is a committed Christian. He reported that there were seventeen government ministers, some Roman Catholic, some from an Anglican background, and others who were seeking God. These were encouragements that the political structures could also be transformed if his people would really pray. He also mentioned a very active prayer group meeting in the center of the city of Kigali at lunchtime. Seven hundred gather to join in intercessory prayer!

The lack of organized, coordinated prayer, and the widespread apathy for spiritual things in the years leading up to April 1994 had, Antoine felt, opened the door to the "roaring lion." Just one day before the genocide broke out April 6, he and his predecessor, Israel Havugimana, felt burdened to mobilize the church for prayer and were even working on a leaflet called "Operation Standing in the Gap," taken from Ezekiel 22:30. Unfortunately, it was too late, and before they could do anything more, the genocide erupted with great ferocity the following evening.

As Antoine and I parted, I felt we had a compelling enough rationale to proceed with an internationally coordinated prayer effort for the nation. Antoine also asked for intervening intercession for protection of himself, his family, and the AEE team. They were in danger physically and spiritually, he said. Recently, infiltrators (Hutu extremists) had been caught hiding in the bush near his home. He and his family could have been killed, just as they almost were during the genocide of 1994 when such extremists appeared at his front gate but were driven away just in time by soldiers.

Also, he often wakes up tired and sick—probably, I surmised, due to the spiritual oppression as well as the lingering trauma of all he has seen and experienced. Finally, he told me that in 1995, while fasting and praying for three days, God showed him and his colleagues three things: (1) Darkness was over all the country, but there were small isolated candles of light. (2) If they could get these candles of light together, it would chase the darkness out. (3) In 1996, their top priority was prayer for the return of the refugees (which had now happened). For 1997, they were praying for conviction and confession of sin, then inner healing and readiness to forgive the offenders (those who took part in the killing in 1994). This was the most important prayer request and would bring a solution to every other problem, they felt.

HEALING THE NATION THROUGH PRAYER AND SPIRITUAL WARFARE

Having just read *The World's Most Dangerous Places* (HarperCollins, 1997) and seen the section on Rwanda, it was encouraging to know that many intercessors around the world were with us in prayer as our international team of nine prayer leaders from six countries (Malaysia, Singapore, Sri Lanka, Ethiopia, Kenya, and the United States) departed for Africa. There had been recent reports in the media of foreigners having become the special targets of the Hutu extremists, who now struck without warning from their hideouts. However, on the way, as he so often does, the Lord reassured me with Psalms 121 and 124— he would keep us from all harm, watching over our coming and going. I praised God, sitting there in my airline seat, for his faithful promises.

More than one hundred Christian leaders (pastors, evangelists, and a few development workers) from fourteen denominations and five para-church organizations gathered in Kigali, May 13–16, 1997, to pray for healing, reconciliation, and deliverance of the nation from the cycle of revenge and violence that had plagued it for many years, the worst of which was the explosion of bloodshed in 1994. Church leaders came from every prefecture, and six traveled all the way from the neighboring nation of Burundi, which shares a similar culture, ethnic groups, and the problem of recurring ethnic conflict.

As we so often find in such initiatives, though most of our international team had never met or ministered together, we quickly bonded as we shared the different ways in which God had placed Rwanda on our hearts. Some had even had dreams and visions in which the Lord prompted them to come! We were again amazed at how the Spirit has a way of making his people one.

The major theme for the initiative was the one AEE had already chosen, Isaiah 62:6–7: that God would raise up an army of intercessors who would "give him no rest" until he made Rwanda a "praise of the earth." Due to serious syncretism mentioned earlier, including blatant involvement in occult practices by the majority of those who professed to be Christian, the wall of protection against the demonic had been broken down so that the "liar and murderer" was free to do his work of destruction.

In my presentation, over which I had agonized during a prior retreat in the Californian desert, I spoke on "From Lamentation to Intercession to Transformation." In spite of feeling very unworthy to speak to these leaders, many of whom had suffered greatly for their faithfulness, I felt the Lord wanted me to refer to passages in Jeremiah and Lamentations that described the judgment that befell God's people for their syncretism and idolatry. I discussed three main points: (1) We need to understand who the real enemy is (not human, but spiritual). (2) We need to take responsibility for human wickedness, which opens the door to the enemy. (3) Our repentance and intercession as God's people can bring liberation, healing, and future protection.

Leading up to the genocide, the church had by and large lost its prophetic role because church leaders had become toadies to the government line of ethnic chauvinism. During our time together, however, there was a deep sense of guilt and identificational repentance for the failure of the church to stop the slide toward the horrific events of '94. Messages from our team on the themes of forgiveness, reconciliation, the love of God, and strategic intercession (spiritual warfare) for dealing with principalities and powers were interspersed with times of deep intercession and travail as we poured out our hearts for the nations of Rwanda and Burundi.

As everyone fell to their knees, Helen Melahouris, one of our team members, led us in an impassioned corporate cry to God: "We have come full of pain and need. We have no answer apart from you. Do the impossible in us. Help us to forgive those who killed our families and friends. Restore hope in us. Now, Lord, in faith and obedience we speak forgiveness to those who have wounded us—our homes and families, our churches, our land, and Africa. We forgive our enemies. Help us now to be healed. Pour your oil of healing into us. Feed us the bread of life. Fill us with your breath, O God, and give us new life, we pray."

Dr. Joe Ozawa, psychologist and team member, received a word from the Lord: "'I am going to change people from hate to love.' God wants Rwanda to be a nation of prayer and love so that the world will be shocked at this greatest of all miracles—the peoples of Rwanda becoming a people of love." He also outlined three practical steps for the pastors to follow as they help the victims of genocide cope with trauma:

1. Spend time with them.
2. Let people tell their stories, and weep with them.
3. Love them.

Our Sri Lankan team member, Reverend Leslie Keegel, gave a prophetic word based on Ezekiel 37:1–14, the valley of dry bones:

The Lord will cause the nation to live. The church will rise up as an army of authoritative prayer warriors to pull down satanic strongholds based on the arrogance of ethnic superiority. It will build godly values and sow the seeds of healing and reconciliation. It will be a combative army against the chief principalities. It will focus on the Lord, who is the Commander in Chief, not fearing to be confrontive through prayer and engaging in conflict with the evil one. It will move in God's timing and fullness. It will not be a destructive army but a creative one, recreating beauty and abundance of hope and life throughout the nation. Wherever their feet will tread, that area will blossom with God's creativity and love. The church will dethrone Satan everywhere and enthrone Jesus Christ. The kingdom of God will be established, and his will shall be done. (abbreviated version)

One of the local participants shared the story of Mozambique and the cessation of its long civil war. Believers there prayed together in 1990 for the healing of the land according to 2 Chronicles 7:14. They then went to the president and rebels as intermediaries, and the Lord brought peace. He said, "Our responsibility is to reach leaders and change structures of authority through the initiative of the church." Genet Kebede, our team member from Ethiopia, shared the experience of her nation's church under the Marxist regime of Mengistu. She testified that God used the difficult days of suffering to save many, even government officials who had been involved in killing the believers. Now the church has grown immensely.

On the final morning of the initiative, participants wrote on paper their plan to raise up a force of intercessors back in their own areas. Among the ideas suggested for follow-up were to have such conferences in various parts of the country and to pick a common day to pray for peace and reconciliation each month. I suggested that each participant find two others in his or her hometown with whom to pray regularly and for members of both ethnic groups to observe communion together at the massacre sites in faith that the blood of Jesus can absorb the cry for revenge and ongoing violence.

We visited two massacre sites along with the conference participants, including the church at Ntarama where several thousand men, women, and children were slaughtered in the church sanctuary as they hid from the extremists. Bones and clothing still lay in heaps everywhere because the government wants to keep this as a memorial. Amidst the gloom and sorrow of the place, I was reminded of humanity's only hope expressed in Jesus' words: "I am the resurrection and the life"(John 11:25). A group of little children spontaneously gathered around us during the ceremony as we prayed for the breaking of the cycle of violence and revenge. We also prayed for the protection and well-being of these children, representatives of the next generation, and the four hundred thousand others orphaned by the genocide.

Some of our team members also met and prayed with the Speaker of Parliament, an enthusiastic Christian. All in all, our team was humbled and blessed to be with the Rwandan and Burundian brothers and sisters in Christ who have suffered and borne so much. We heard many stories of great heroism by ordinary Christians during the genocide as they sought to protect members of the rival ethnic group, often at the cost of their own lives.

The prayer initiative seemed to deeply encourage those who took part. Here are some of the comments:

"Your team is a gift of God to Rwanda."
"Your team brought the 'oil of anointing' to soften hardened hearts."
"You were God's messenger who brought joy to my heart and healing to my soul."
"We have learned so much from you, and we hope you will come back."
"You are a blessing for our land."

One participant, while still in a refugee camp in Zaire, had seen a vision of a team coming and speaking on reconciliation and intercession. Everything happened according to what he had seen: "This is what I've been waiting for in my spirit and for which my spirit was restless. Now we know what to do." Many said, "You have brought hope to our land."

We were so grateful to God and all of his people who supported the initiative in their prayers. On my return, I sent out a report to these faithful people:

> Thank you for letting the Lord use you and your intercession to bless the peoples of Rwanda and Burundi. Please keep praying that true healing, reconciliation, and deliverance from hatred, fear, and revenge will come to these tortured countries. Pray for the raising up of an army of intercessors in every area of the land so that this transformation will come. Hallelujah! Our God is going to bring it to pass!

ONGOING IMPACT OF UNITED PRAYER

Throughout the past two years we have continued to pray for Rwanda and have heard reports from time to time that significant change is happening in the nation. True, there is still a long way to go as they travel back from the brink of hell after the genocidal destruction that engulfed the land to full healing and development. In November and December 1997, Amnesty International relayed dismaying reports of new massacres of hundreds of civilians in the northern provinces of Ruhengiri and Gisenyi by both Hutu extremists and government soldiers.[21] Three of our own World Vision staff lost their lives as well, and World Vision had to close its work in the north for a time because the situation was so unstable and dangerous. John Steward, an Australian colleague with World Vision who was working in Rwanda on reconciliation and peace building, wrote: "The country here continues to stagger along; many believe that it will get worse in the near future and then God will step in. We are holding on. God continues to work against the obstacles here—prayer is being tangibly answered in the midst of the deepening mire."[22]

In May, John Steward with his Rwandan coworker, Solomon Nsabiyera, visited our office in California and gave a more extensive and upbeat report of what God was doing in response to prayer.[23] It seemed to bear out the truth of Robert Schreiter's words: "Reconciliation is more spirituality than strategy."[24] Antoine Rutayisire and AEE had started the "Prayer Network over Rwanda" project, consisting of weeklong seminars followed by weekend crusades, with all churches in an area taking part. Their objectives to be reached by the end of 1999 were:

1. First to mobilize all churches in main towns, and then in every village for intercession for the healing of the nation
2. To raise up an army of prayer warriors all over the country and train them
3. To produce material on a number of related topics, including audio tapes and handouts

African Evangelistic Enterprise and World Vision had been partnering for workshops on healing, forgiveness, and reconciliation in various parts of the country. In February, eighty-five people attended in Ruhengiri, perhaps the most violence-prone area of the country. Both Hutu and Tutsi repented of their own sins and those of their ancestors, forgiving each other with a lot of weeping. Christians from thirteen denominations took part as they focused on the role of a Christian in peace restoration, spiritual warfare, God's promises and purposes for Rwanda, and healing inner wounds. They identified operating powers of darkness in this region—which is "the purest place of violence and ethnic hatred"— as terror, xenophobia, tribalism, insubordination, and idolatry. The local spirit, Nyabingi, oppresses people with fear and drives them to violence and ethnic killing. However, the principal reason why violence has continued is: "Rwandan hearts are full of hatred, fear, anger, guilt, sorrow, and anguish that trigger them to murder and vengeance." Some who attended said they had never heard such spiritual warfare teaching in their churches and now realized they needed to stand together against the evil one, not against those of another ethnic group.

Also during this seminar, three thousand gathered to pray for peace in the stadium. Antoine Rutayisire shared promises for the restoration of peace in Rwanda from Jeremiah 25:5 and 22:3 having to do with repentance, righteous living, and abhorring violence and the shedding of innocent blood. There was a major impact from this seminar and prayer for peace. Many gave testimonies of being delivered from bitterness and being able to forgive enemies for the first time. One woman who had lost all four of her children during the war and used to dread even seeing soldiers is now ready to forgive them. Another woman whose son was murdered actually adopted the repentant murderer as her own son rather than turn him over to the authorities to be executed!

After this encouraging meeting, I reported to the prayer team: "God is clearly at work bringing transformation and healing to the nation. Let us keep praying for the peacemakers like AEE and World Vision and the churches. Pray for the complete binding and overthrow of Nyabingi and other powers of darkness." From time to time since, I have heard stories in bits and pieces coming out of the country. Later in 1998, a filmmaker who was shooting film for World Vision called me. He said he had visited Rwanda originally after the heartbreaking events of 1994 when a heavy, oppressive gloom hung over the land. He now reported that he had just come back from a second visit and could not believe the difference. He excitedly told me, "John, the atmosphere has changed! People seemed friendly and hopeful about the future. Even the soldiers who used to glower at me smiled and waved!"

For the purposes of this book, which was being finished in the summer of 1999, I decided to contact Antoine Rutayisire and two of our Rwandan World Vision colleagues to hear a more complete, inside account of what has happened in Rwanda. George Otis Jr., in his research on communities transformed through united prayer and social reconciliation, maintains correctly that a crucial ingredient is "persevering leadership."[25] These men and other people like them have provided this kind of leadership to the prayer movement in the nation. I wrote to them asking them to describe what impact they had seen from the united prayer efforts the last two years; to share some of the changes politically, socially, and spiritually; and to comment on the role prayer has played in the reconciliation and peace-building process.

First, let me allow Antoine, the main organizer of the prayer effort nationally and of the 1997 initiative in particular, to tell his story. In June 1999, he wrote a lengthy letter of which I include excerpts:

> I have been dreaming of writing an article on this topic of "The Role of Prayer in the Healing of a Nation," but as I have not done it yet, I will try to give you just some elements. The idea of starting a prayer network in the country started just some days before the beginning of the genocide. At the time, the tension in the country had become so threatening that we as Christians had started wondering what we could do. AEE had been organizing reconciliation meetings and seminars all over the country since 1991, but it seemed as if no results were being achieved and the situation was going from bad to worse, with prophecies warning of bloodshed of unforeseen dimension. (Don't let anyone tell you that the Lord had not warned his people, we simply did not know what to do with the warnings we were receiving, no one having ever taught us about spiritual warfare and the use of prophecy in that.)
>
> There are times I regret not having known what I now know on the two topics of spiritual warfare and the use of prophetic warnings (they are now part of our teachings on spiritual warfare). Tuesday 5th April 1994, we took an evening to inquire of the Lord what we should do and what we could have done that we did not do, and the answer was 2 Chronicles 7:13–14. We read that passage and we immediately, the same evening, wrote a leaflet to be spread in all the churches in the country, mobilizing them for prayer along that Bible reference. The draft was taken to a printer on Wednesday, April 6; the presidential plane was shot the same day in the evening and the genocide started. The devil had been quicker with his plans!
>
> Of all the members of the group that had prayed that evening and had worked on the leaflet, I was the only one to survive, and I have taken over where we left in April. Since the end of the war and genocide, AEE-Rwanda came under my leadership, and I have taken intercession for the healing of the nation as one of our main thrusts in the ministry.

Already in 1995, during a three-day fasting and prayer meeting, the Lord revealed to us his priorities in the process of healing the nation:

1. First, we had to pray for a peaceful return of the refugees that were in the surrounding countries (Zaire, Burundi, Tanzania, and elsewhere). We did organize all the churches from North to South and from East to West and even those who were in the camps, and we all prayed for that. 1996–97 saw most of the refugees home and even the government (listen well to this) called for an afternoon of thanksgiving to the Lord on December 31, 1996. The announcement on the radio read like this: "In order to thank the Lord for the miracle He had done bringing back the Rwandan refugees, the Ministry of Social Affairs, on behalf of the Rwanda government, invites all the religious leaders to an afternoon of thanksgiving in the national stadium." . . .

2. The Lord had also revealed that this return would be followed by some instability in the country but called us to pray for peace during that time. This did indeed materialize as most of 1997–98 insecurity ravaged the Northern Prefectures of Ruhengeri and Gisenyi and did even overspill into other regions neighbouring the two. In the midst of all that, the Lord sent us to Ruhengeri to pray for the people there. He revealed to us in prayer all the spiritual mapping of the area, and this was real warfare strategy. The Lord revealed to us that the region was plagued by demons of rebellion in links with the Nyabingi female demon that has been given the northern part of the country as its dominion. He also revealed to us that the northern range of volcanoes/mountains called Birunga has been given to spirits as their abode, and even now, when Christians cast out a demon, they still send it into the Birunga which shows that even now we recognize the covenant that was made with the evil spirits to live on our highest points. The Lord revealed also that evil spirits Fear, Hatred, and Terror have been dominating the area as can be seen in the names they give to their children. Names like Ntibanyendera (they don't wish me well), Ntahondi (I'm on

my own), Ntanshuti (no friends) and others of that spirit are known to be common in the region. . . .

3. We were led to bind all those evil spirits if we were to see results in the region in terms of peace and stability. We prayed for a whole week, fasting with the Christians of the region, and we had promises that the Lord was going to do something. When we left, nothing special had happened, but when we returned for three days of fasting and prayer in May, the reports from different corners of the regions were astounding. Here is an excerpt from a letter Augustin Ahimana of World Vision . . . wrote calling for support in prayer:

> People of God had prayed for the security situation in the Northwestern Prefectures of Ruhengeri and Gisenyi, and God answered prayer. Recently, many of those who had been kept captives by the rebels in the forests started returning massively to their home communes. They continue to come back every day. Besides, rebels are surrendering to the security forces and are asking for forgiveness, and this happens daily.

Wonderful reports were given during that time of people inviting Christians to destroy the shrines of Nyabingi, of rebels surrendering, of people getting converted, and churches resuming their activities. Today, the whole region is at peace. Maybe the politicians do not acknowledge the impact of prayer on the turn of events, but we as intercessors know, and I still have my notebooks with all the promises of what was going to happen. What a mighty God we have!

4. The Lord has also disclosed his plans for reconciliation between the victims and the genociders. We now have around 150,000 people in jail because of the participation or suspicion of participation in the genocide. It has been evaluated that it would take more than 300 years if those people are to be judged fairly. But the Lord has told us to pray for repentance (recognition of the sin, confession of the sin, asking for forgiveness, and restitution) on the part of the offenders and healing and a spirit of forgiveness on the part of the offended. This has been the most difficult topic to pray

for. The wounds on the hearts of the people are still very fresh and that's probably why the results are still meager. But we have seen wonderful miracles in that area too. Many prisoners are now repenting and asking for forgiveness and even some of the survivors of the genocide who are healed now go to the prisons to extend their forgiveness. We see a cloud as "big as the hand of a man," and I'm praying that more will see clearly the benefit for the nation and will submit to the Lord and pray for his mighty intervention in that area too.

Prayer is definitely a powerful tool in bringing about reconciliation. In all our evangelistic crusades we have included a day of fasting and prayer and very often people will spontaneously go to their "enemy" to extend forgiveness or ask for it. In one of our crusades (Rwamagana Town), one lady stood up and confessed during the day of fasting and prayer that she had stopped taking communion since the time of the genocide because she did not want to share the same cup with the Hutus. This happened when we were praying for healing and reconciliation after teaching on a wounded heart as a hindrance to prayer. Another lady stood up, went and hugged another lady saying, "I want to repent to God and to ask for your forgiveness. I used to come to this church, but I have now shifted to another church because I could not bear to see your face among the deacons. You were very nice to me but I could not bear that. I know you have been in the camps, and I have always resented you as an *interahamwe* (militia). Forgive me for my prejudices and may the Lord forgive me also." Such stories are frequent in our prayer meetings now. They are part of the result of prayer and teaching.

5. The Lord is still warning that our situation is still fragile, and the devil may come back in strength if we close our eyes or become complacent because of what has been achieved. But Isaiah 62:6–7 has become our motto now, and we are determined to train and empower intercessors to pray for the nation until we become a blessing among the nations. . . . We are now building a house of prayer that will

serve as a training place for the intercessors from different areas of the country but also as a documentation center on intercession. . . .

Yours in Christ, Antoine Rutayisire[26]

World Vision colleague, Solomon Nsabiyera, in an E-mail message on May 12, 1999, said succinctly: "I am always delighted to share God's wonders here in Rwanda with partners. . . . The ultimate impact of our prayer today is the peace that is prevailing in the entire country." Peace, restoration, repentance, healing, forgiveness, reconciliation, spiritual revival, hope for the future—these are some of the many words that could be used to describe what God has done and continues to do through the united prayers of his people, both inside and outside the nation. How encouraging to hear that, based on their experience of all he has done, the Rwandans are building a special "House of Prayer." In so doing, they are taking seriously Jesus' promise: "My house will be called a house of prayer for all nations" (Mark 11:17). (One church of intercessors in Malaysia just notified us that they are sending $10,000 to help with its cost and want to partner in prayer with Rwandans for the future!) Surely the rest of Africa and other nations torn by ethnic conflict and warfare also need the prayers of Rwandan Christians who know firsthand what intercession and spiritual warfare are really all about. Praise God that his salvation and transformation are not just for individuals but also are national and international in their impact. Truly, Jesus Christ is the one who heals the nations and makes us one in him.

Rwandan pastors crying out to God for the healing of the nation during a prayer initiative in Kigali.

Team members ministering to local leaders.

Hilltop massacre site near Kigali.

Unburied bodies from Ntarama Church massacre site.

Some of the remains of those killed at Ntarama.

Being introduced to the local children at Ntarama.

CONCLUSION: A CALL FOR A
PREEMPTIVE PRAYER STRATEGY

We have seen the role of the powers in human conflict and the need for a spiritual response as well as just a diplomatic or military one. Special prayer initiatives have an essential role to play in bringing healing to conflicts such as the ones featured in this book. It is likely that there will be many more Bosnias, Kosovos, Cambodias, and Rwandas. Leon Wieseltier, without knowing what was to come in Kosovo, wrote, "But now we know that the Holocaust was not received as a warning. It was received as a precedent. . . . It is one of the consequences of the Serbian terror in Bosnia that we may never again say, 'never again.' . . . It is only a matter of time before we learn the name of the place that will be the new Srebrenica. The destiny of Bosnia has given heart to the wicked. We will be tested again."[1]

Holbrooke bluntly predicts, "There will be other Bosnias in our lives." He argues for early outside involvement in which American leadership will be required.[2] Our response is that without *spiritual* leadership, no matter what nation or nations help comes from, such outside attempts may turn out to be as ineffective as those undertaken during the first years of Bosnia's war.

In war, there is such a thing as a preemptive first strike which seeks to destroy the enemy's capacity before he is able to unleash his own assault. Sun Tzu's *The Art of War*, an ancient Chinese classic on military strategy still read by war planners today, says: "What is of supreme importance in war is to attack the enemy's strategy. . . . Attack plans at their inception."[3] We believe that in spiritual warfare, the same principle pertains. It is much better to be proactive rather than reactive. Knowing full well that the number of complex humanitarian emergencies is on the rise, God's people need to have a preemptive prayer strategy to deal with them.

In 1997 and before, ominous warnings were being issued about the crisis in Kosovo and its potential to become an even more explosive, destructive conflict, spilling over into surrounding nations—but there was little or no preemptive prayer action taken. In 1998, Angola and Congo again erupted in civil wars that threatened to become a regional struggle as other nations got involved. The recent standoff between the Pakistanis and Indians that involved tit-for-tat nuclear testing raised the stakes of such conflicts far more dramatically. But lest we in the comfortable West think we are somehow exempt because these conflicts are "over there," we had better think again. Through electronic mail we received the following urgent request for prayer entitled "Local racial war emerging." It came not from Bosnia or Rwanda but from the U.S.A.:

> I am the pastor of the only Indian church in town. Two of the sons of members of our congregations—ages nineteen and fifteen—with eight other Indian youth (one female) were arraigned today for [first degree murder] and they may seek the death penalty. In a small congregation, in a small town, this is very bad.
>
> The Indian boys were reacting to a situation where their female cousin was beat up by a guy from a local Hispanic gang. The police were notified but did not take action so the Indian youth returned en masse and beat up the twenty-five-year-old Hispanic male who died and one other Hispanic male.
>
> The American Indian Movement is here and becoming involved. The gang, "the Tokers," are fueled by outside bigger gangs, and it appears we may be on the verge of a race war between Hispanics and Indians with the first day of school beginning tomorrow.

Please pray for peace in Carson City as well as justice, since it was not the boys' intentions for anyone to die, and injustice is the norm here for Indians. Ask God to turn this nightmare into a revival. Also for me, Pastor Randy Woodley and Pastor Victor Romero of the local Hispanic church to be used as agents of peace between our communities.

Such developments, whether they occur across the seas, in another city, or in our own community, demonstrate that we as God's people need to be vigilant, to "watch and pray" as Jesus commanded us, so that the possibility of a more serious conflict can be averted.

In order to preempt destructive human conflict, we need a workable prayer strategy. *Strategy* has been defined as "skillful management in getting the better of an adversary or attaining an end." The essence of good strategy is the concentration of force. As the renowned Prussian military strategist Clausewitz put it, "All forces which are available and destined for a strategic object should be *simultaneously* applied to it . . . compressed into one act and into one movement."[4] In the same way, an effective prayer strategy coordinates and concentrates the combined, simultaneous spiritual force of the Body of Christ around the world.

This must be done speedily. As affirmed in *The Art of War*, "What is of the greatest importance in war is extraordinary speed; one cannot afford to neglect opportunity. . . . An attack may lack ingenuity, but it must be delivered with supernatural speed."[5] Through electronic mail and fax machines, networks of praying people can be alerted quickly and guided to intercede with specificity and accuracy to deliver a powerful, concentrated punch. This is part of the mandate for the new World Prayer Center that has been established in Colorado Springs, Colorado. It incorporates state-of-the-art telecommunications to link intercessors around the world to pray in this way.

In addition, experienced prayer teams can be dispatched at the first rumblings of a conflict or other potential human disaster to stand with the local believers and provide ongoing direction from the frontlines to external networks of home-based intercessors who will need regular information updates. We propose that several teams of gifted prayer warriors be created for this purpose; a kind of rapid deployment force that would be international, interdenominational, and made up of both men and women who have cross-cultural sensitivity along with knowledge and experience in at least one region of the world other than their own. Funds can be sought from foundations and churches to create a standing reserve that would provide financial support to these prayer leaders while they are away from their jobs and families on special assignments. Teams like this can then be quickly moved into position to support the local believers and to provide on-site intelligence to electronically linked prayer networks throughout the world. Such a rapid deployment force could be coordinated by the World Prayer Center or another willing agency.

By employing this kind of approach, we believe that crises and conflicts with the potential for destroying large numbers of people can be averted. Such a global prayer strategy will also be used by God to bring his peace, healing, and transformation to peoples already engulfed in destructive clashes.

APPENDIX A:

PERCEIVING SATAN'S
AGENDA AND OPERATION

The third floor of my (John's) grandparents' ancient, colonial-style summer home was a dark, dank attic into which we visiting grandchildren would only seldom dare to enter during our playful summer explorations. The overgrown woods and lake out back, the vast barn with its piles of forgotten hay, as well as the nearby ocean waves were all frequented often, without any hesitation and with much childlike exuberance. Only on rainy days, after the fifth game of Monopoly and while suffering from abject boredom, did we ever venture up into that forbidden zone. Perhaps it was the darkness, the cobweb-filled unfamiliarity of it all, that kept us away. But once we had climbed those creaking stairs and pulled the lightbulb string, our fears departed, and we enjoyed looking through antique dresser drawers, discovering relics of our parents and grandparents' own childhoods. Because the light shone, there was nothing to fear, and a whole new realm of experience opened before us.

Most Christians feel a similar kind of reticence in considering the operation of Satan and his kingdom. There is a hesitation, a trepidation, on our part to delve into this unknown dark area of reality we would prefer to avoid. Nonetheless, it is part of the spiritual warfare with which we must daily contend as believers, and so we would do well to understand as much as we can. In war, it may prove disastrous to be without accurate intelligence of the enemy and his forces. Granting that we do not want to give way to an unhealthy fascination with this realm, we must still be willing to venture into it with the light of Scripture, the leading of the Holy Spirit, and without fear because we have nothing to fear. Jesus said, "I have given you authority to tread upon serpents and scorpions, and over all the power of the enemy; and *nothing* shall hurt you" (Luke 10:19, RSV, italics added). His disciples returned from their first encounter with the demonic realm joyfully exclaiming, "Even the demons are subject to us in your name!" (Luke 10:17, RSV). And the apostle John encourages us that "greater is he that is in you than he that is in the world" (1 John 4:4, KJV). True, we can live in blissful ignorance of our enemy and his tactics, like children too afraid to venture into a darkened attic. But with the light of God's Word and faith in his guidance and protection, we will discover in a new way the power and prerogatives Jesus has given his followers to joyously and victoriously deal with the forces of darkness. In this chapter we will endeavor to understand better this opaque dimension in order to combat it more effectively through the light of Scripture and the experience of God's servants around the world.

SATAN'S OVERALL PROGRAM

Satan is a highly organized, intelligent spirit-being dedicated to destroying human beings made in the image of the Creator he hates. He is the master deceiver and the author of idolatry, seeking to bring the whole world under his dominion by undermining faith in God, twisting values, and promoting false ideologies. He does this through infiltrating institutions — government administrations, communications media, educational systems, and religious bodies. He seeks to divert humankind's attention from worship of their Creator through substitution of money, fame, power, pleasure, science, art, politics, or religious idols. His three-point agenda is deception, dominion, and destruction. The ultimate objective is to gain such control over nations and governments that he can turn them against one another for the destruction of war and/or to turn them against their own citizens in selective murder. Some examples of his successes, other than the examples already referred to earlier in this book, include the genocide crimes of Hitler, Stalin, and Saddam Hussein, or the massive killing of the unborn through abortion practiced increasingly in many societies.

SATAN WORKS THROUGH CONTROLLING SPIRITS

He is not omnipresent or omniscient, but as a master "networker," he works through a vast organization of spirit-beings who apparently communicate with one another and work in some sense cooperatively to undermine humanity's encounter with the kingdom of God in every way they can. Toward this end these spirits attempt to get influence over government leaders, legal systems, educational systems, and religious movements. Admittedly, Scripture is not entirely lucid as to how these spirits are organized and how they operate, but there is enough scriptural warrant to make some conclusions.

Both Israel and the early church perceived that God had given his angelic hosts a special role in the administration of human affairs. The Septuagint rendering of Deuteronomy 32:8 says, "He set the bounds of the peoples according to the number of the angels of God." Biblical scholar F. F. Bruce writes, "The biblical evidence for the angelic government of the world is early: it goes back to the song of Moses in Deuteronomy 32. . . . This reading implies that the administration of the various nations has been parceled out among a corresponding number of angelic powers."[1] In Daniel, these powers reveal themselves as both good and evil. Michael the archangel is "the great prince" who has charge of the people of Israel, looking after their interests in the unfolding of history (Dan.12:1). The messenger of the Lord, presumably Gabriel, is detained by the "prince of Persia" against whom he must fight (Dan. 10:13). The "prince of Greece" is also mentioned (Dan. 10:20). Apparently these last two high-level angelic powers were standing in resistance against the revelation made to Daniel about the future of God's people, Israel.

Theologian Walter Wink wonders at the power of these evil beings who are able to hold God's messenger back for twenty-one days: "The angels of the nations have a will of their own and are capable of resisting the will of God. God is perhaps omnipotent but certainly not able to impose the divine will on recalcitrant powers due to God's own self-limitation: God will not violate the freedom of creatures."[2]

How and why did some of the angels turn against the Lord their Creator? We don't know exactly but may surmise that they joined Satan in his rebellion, and since that time they have become foes of God and the nations of humankind whom they seek to hinder rather than to help. In much of the Old Testament we probably see their baleful influence as the false "gods" of the nations—the gods of Egypt, the Amorites, Canaanites, Edomites, etc.—whose worship, Israel was warned, would bring oppression, slavery, foreign invasion, and poverty (Judg. 10:6–16). The Lord is portrayed as bringing judgment upon the gods of Egypt under Moses (Exod. 12:12) and "driving out nations and their gods" from before Israel during the conquest (2 Sam. 7:23).

Of course, in relation to Yahweh, the incomparable Creator, they are not really gods but only demons impersonating deities worshiped through the medium of idols. "For all the gods of the nations are idols, but the LORD made the heavens"(Ps. 96:5), and in Psalm 95:3 he is referred to as "the great God, the great King above all gods." Later, the apostle Paul acknowledges the reality of these spirit-beings and their deception of the Gentiles (the nations), whose sacrifices to idols are made to demons (1 Cor. 10:20) and who are "slaves to those who by nature are not gods" (Gal. 4:8). Scripture, therefore, seems to indicate that these corrupted angels have joined Lucifer in seeking to deceive the nations so that they will not recognize the true God.

THEIR AGENDA: DOMINANCE

Domination and control appear to be the main objectives of these demon gods whom the apostle Paul appropriately calls "principalities," "powers," "thrones," and "dominions" (see Col. 1:16, KJV). The acquisition of power and influence over human beings and their societies must be their obsession. This dominating nature may be revealed in their very names. For example, the meaning of Molech, god of the Ammonites, is "ruler." He managed to get such control over the people of Ammon that they offered their firstborn children to him as sacrifices by fire.[3] *Chemosh*, the national god of Moab, may mean "subduer," perhaps a reflection of the degree of dominion he had obtained over this people, as well as of the successes he gave Moab in wars against their enemies.[4]

Heinrich Schlier writes of these fallen spirit beings: "Principalities . . . exercise their being by taking possession of the world as a whole and of individual men, the elements, political and social institutions, historical conditions and circumstances, spiritual and religious trends."[5]

In referring to Paul's teaching in Romans 8, theologian Hendrik Berkhof concurs with the idea that the principalities and powers seek a totalitarian form of control: "Paul observes that life is ruled by a series of Powers. He speaks of time (present and future); of life and death; of politics and philosophy; of public opinion and Jewish law; of pious tradition and the fateful course of the stars. Apart from Christ, man is at the mercy of these Powers."[6]

Missionaries of today can also give testimony to the kind of control that these spiritual beings have over pagan peoples. The late Ernest Heimbach, formerly a pioneer missionary to the Hmong tribe in Thailand, described how the chief spirit of the tribe dominated it for centuries, using the fear of sickness, death, attack by evil spirits, and also opium addiction to keep the people in his grip.[7]

Lest we think these demon gods, these controlling spirits, these principalities and powers, are still operative only in far-off pagan tribes, we need to take a harder look at our own society. Aside from Charles Manson, Jim Jones, and the Branch Davidians (who seem more obvious examples of demonic deception), what about our own national policy and culture? Walter Wink urges us to discern the demonic installed at the heart of our own national policy, infiltrating the CIA, government administration, and armed forces to ensure continued American political and economic dominance over weaker nations. Commenting on the blind allegiance so many citizens give to their national self-interest, he writes: "What makes nationalism so pernicious, so death-dealing, so blasphemous, is its seemingly irresistible tendency towards idolatry. In the name of this idol, whole generations are maimed, slaughtered, exiled and made idolaters. One hundred million lives have been offered on the altar of this Moloch, thus far in the 20th Century."[8]

Wink, Berkhof, and others help us to see that the powers are still very much with us, injecting their influence over culture, public opinion, and ideology while coloring our assumptions, worldviews, values, and behavior. As Christians who rightly want to discern the activity of the powers of darkness in our society, Berkhof helpfully suggests, "The church's great question is always which Powers are now attempting to get life under their control."[9]

ARE THEY "TERRITORIAL SPIRITS"?

Are these spiritual powers "territorial spirits" as they have been almost faddishly described lately? Certainly geographical territoriality is part of how Scripture describes their influence. The Canaanite god, Baal, who was a continual scourge to Israel because of Israelite involvement in Baal worship, had several localities named after him, e.g., Baal-Peor, Baal-Gad, Baal-Hermon, etc. "The etymology suggests that Baal was regarded as the owner of a particular locality . . . [since] these local Baals were believed to control fertility in agriculture, beasts and mankind. It was highly important to secure their favor."[10] This was accomplished through ritual prostitution, child sacrifice, and other detestable activities (Judg. 2:17; Jer. 7:9; 19:5).

Continually the Lord warned Israel through his prophets to forsake worshiping foreign gods like these if they wanted to remain in their land; otherwise God would bring the peoples against them in judgment "against this land and its inhabitants. . . . this whole country will become a desolate wasteland" (Jer. 25:9, 11). When judgment finally came upon them, a primary reason God gave for this judgment was that "they have defiled my land with the lifeless forms of their vile images and have filled my inheritance with their detestable idols" (Jer. 16:18). Other nations who were guilty of enshrining false gods on their territory also incurred his wrath. The prophet Zephaniah mentions how God will be awesome to the Moabites and Ammonites when he "destroys all the gods of the land" (Zep. 2:11). Philistine lords were told that if they returned the ark of the covenant to Israel, the Lord might "lift his hand from you and your gods and your land" (1 Sam. 6:5). At least in the understanding of Yahweh's prophetic spokesmen, there was a link between the "gods" and the land that was activated by or reinforced by the worship of people.

In the New Testament, geographical territoriality is only hinted at. The mob of demons speaking out of the Gadarene demoniac begged Jesus that they "not be sent out of the country," perhaps because that was the territory to which they had been assigned (Luke 8:26–39). In Acts 19:35 the Ephesian city clerk attempted to quiet the screaming mob by affirming: "The city of Ephesus is the guardian of the temple of the great Artemis and of her image, which fell from heaven." The fact that the mob had been shouting in irrational unison for about two hours: "Great is Artemis of the Ephesians" (v. 34), may indicate some kind of collective possession by a "territorial spirit," though Scripture itself does not make this analysis.

Other cities mentioned in the Bible are described as having connections with Satan or demonic gods. Pergamum, location of one of the seven churches of Revelation, was "where Satan has his throne" and "where Satan lives" (Rev. 2:13). It was a known center in the ancient world for the worship of the spirit of Rome. In declaring allegiance to the emperor, citizens burned incense at the foot of his statue. Also, Dionysus, god of wine, and Asklepios, god of healing, were worshiped locally. Snakes and the handling of reptiles were associated with the cults of both these gods. An ancient coin from Pergamum shows the emperor, Caracalla, standing before a great serpent twined around a tree and saluting it in the manner for which the Nazis later became known.[11]

Spiritual territoriality probably does take an urban form, but a more subtle form than is often recognized in the spiritual warfare movement.

Whether we can identify the spirits over cities as "greed" for New York City, "power" for Washington, or "pornography" for Los Angeles, as one American evangelist did, is highly questionable. After all, aren't these just the sins of some of the people who live in those places? Couldn't greed be equally applied to Los Angeles as to New York? Or pornography to Washington as to Los Angeles? Undoubtedly, much of the discerning of "territorial spirits" is both oversimplified and extremely naive. Satan could be having a good laugh at us!

Can science give us any help? Dr. Hugh Ross has written about the latest discoveries in astrophysics that demonstrate the existence of additional higher dimensions of reality. Altogether there are two to three dimensions of time and eight dimensions of space, some of which are beyond our own experience in the four dimensions of space-time in which we live. Of course, God and other spiritual beings are not subject to the limitations of our more circumscribed space-time reality because they are "extradimensional," able to operate in more and higher dimensions. In a 1993 conversation, Dr. Ross speculated about the application of science's latest findings to the issue of territorial spirits. He felt the issue of territoriality could be a lot more complicated than many realize and raised the possibility that a spirit-being could, due to extradimensionality, maintain several responsibilities and locations on earth simultaneously.[12] Perhaps in our desire to understand the operation of such spirits, we have made the mistake of conceiving of them in static time and space-bound ways that may not be the whole story.

HOW ARE THEY ORGANIZED?

We must be careful of making unwarranted assumptions about the way in which the principalities and powers are organized. One of the most frequent such assumptions is that they compose a hierarchy in a pyramidal sense, with Satan at the top and various gradations of spirit-beings ranked in descending order down to "ground-level spirits," the kind that oppress and possess individuals. The idea of a possible hierarchy stems from attempts to decipher the apostle Paul's understanding of the principalities and powers. Berkhof argues that the apostle was influenced by Jewish apocalyptic writings that conceived of classes of angels on higher and lower levels who influenced events on earth. He also points out that Near Eastern nature religions of Paul's day also believed in a hierarchy of demonic beings arrayed at various levels between God and the world. But he stops short of identifying a definite hierarchical structure in Paul's depiction of the powers since the functions and names of the various terms Paul uses ("principalities," "powers," "thrones," and "dominions") are never clarified: "We rather have the impression that Paul means to suggest broadly by the variety of expressions the number and diversity of the powers."[13] F. F. Bruce agrees. Commenting on Colossians 1:16, he says, "They probably represent the highest orders of the angelic realm, but the variety of ways in which the titles are combined in the New Testament warns us against the attempt to reconstruct a fixed hierarchy from them."[14]

Walter Wink has demonstrated that the terms Paul used in describing the powers were the same ones used to describe human authority in the New Testament.[15] Because human authority is generally organized in a hierarchical manner, perhaps Paul also conceived of the spirit world in a hierarchical manner, but we must not categorically assume this to be the case. Are there other models that may give us a better handle on understanding their organizations? Given their anarchic self-centeredness and total depravity as fallen spirit-beings, could they instead operate like a band of unruly guerrillas or an urban street gang—terrorizing, vandalizing, and running on to the next place where an opportunity presents itself to do destructive things? In this case they would be constantly deploying and redeploying to take advantage of unfolding situations. Just as terrorists' or vandals' activities are affected by the arrival of soldiers or the police, so these roving bands of evil spiritual forces are put to flight by the intervention of God in answer to the prayers of his people. Wouldn't this characterization fit more with the apostle Peter's description of Satan as prowling "around like a roaring lion, looking for someone to devour" (1 Pet. 5:8–9)?

Clearly, as Heinrich Schlier has demonstrated, the apostle Paul had no interest in speculating about the spiritual powers' organization and operation (perhaps that should serve as a caution to us as well). He finds that the names Paul gives to the powers are "to a large extent interchangeable," that is, principalities, spirits, demons, gods, princes, etc., are all used of one another. Schlier finds only one distinction emphasized among them. Whether demons, spirits, or principalities, they are all subordinate to Satan and manifest his power: "The numerous powers all derive from one fundamental power which is called Satan; they may be regarded as emanations and effects of that power."[16] He may be right. Perhaps we should think of Satan and the demons as being more closely joined together. Most likely, given their extradimensionality, they can be both many and one at the same time. How else could up to six thousand demons (the size of a Roman legion) inhabit the Gadarene demoniac and speak with one voice, "My name is Legion, for we are many"(Mark 5:9)?

Though we must be careful of constructing a theology of the spirit world based on pagan belief systems, the possibility of a hierarchy of spirits may be borne out by the perceptions of animistic peoples. Animists believe in a hierarchy headed by a supreme god, who is remote and unknown, and in a pantheon of lesser deities, superior spirits who exercise great power over a wide range of affairs. Beneath these are the lesser and the more immediate spirits of their ancestors, and finally, the evil spirits.[17] The Burmese believe in *nats*, supernatural beings arranged hierarchically with control over natural phenomena, villages, regions, and nations.[18] The cult of guardian spirits in northeast Thailand involves both village and regional spirits, the village ones being subordinate to the regional.[19] In India, Hindu goddesses serve as "guardians" of villages and regions. They are often associated with disease, sudden death, and catastrophe.[20] Kali, goddess of destruction, is a regional deity widely recognized to be over West Bengal and the Bengali people.

A missionary in Thailand believes he has identified the national principality that reigns over the whole country. It is a being known as Phra Sayam Devadhiraj, which means "greatest of the guardian angels of Siam." It is believed this deity has kept Thailand from being overrun by invaders. The king and queen preside over a royal homage-paying ceremony, with the whole nation joining in the worship of this spirit, whose image resides on a throne in the royal palace.[21]

We can conclude that Satan works to exercise dominion through a vast organization of other spirit-beings. But whether he and his spirit henchmen operate as a network, hierarchy, or a more free-flowing operation, we cannot definitively surmise from Scripture, though the beliefs of animistic peoples support a hierarchical point of view. Certainly they are "territorial," but we prefer to use the term *controlling* since the achievement of control is the essence of their purpose and since they seek control not primarily over geographical areas but first and foremost over people and all that concerns them politically, institutionally, culturally, religiously, etc. In other words, they do not care about real estate but those who own and live on it. Both as many and as one, they participate in the destructive agenda of the one whom Jesus said was a "liar" and "a murderer from the beginning" (John 8:44). For this reason alone we need to gain a better understanding of how they get control over individuals and societies.

THE ACTIVE COMPLIANCE
OF HUMAN BEINGS

From the original episode in the garden where the original humans allowed Satan to get control over them through deception (Gen. 3), sadly the whole history of our race attests to human cooperation with Satan and his evil spirits to gain control over individuals and societies. Indeed, one theologian places the blame for the fall of angels on humanity rather than the other way around: "The fall of angels must not be seen independently from the sin of man . . . the two are interwoven. The angels fell because they were tempted by man who was prepared to sell his soul to authorities other than Yahweh."[22] Instead of saying, "The devil made me do it," we may need to change the saying to "We made the devil do it."

The Israelites not only forgot their God and served the Baals and Ashteroth, the gods of other nations, they refused to listen to God's prophets, despised his statutes and covenant and stubbornly opened the door for satanic occupation of their society. The Bible lays the blame squarely upon the Israelites themselves rather than on Satan:

> All this took place because the Israelites had sinned against the LORD their God. . . . They worshiped other gods and followed the practices of the nations. . . . They did wicked things that provoked the LORD to anger. They worshiped idols, though the LORD had said, "You shall not do this." . . . They would not listen and were stiff-necked. . . . They rejected his decrees and the covenant he had made. . . . They followed worthless idols and themselves became worthless. . . . They forsook all the commands of the LORD their God. . . . They bowed down to all the starry hosts. . . . They sacrificed their sons and daughters in the fire. They practiced divination and sorcery and sold themselves to do evil in the eyes of the LORD. (2 Kings 17:7–17)

John Dawson sees the same principle operating today: "Satan is an invader and usurper operating in our territory. God did not give demons authority over your city. Demons have infested the earth's atmosphere since before the creation of mankind, but they can only extend their authority into a town or institution when people sin."[23]

One Christian worker who served in Mauritania thinks the people there have opened the door to a "spirit of divorce" through serial polygamy and adultery. The tragic result is child abandonment, leading to the severe malnutrition and death of many children. The main obstacle to spiritual growth for the tiny number of Christians is temptation through divorce and adultery. Three believers of the estimated twenty in the country have already fallen away from the faith for this reason, and the marriages of expatriate Christians have also been troubled.

As mentioned earlier, after World War II, German Christian leaders reflected on the role of the demonic in the events that befell their fatherland. One said, "You cannot understand what has happened in Germany unless you understand that we were possessed by demonic powers. . . . *We let ourselves be possessed*" (italics added).[24] Theologian Walter Wink believes that demons became "the actual spirituality of Nazism—manifested in the political forms of the Hitler Youth, the SS [Hitler's bodyguard], Gestapo, the unwitting cooperation of churches, the ideology of Aryan racial purity and the revival of Norse mythology." He also mentions the "collective possession" prevalent in modern times in which "the demonic has taken the form of mass psychosis," when humankind en masse gives itself up to evil.[25]

The reverse of the above is also true. McCandlish Phillips writes: "Fidelity to God and his Word breaks the power of evil spirits and erects barriers to Satan. This can be true in a life, in a home, in a nation." He relays the story of the failed attempt by the Theosophical Society in 1926 to bring the Hindu guru Krishnamurti to prominence in America as a "world teacher" who would combine all religions into one and make radical changes in American civilization. After Krishnamurti arrived in New York harbor, he complained of "electrical atmospheric intensity" and said he doubted he would be able to meditate successfully. Plans to speak throughout the country were canceled when he became incoherent—stripped of the powers that had worked for him in India—and complaining of "bad atmospheric conditions prevailing in this country." He ultimately went into seclusion and renounced his pretensions as a new messiah. God had put a hedge about America because of his people's faithfulness and the general commitment of the wider society to keeping his ways.[26]

Would that this were still the case in our society! Unfortunately, the general unfaithfulness and disobedience to God's ways have opened the way for a literal invasion of evil spirits in various forms of Eastern mysticism, the New Age Movement, and especially through declining moral standards relating to honesty, integrity, and sexual purity. We must not think that America is exempt from what has happened in the Balkans or Africa. It can happen here, too, if we allow it!

DECEPTION AND FALSE MIND-SETS

In keeping with his character as the arch liar and the father of lies, Satan's major strategy for the world involves massive deception. He "has blinded the minds of unbelievers, so that they cannot see the light of the gospel of the glory of Christ" (2 Cor. 4:4). His most pernicious attacks are directed at the minds of people, and in this effort he "masquerades as an angel of light" (2 Cor. 11:14). *Time* magazine, in reviewing the film *The Exorcist*, observed that the devil presented therein was an "easy devil."[27] Far more dangerous and destructive are the shared wrong notions about reality with which hundreds of millions of human beings live. The apostle Paul warns both the Galatians and Colossians about being taken prey by deceptive philosophies and becoming slaves again to the "elemental spirits" (Gal. 4:3; Col. 2:8–9, RSV). The book of Revelation depicts worldwide Satanic deception that results in gathering all the nations for that last great battle of Armageddon (Rev. 16:12–14).

Richmond Chiundiza describes how in Zimbabwe the demonic powers came to inhabit the Shona people's legends concerning the Nehanda and Chaminuka, two of their heroes from the past. Through the phenomenon of spirit possession, the spirits of these heroes are now being consulted by Zimbabwean government officials. Other demonic spirits inhabit the legends of the Shona clans, requiring animal sacrifices, festivals, and the possession of individuals to speak their will. Clan members fear to leave the clan territory without asking the permission of these spirits, and they must wear charms for protection and continue appeasing the spirits daily wherever they happen to be living.[28]

Referring to 2 Corinthians 10:3–5, Francis Frangipane says, "There are satanic strongholds over countries and communities. There are strongholds which influence churches and individuals. Wherever a stronghold exists it is a *demonically induced pattern of thinking* . . . a 'house' made of thoughts which has become a dwelling place of satanic activity" (italics added).[29] Culture is made up of many commonly held patterns of thinking, developed through generations and passed down to children as the normative way in which a society operates. For example, the Japanese, though outwardly highly technological and materialistic, are still bound up with occultism. Two-thirds of the population attend Shinto shrines, every schoolchild carries an amulet, and Shinto priests dedicate each new building.[30]

The recent coronation of the new emperor called for ritualized intercourse with the sun goddess, the national deity of the country.[31]

The Bozo people of Mali believe it is necessary to sacrifice animals and deformed people, such as albinos, to ensure the blessings of the spirits for abundant harvests. When twins are born, they kill one or both of them since, in their belief system, two people cannot share one spirit. An animistic Bantu population in Somalia believes the land will not yield an abundant harvest without the shedding of human blood. To guarantee the fertility of a field, all the men rush to meet one another at its center to beat one another with clubs. Thus, numerous injuries and deaths provide enough blood to bring a good harvest.[32]

Cindy Jacobs, a noted intercessory prayer leader, characterizes the "Western mind-set" as being "a stronghold that Satan has built within the culture of the United States and other countries that denies the supernatural and relegates reality to what can be proven scientifically or what can be known by the physical senses. The result upon the Western church is one of disbelief of the work of territorial spirits, thus Satan's kingdom is protected from attack by disbelieving Christians."[33] Indeed, this may be one of the devil's most effective subterfuges, blinding the Western church to the way he operates by getting us to buy into an unbiblical, materialistic worldview held by the rest of our culture.

APPENDIX B:

STRATEGIC PRAYER RESOURCES

If you are interested in taking part in an ongoing prayer network for a particular region of the world, would like more information on strategic intercession, or would actually like to go on a prayer journey yourself, feel free to contact the following agencies that will be glad to assist you:

1. World Prayer Center, 11005 State Highway 83, Colorado Springs, CO., 80921. Phone: 719-536-9100; fax: 719-262-9920. Websites: www.globalharvest.org, www.wpccs.org

This newly established center connects churches and prayer groups with prayer needs from around the world through 120 national prayer networks and other sources.

2. World Vision, Attention: "Prayer Guide," P. O. Box 9716, Federal Way, WA., 98063-9716. Phone: 253-815-1000; fax: 253-815-3140. Website: www.wvus.org

World Vision provides prayer requests concerning its humanitarian efforts throughout the world on its website and through a monthly *Prayer Guide* to those who request it.

3. International Reconciliation Coalition, P. O. Box 3278, Ventura, CA., 93006. Phone: 805-642-5327; fax: 805-642-2588. E-mail: ircio@pac-bell.net. Website: www.reconcile.org

IRC focuses on bringing healing and reconciliation to peoples in conflict through a number of initiatives worldwide. They provide training resources, both written and video, as well as access to networks and a database of people involved in this ministry. They also put out a prayer bulletin and a quarterly *Reconciliation World Watch.*

4. Bethany World Prayer Center, 13855 Plank Road, Baker, LA., 70714. Phone: 504-774-2002; fax: 504-774-2001. Website: www.bethany-wpc.org/profiles

Bethany has produced excellent prayer profiles for the unreached peoples of the AD2000 and Beyond Movement's Joshua Project, an effort to plant Christ's church among those peoples without a viable Christian presence. These can be ordered by phone or fax or downloaded from their website.

5. PrayerWave Asia, 250 Tanjong Pagar Road, St. Andrew's Centre #11-01, Singapore 088541. Phone: 226-4191. 475-2124; fax: 472-1163. E-mail: visioncity@pacific.net.sg

As described in their brochure: "Launched July First 1997, the vision of PrayerWave Asia is to unite prayer networks across Asia to contend for the spiritual future of this vast continent.

PrayerWave Asia is a pioneer project of the AD2000 Joshua Project 2000 movement in Singapore. The focus of PrayerWave Asia is the unfinished task among unreached people groups, most of whom live in Asia. Twice a year—January First and July First—PrayerWave Asia invites the Church across Asia to join in a chorus of prayer on behalf of unreached people groups groaning in their enslavement to the oppressive pharaoh-powers dominating their lives."

6. National Prayer Committee, P. O. Box 770, New Providence, NJ, 07974. Phone: 908-771-0146; fax: 908-665-4199. E-mail: natlpray@aol.com. Website: www.nationalprayer.org

The NPC fosters a number of projects, including the National Day of Prayer, the Nationally Broadcast Concert of Prayer, *Pray!* Magazine, the Denominational Prayer Leaders Network, and others.

7. Intercessors for America, P. O. Box 4477, Leesburg, VA, 20177. Phone: 800-872-7729. Website: www.ifa-usapray.org

Intercessors for America serves the Church of Jesus Christ by encouraging effective prayer and fasting for the church, our nation, and our leaders.

8. European Prayer Link (EPL): www.hfe.org/epl/eplbroch.html

European Prayer Link desires to serve and support God-ordained prayer initiatives in Europe and the CIS. Specifically these prayer initiatives will develop prayer strategy among praying people and churches for a spiritual awakening throughout Europe.

9. Intercessors International, P. O. Box 390, Bulverde, TX, 78163. Phone: 830-438-2615. E-mail: intercessors_intl@compuserve.com

Intercessors International is a ministry committed to teach, train, and mobilize the body of Christ worldwide in the principles of prayer for the purpose of enhancing spiritual growth as well as furthering world evangelism and to strengthen Christian leaders through prayer, encouragement, and restoration.

ENDNOTES

INTRODUCTION

1. Daniel Patrick Moynihan, *Pandemonium: Ethnicity in International Politics* (New York: Oxford University Press, 1993), xiii.

2. Samuel P. Huntington, *The Clash of Civilizations and the Remaking of the World Order* (New York: Simon & Schuster, 1996), 19.

3. Ibid., 20.

4. Gojko Vuckovic, *Ethnic Cleavages and Conflict: the Sources of National Cohesion and Disintegration, the Case of Yugoslavia* (Brookfield, Mass.: Ashgate, 1997), 151.

5. Tom Morganthau, "The Face of the Future," *Newsweek*, 27 January 1997, 59.

6. Vuckovic, *Ethnic Cleavages and Conflict*, 2.

7. Huntington, *Clash of Civilizations*, 35.

CHAPTER 1

1. E. M. Bounds, *Purpose in Prayer* (New Kensington, Penn.: Whitaker House, 1997), 139.

2. Hugh Ross, *Beyond the Cosmos* (Colorado Springs: NAV Press, 1996), 123.

3. Quoted in Richard Foster, *Prayer: Finding the Heart's True Home* (San Francisco: Harper-Collins Publishers, 1992), 229.

4. Ibid., 50–51.

5. Karl Barth, *Prayer* (Philadelphia: Westminster Press, 1985), 83.

6. Joe Nangle, "In the Face of Evil: The Strength of Community," *Sojourners*, Dec.1994–Jan. 1995, www2.ari.net/home/esabath/941243.html

7. Bounds, 27–28.

8. Ross, *Beyond the Cosmos*, 101.

9. Walter Wink, *Engaging the Powers: Discernment and Resistance in a World of Domination* (Minneapolis: Fortress Press, 1992), 303.

10. Larry Dossey, *Healing Words: the Power of Prayer and the Practice of Medicine* (San Francisco: Harper-Collins, 1993), xv, xiii-xix, 45.

11. Terry LeFevre, *Understandings of Prayer* (Philadelphia: Westminster Press, 1981), 173.

12. Wink, *Engaging the Powers*, 299.

13. Ellul, *Prayer and Modern Man*, 172–73.

14. Naomi Frizzell, "A Tale of Three Cities: What God Is Doing through United Prayer across the Country," *Pray!* 6 May 1998, 23.

15. Wink, *Engaging the Powers*, 298.

16. Quoted in Foster, *Prayer*, 238.

17. Quoted in Frizzell, "A Tale of Three Cities," 28.

18. Peter Wagner, *Churches That Pray* (Ventura, Calif.: Regal Books, 1993), 210.

CHAPTER 2

1. "Both Sides Suffer Consequences of Ethnic War in Central Bosnia," United Methodist Committee on Relief Home Page. www.gbgm-umc.org/units/umcor/bosnia/bosnia5.html
2. Peter Wagner, *Warfare Prayer* (Ventura, Calif.: Regal Books, 1992), 77.
3. Heinrich Schlier, *Principalities and Powers in the New Testament* (New York: Herder and Herder, 1962), 19–20.
4. Gerhard Friedrich, *Theological Dictionary of the New Testament* (Grand Rapids: Erdmans Publishing Co., 1972), 614.
5. Francis Frangipane, *The Three Battlegrounds* (Marion, Iowa: River of Life Ministries, 1989), 14–15.
6. Schlier, *Principalities and Powers*, 19–20.
7. Wink, *Engaging the Powers*, 8.
8. Ibid., 3.
9. Quoted in Walter Wink, *Unmasking the Powers* (Philadelphia: Fortress Press, 1986), 54.

CHAPTER 3

1. Richard Holbrooke, *To End a War* (New York: Random House, 1998), 367.
2. Hendrick Berkhof, *Christ and the Powers* (Scottsdale, Pa.: Herald Press, 1977), 147.
3. David Manuel, *Bosnia: Hope in the Ashes* (Brewster, Mass.: Paraclete Press, 1996), 26.
4. Sabrina P. Ramet, *Balkan Babel: The Disintegration of Yugoslavia from the Death of Tito to Ethnic War* (Boulder, Colo.: Westview Press, 1996), 23, 44.
5. Peter Kuzmic, "A Historical Context: How Did We Get Here?" *World Vision: Bridges of Reconciliation*, 1996, 3.
6. Holbrooke, *To End a War*, 23.
7. Kuzmic, "A Historical Context," 7–8, and "Worldviews in Conflict: Report on Bosnia," in *Strategies for Today's Leader*, 28, an undated, photocopied attachment to his personal newsletter of September 1997.
8. Paul Mojzes, "Radovan Karadzic Talks Religion: Confessions of a Serb Leader," *Christian Century*, 16-23 August 1995, 764–66.
9. Philip J. Cohen, "The Complicity of Serbian Intellectuals in Genocide in the 1990s" in Thomas Cushman and Stephan G. Mestovic, eds., *This Time We Knew: Western Response to Genocide in Bosnia* (New York: New York University Press, 1996), 49.
10. Terry Moffitt, "Love Among the Ruins," *Charisma*, July 1997, 65.
11. Warren Zimmerman, "Origins of a Catastrophe: Yugoslavia and its Destroyer," *New York Times Books*, 1996, quoted in Holbrooke, 24.
12. Paul Mojzes, *Yugoslavian Inferno: Ethnoreligious Warfare in the Balkans* (New York: Continuum Publishing Co., 1994), 39–41.
13. Michael Sells, "Religion and War in Bosnia," *New York Times on the Web*, 12 June 1996.
14. Mojzes, *Yugoslavian Inferno*, 46.
15. Ibid., 32–33.
16. Ibid., 32.
17. Ramet, *Balkan Babel*, 40.
18. Michael Sells, *The Bridge Betrayed* (Los Angeles: University of California Press, 1996), 61.
19. Mojzes, *Yugoslavian Inferno*, 172.
20. Manuel, *Bosnia: Hope in the Ashes*, 82.
21. Ibid., 135.
22. Sells, *The Bridge Betrayed*, 65.

23. Wink, *Engaging the Powers*, 87, 94.

24. Paul Marshall, "Nationalism," *AIM* magazine, Evangelical Fellowship of India, June 1998, 35.

25. Holbrooke, *To End a War*, xx.

26. Ramet, *Balkan Babel*, 277.

27. Sells, *The Bridge Betrayed*, 79.

28. The Holy Assembly Bishops Serbian Orthodox Church, *Message to the Public*, Assembly No. 70. Belgrade. May 1995, 1.

29. Sells, *The Bridge Betrayed*, 15, 50–51.

30. Ibid., 29–31.

31. Ibid., 37, 51, 103.

32. Ibid., 31.

33. Ibid., 41.

34. Ibid., 24.

35. Ibid., 86.

36. Ibid., 75.

37. Ibid., 17–22.

38. Ibid., 73, 75.

39. Manuel, *Bosnia: Hope in the Ashes*, 194.

40. Irvin Staub, "Healing and Reconciliation: Highlights," *New York Times on the Web*, 7 June 1996.

41. Holbrooke, *To End a War*, xv, 26–28.

42. M. Elliott, "The Lessons of Bosnia's War," *Newsweek*, 20 April 1998, 35.

43. Fouad Ajami, "Beyond Words," in Nader Mousavizadeh and Leon Wieseltier, eds., *The Black Book of Bosnia* (New York: Basic Books, 1996), 150–51.

44. Kuzmic, "Historical Context," 10–11.

45. Thomas Cushman and Steven G. Mestovic, eds., *This Time We Knew: Western Response to Genocide in Bosnia* (New York: New York University Press, 1996), 10.

46. Sells, *The Bridge Betrayed*, 116–17.

47. Quoted in Sells, *The Bridge Betrayed*, 124, 141.

48. Cushman and Mestrovic, *This Time We Knew*, 11.

CHAPTER 5

1. M. Elliott, "The Lessons of Bosnia's War," *Newsweek*, 20 April 1998.

2. Holbrooke, *To End a War*, 69.

3. Ibid., 70.

4. Ibid., 81.

5. John Robb, unpublished trip report of Bosnia visit, August 1995.

6. Holbrooke, *To End a War*, 93.

7. Ibid., 105–16.

8. Ibid., 215.

9. Statement by President Clinton on the Bosnia Peace Agreement, 21 November 1995, www.state.gov/www/regions/eur/Bosnia

10. Manuel, *Bosnia: Hope in the Ashes*, 90–91.

11. Kuzmic, "A *Historical Context*," 4.

12. Ibid.

13. Kuzmic, "World Views in Conflict," 26.

14. Kuzmic, "Afterword," in his personal newsletter, September 1997.

CHAPTER 7

1. Miranda Vickers, *Between Serb and Albanian* (New York: Columbia University Press, 1998), 300.

2. Richard Johnson, "Serbia and Russia: U.S. Appeasement and the Resurrection of Fascism" in Stejepan G. Mastrovic, *The Conceit of Innocence* (College Station: Texas A&M University Press, 1997), 181.

3. Johanna McGeary, "Why He Blinked," *Time,* 14 June 1999, 46.

4. Steven Erlanger, "For Serbs in Kosovo, Frustration and Anger," *New York Times,* 10 June 1999, A17.

5. George Otis Jr., *The Twilight Labyrinth* (Grand Rapids: Chosen Books, 1997), 141.

6. Noel Malcolm, *Kosovo: A Short History,* (New York: New York University Press, 1998), 24.

7. "Albanian History," Http:www.albanian.com/main/history/byzantine.html

8. Malcolm, *Kosovo: A Short History,* 41.

9. Vickers, *Between Serb and Albanian,* 9.

10. Malcolm, *Kosovo: A Short History,* 3.

11. "Online Extra: Slobodan Milosevic, " www.newsweek.com (from 21 December 1998 issue of *Newsweek* magazine).

12. Otis, *The Twilight Labyrinth,* 163.

13. Ibid.

14. Ibid., 164.

15. Malcolm, *Kosovo: A Short History,* 59.

16. Vickers, *Between Serb and Albanian,* 12.

17. Hugh Poulton and Miranda Vickers, "The Kosovo Albanians: Ethnic Confrontation with the Slav State," *Muslim Identity and the Balkan State,* eds. Hugh Poulton and Sahu Taji-Farouki (New York: New York University Press, 1997), 141.

18. "Kosovo and Medieval Serbia," http://kosovo.serbhost.org/kossaga.html

19. Otis, *The Twilight Labyrinth,* 165.

20. Ibid., 166.

21. Vickers, *Between Serb and Albanian,* 28.

22. Mojzes, *Yugoslavian Inferno,* 19.

23. Miron Rezun, *Europe and War in the Balkans: Toward a New Yugoslav Identity* (Westport, Conn.: Praeger, 1995), 30.

24. Vickers, *Between Serb and Albanian,* 76.

25. Ibid., 77.

26. Mojzes, *Yugoslavian Inferno,* 21.

27. Rezun, *Europe and War in the Balkans,* 44.

28. Malcolm, *Kosovo: A Short History,* 268.

29. Otis, *The Twilight Labyrinth,* 224.

30. Malcolm, *Kosovo: A Short History,* 288.

31. Mojzes, *Yugoslavian Inferno,* 75.

32. Rezun, *Europe and War in the Balkans,* 77.

33. Istvan Deak, "The One and the Many," *The Black Book of Bosnia,* ed. Nader Mousavizadeh (New York: BasicBooks, 1996), 17.

34. Aleksa Djilas, "The Nation that Wasn't," *The Black Book of Bosnia,* ed. Nader Mousavizadeh (New York: BasicBooks, 1996), 24–25.

35. Malcolm, *Kosovo: A Short History,* 314.

36. Vickers, *Between Serb and Albanian,* 158.

37. Robert Howse, "A Horizon beyond Hatred? Introductory Reflections," *Yugoslavia the Former and Future,* ed. Payam Akhavan (Washington: The Brookings Institution, 1995), 7.

38. Vuckovic, *Ethnic Cleavages and Conflict,* 155.

39. Vickers, *Between Serb and Albanian,* 194.

40. Vuckovic, *Ethnic Cleavages and Conflict,* 155.

41. Malcolm, *Kosovo: A Short History,* 334.

42. Rezun, *Europe and War in the Balkans,* 126.

43. Ibid., 127.

44. Anna Hursarska, "Dateline Pristina: The Next Bosnia," *The Black Book of Bosnia,* ed. Nader Mousavizadeh (New York: BasicBooks, 1996), 94.

45. Rezun, *Europe and War in the Balkans,* 127.

46. Vickers, *Between Serb and Albanian,* 239.

47. Holbrooke, *To End a War,* 26.

48. Rezun, *Europe and War in the Balkans,* 128.

49. Walter Wink, *Naming the Powers* (Philadelphia: Fortress Press, 1984), 140.

50. Malcolm, *Kosovo: A Short History,* 350–51.

51. "War with Milosovic," 3 April 1999, www.economist.com

52. Ramnet, *Balkan Babel,* 180.

53. Mojzes, *Yugoslavian Inferno,* 136.

54. Carlotta Gall, "Serb Orthodox Leaders Denounce Milosovic's Policies as Criminal," *The New York Times on the Web,* 29 June 1999, http://nytimes.com.

55. Tihomir Loza with Anthony Borden, "Transitions, May 1998: Kosovo Albanians — Closing the ranks," www.iwpr.net, 10.

56. Chris Hedges, "Kosovo's Next Masters?" *Foreign Affairs,* May/June 1999, 26.

57. Ibid., 32.

58. Massimo Calabresi, "Kosovo Smolders," www.time.com, 11 May 1998.

59. "Kosovo in Crisis," *The NewsHour with Jim Lehrer* transcript, 12 June 1998, http://pbs.org/newshour/bb/europe/jan-june98/kosovo_6-12.html

60. Peter Finn, "NATO Fears Serb Exodus after Killings," Washington Post Foreign Service, Washingtonpost.com/wp-srv/wp;ate/1999-07/25/2481-072599-idx.html, A01.

61. Hedges, "Kosovo's Next Masters?" 38.

62. Ibid., 42.

63. "Online Extra: Slobodan Milosovic," www.newsweek.com

64. Otis, *The Twilight Labyrinth,* 216.

65. "Albania's Evangelicals Rush to Aid Kosovo Refugees," *Religion Today,* 13 April 1999. http://religionnewstoday.net/Archive/FeatureStory/view.cgi?file=19990413.sl.html

66. Tomas Dixon "Bridging Kosovo's Deep Division," *Christianity Today* online, www.christianity.net, 8 February 1999.

67. "Serb and Kosovo Christians Preach Peace Amid War," *Religion Today,* March 25, 1999, http://religionnewstoday.net/Archive/FeatureStory/view/cgi?file=19990325.s1.html

68. "Serbian Diary: Bombs Makes Prayers Run Deeper," *The Orange County Register* Online Archives, Tuesday, 30 March 1999 from News section A09 id: 1999089058.

69. "Pray for Kosovo, Christians Plead, "*Religion Today,* 28 January 1999, http://www.religionnewstoday.net/Archive/FeatureStory/view.cgi?file=19990128.s1.html

70. Ibid.

71. *Religion Today,* 13 April 1999.

72. Ibid.

73. Dwight Gibson, "Balkan Churches in Time of Need, " E-mail from World Evangelical Fellowship dated 8 April 1999.

74. Eugen Begu, "Albanian Churches Seek Guidance—Prayer Day, May 16," www.worldevangelical.org/noframes/2newsold.htm#albania-May16

75. "Christians on the Front: A Call for Prayer," 25 March 1999. www.cbn.org/living/christianwalk/lettersofaffliction.html

76. *Religion Today*, 28 January 1999.

77. "Agencies Assisting Kosovo Refugees," 4 May 1999, http://www.washington post.com/wp-srv/inatl/longterm/balkans/kosovorelief.html

78. "Chenoweth Asks Congress to Call for Solemn Assemblies," May 29, 1999, www.prayeralert.org/alerts5-29-99.html

79. Drs. Mark and Betsy Neuenschwander, E-mail newsletter, "Plans for Albania, Prayer Focus," DrsNeu@aol.com, 31 May 1999.

80. Sonja Nowack in an E-mail to Jim Hill, 5 July 1999.

81. Neuenschwander, E-mail newsletter.

82. Nowack, 2.

CHAPTER 8

1. Michael Freeman and Roger Warner, *Angkor: the Hidden Glories* (Boston: Houghton Mifflin, 1990), 64.

2. George Otis Jr., *Cambodia Profile*, a prepublication report sent by the Sentinel Group in 1995.

3. Freeman and Warner, *Angkor*, 80.

4. Margot Sluka and Tri Budiardjo, "Oudong Rural Health Project: Drama of an Emerging Church in Rural Cambodia," unpublished paper, 24 March 1995.

5. David Chandler, *A History of Cambodia* (Boulder, Colo.: Westview Press, 1992), 18.

6. Seanglim Bit, *The Warrior Heritage: A Psychological Perspective of Cambodian Trauma* (El Cerrito, Calif.: privately printed, 1991), 66–67.

7. Ibid., 65.

8. May Ebihara, ed. *Cambodian Culture Since 1975: Homeland and Exile* (Ithaca, N.Y.: Cornell University Press, 1994), 153.

9. Ibid., 1.

10. Ibid.

11. Ibid., 13.

12. P. Dyphon, quoted Ibid., 2–3.

13. Ibid, 3.

14. Ibid., 18.

15. Don and Margaret Cormack, personal newsletter, April 1994.

16. Kjell and Lena Sjoberg, "Newsletter," 28 March 1995, 1–2.

17. Ibid., 2.

18. Ibid.

19. Ibid., 3.

20. Ibid., 4.

21. Ibid., 5.

22. Ibid.

23. Associated Press news release, 17 April 1995.

24. *The Daily Breeze*, Madras, India, 14 June 1997, A6 and 15 June 1997, A7.

25. *Far Eastern Economic Review*, 13 May 1999, 20; *Friday Fax*, issue 23, 11 June 1999.

26. E-mail letter from Barnabus Mam, 24 June 1999.

27. Ibid.

28. Undated letter from Joye Alit.

CHAPTER 9

1. Carl Lawrence, *Rwanda: A Walk through Darkness into Light* (Sisters, Ore.: Multnomah Publishers, 1995), 135–36.

2. Augustin Karakezi, "Report from Rwanda," *America*, 7 December 1996, 15.

3. Eric Ransdall, quoted in Lawrence, *Rwanda: A Walk through Darkness*, 135.

4. Gerard Prunier, *The Rwanda Crisis* (New York: Columbia University Press, 1995), 141.

5. Ibid., 142.

6. Ibid., 4.

7. E. M. Kolini, "A Tutsi's Hope," *Christianity Today*, 7 April 1997, 11.

8. Prunier, *The Rwanda Crisis*, 39.

9. Ibid., 7–9.

10. Ibid., 40.

11. Human Rights Watch, "Leave No One to Tell the Story: Genocide in Rwanda," March 1999 report on the failure to prevent the Rwanda genocide, http://www.hrw.org/reports/1999/rwanda.

12. ABC News "20/20," 28 July 1999.

13. Prunier, *The Rwanda Crisis*, 31–32.

14. Kolini, "A Tutsi's Hope," 11.

15. Lawrence, *Rwanda: A Walk through Darkness*, 137.

16. Ibid., 142.

17. Ibid.

18. Interview with Antoine Rutayisire in Washington, D.C., April 1997.

19. Interview with Faustin Uzabakiliho in Los Angeles, April 1997.

20. Faustin Uzabakiliho, undated report, April 1997.

21. Amnesty International, "Rwanda: 'The Dead Can No Longer Be Counted,'" 19 December 1997, http://www.africanews.org/east/rwanda/19971219_feat2.html

22. John Steward, in an E-mail letter, 23 January 1998.

23. Conversation with John Steward and Solomon Nsabiyera at World Vision International, May 1998.

24. Robert Schreiter, *Reconciliation: Mission and Ministry in a Changing Social Order* (New York: Orbis Books, 1992), 26.

25. George Otis Jr., "Community Transformation through United and Persevering Prayer," *International Journal of Frontier Missions*, vol. 15:4, October–December 1998.

26. Antoine Rutayisire, in an E-mail letter, 16 June 1999.

CONCLUSION: A CALL FOR A PREEMPTIVE PRAYER STRATEGY

1. Leon Wieseltier, "Afterword" in *The Black Book of Bosnia*, ed. Nader Mousavizadeh (New York: Basic Books, 1996), 196.

2. Holbrooke, *To End a War*, 368–69.

3. Sun Tzu, *The Art of War*, trans. Samuel B. Griffith (New York: Oxford University Press, 1963), 77.

4. Anatol Rapoport, ed., *Clausewitz on War* (New York: Penguin, 1968), 183.

5. Sun Tzu, *The Art of War*, 69–70, 73.

APPENDIX A

1. F. F. Bruce, *The Epistle to the Hebrews* (Grand Rapids, Mich.: Eerdmans, 1990), 32–33.

2. Wink, *Unmasking the Powers*, 90–91.

3. Merrill C. Tenney, ed., "Molech," *Zondervan Pictorial Encyclopedia*, vol. 4 (Grand Rapids, Mich.: Zondervan Publishing House, 1975), 269.

4. "Chemosh," *Zondervan Pictorial Encyclopedia*, 1:786.

5. Schlier, *Principalities and Powers*, 19–20, 67.

6. Berkhof, *Christ and the Powers*, 22.

7. Ernest Heimbach, conversation with author, 27 November 1990.

8. Wink, *Unmasking the Powers*, 50–52.

9. Berkhof, *Christ and the Powers*, 63.

10. "Baal," *Zondervan Pictorial Encyclopedia*, 1:431–32.

11. Ibid., 4:702.

12. Hugh Ross, conversation with author, 17 September 1993. For discussion of "extradimensionality," see his book, *The Fingerprint of God* (Orange, Calif.: Promise Publishing Co., 1989).

13. Berkhof, *Christ and the Powers*, 14–16.

14. F. F. Bruce, *Commentary on the Epistle to the Colossians* (Grand Rapids, Mich.: Eerdmans, 1965), 198.

15. See Walter Wink, *Naming the Powers*, for an extensive analysis of these terms.

16. Schlier, *Principalities and Powers*, 14–15.

17. Philip Steyne, *Gods of Power* (Houston, Tex.: Touch Publications, 1989), 72.

18. Melford Spiro, *Burmese Supernaturalism* (Philadelphia: Institute for the Study of Human Issues, 1978).

19. S. J. Tambiah, *Buddhism and the Spirit Cults in Northeast Thailand* (New York: Cambridge University Press, 1970), 263–84.

20. David Kinsley, *Hindu Goddesses: Visions of the Divine Feminine in the Hindu Religious Tradition* (Berkeley: University of California Press, 1986), 197–98.

21. In a letter from Frank Schaftner, August 1989.

22. Rob Van der Hart, *The Theology of Angels and Devils* (Notre Dame: Fides Publishers, 1972), 87.

23. John Dawson, *Taking Our Cities for God* (Lake Mary, Fla.: Creation House, 1989), 79.

24. David Robinson, conversation with author, fall 1990.

25. Wink, *Unmasking the Powers*, 54.

26. McCandlish Phillips, *The Spirit World* (Wheaton, Ill.: Victor Books, 1970), 21–24.

27. Quoted in Lynn Buzzard, *Introduction to Demon Possession*, J. W. Montgomery, ed.

28. Richmond Chiundiza, "High-Level Powers in Zimbabwe," *Territorial Spirits*, ed. Peter Wagner (Chichester, England: Sovereign World Ltd., 1991), 123.

29. Francis Frangipane, *The Three Battlegrounds* (Marion, Iowa: River of Life Ministries, 1989), 21.

30. Paul Ariga (a Japanese evangelist), conversation with author, spring 1990.

31. Carl Schoenberger, "Akihito and Final Ritual of Passage," *Los Angeles Times*, 23 November 1990.

32. From a 1990 unpublished paper by Bruce Bradshaw of World Vision International, Monrovia, Calif.

33. From unpublished notes of Cindy Jacobs sent to the author, November 1990.